T0268532

Have you ever wondered what Word of F[...] self-help, and the seeker-sensitive mo[...] *Happy Lies* is a groundbreaking book [...] the little-known yet widely followed movement called New Thought. Melissa Dougherty has given us a valuable resource that is meticulously researched, deeply fair-minded, and thoroughly entertaining. If you are a Christian interested in discerning the times, this is the book for you!

Alisa Childers, author, *Another Gospel?*;
coauthor, *The Deconstruction of Christianity*

If you're wondering why the world looks as it does, and wondering why the church is looking more like the world, Melissa Dougherty's book, *Happy Lies*, will be a welcome addition to your library. Melissa identifies the movement behind the slow corruption of the culture—*and the church*—with her usual wit and poignant analysis. Once you've finished *Happy Lies*, you'll understand the challenge we face and the response we must offer.

J. Warner Wallace, *Dateline*-featured cold-case detective;
senior fellow, Colson Center; adjunct professor of apologetics

It's rare to come across a book that sparks a whole cascade of aha moments, but *Happy Lies* is certainly one of those books. Melissa illustrates how New Thought—essentially a repackaged version of the original lie from the garden—has permeated pop psychology and, more chillingly, has now infiltrated the church. Anyone concerned about the dangerous effects of "almost true" doctrine must read this book.

Hillary Morgan Ferrer, founder/president,
Mama Bear Apologetics; bestselling author/
editor, Mama Bear Apologetics book series

In *Happy Lies*, Melissa Dougherty has unraveled every major deception that has crept into the church in the past century—most of which are hiding in plain sight. I've seen these dangerous ideologies dealt with in separate books before, but never in one book and with such clear, concise language. Every Christian should read this book, especially parents, pastors, and educators. These "happy lies" are targeting the next generation, but they are no match for those who know the truth.

Costi W. Hinn, teaching pastor, Shepherd's House
Bible Church; president/founder, For the Gospel

Modern Christians are probably more familiar with New Age spirituality than the New Thought movement. But the influence of New Thought is everywhere in our culture, including in the church—though we often fail to recognize it. In this important book, Melissa Dougherty explains the origins and beliefs of this movement, calling Christians to biblical discernment. *Happy Lies* will help you understand spirituality in modern culture, how to distinguish truth from lies, and why the gospel is better than the cheap substitutes that compete with it.

Gavin Ortlund, author; theologian

Sometimes old lies dressed up in new lingo sound like new truth, or like a new twist on old truth if baptized with biblical language. Melissa Dougherty's *Happy Lies* reveals that, in spite of its cheerful face, New Thought is just an old deception—an ancient falsehood going back to the garden. *Happy Lies* provides a thoughtful tutorial on the origins, the teachings, and the dangers of New Thought, made completely accessible by Dougherty's readable—sometimes whimsical—style. Dougherty's work provides insight and instruction vital to Christians seeking to avoid the pitfalls of an old lie that continues to deceive and destroy.

Gregory Koukl, president, Stand to Reason; author,
Street Smarts, Tactics, and *The Story of Reality*

The happy lies you've been told about God eventually lead to unhappy lives, but many don't recognize the deceit until it's too late. Melissa Dougherty brilliantly exposes these New Thought lies that are infiltrating the church. She'll lead you back to the true Jesus and rescue you from the pretend Jesus that "MEologians" have created in their own image. Don't fall for their pretend Jesus. Get this enlightening book!

Frank Turek, author; speaker; president,
CrossExamined.org ministries

Happy Lies is the most important book that Christians don't know they need. Melissa connects dots that give readers a wealth of aha moments and provides invaluable insights that bring clarity to some of the most pervasive errors in the church. As a bonus, she does it all in a writing style that makes it fun and engaging to read. I loved this book and highly recommend it!

Natasha Crain, speaker; podcaster;
author, *When Culture Hates You*

Happy Lies is a wake-up call. I've studied New Age for years but was not as aware of how deeply New Thought has infiltrated the church. This book is a huge service for Christians today. I hope you will get a copy, read it, and share it with others.

Sean McDowell, PhD, professor of apologetics at Biola;
popular YouTuber; coauthor, *End the Stalemate*

In *Happy Lies*, Melissa Dougherty draws from personal experience of being within New Thought, skillfully and poignantly diagnoses the issue, highlights its key characteristics, and provides the cure: the authentic, intellectually robust, and life-giving truth of the Christian worldview.

Wesley Huff, historian; biblical scholar; Central
Canada director, Apologetics Canada Ministries

Satan's primary scheme is lies. With them, he takes people captive. It happened in the garden of Eden, and it's happening today. In *Happy Lies*, Melissa Dougherty brilliantly uncovers the deceptive teachings that many Christians unknowingly embrace—teachings that promise happiness but only lead to despair. Drawing from her personal experience and extensive research of New Thought spirituality, Melissa exposes the seductive spiritual lies that have infiltrated our culture and points readers back to biblical truth. This unique book isn't just an eye-opener—it's essential for anyone serious about discerning the deceptive teachings taking people captive today. If you care about understanding truth in a world full of spiritual confusion, *Happy Lies* is a must-read.

Tim Barnett, creator, Red Pen Logic with Mr. B;
coauthor, *The Deconstruction of Christianity*

HAPPY LIES

HAPPY
LIES

How a Movement
You (Probably) Never
Heard Of Shaped Our
Self-Obsessed World

MELISSA
DOUGHERTY

ZONDERVAN
BOOKS

ZONDERVAN BOOKS

Happy Lies
Copyright © 2025 by Melissa Dougherty

Published in Grand Rapids, Michigan, by Zondervan. Zondervan is a registered trademark of The Zondervan Corporation, L.L.C., a wholly owned subsidiary of HarperCollins Christian Publishing, Inc.

Requests for information should be addressed to customercare@harpercollins.com.

Zondervan titles may be purchased in bulk for educational, business, fundraising, or sales promotional use. For information, please email SpecialMarkets@Zondervan.com.

ISBN 978-0-310-36886-1 (softcover)
ISBN 978-0-310-36889-2 (audio)
ISBN 978-0-310-36887-8 (ebook)

Published in association with William K. Jensen Literary Agency, 119 Bampton Court, Eugene, Oregon 97404.

Cover design: Micah Kandros
Cover photos: Shutterstock
Interior design: Denise Froehlich

Printed in the United States of America

24 25 26 27 28 LBC 5 4 3 2 1

To my Lord and Savior,
Jesus Christ, the only one
who can truly make us whole

Contents

Acknowledgments

I've learned that writing a book is not a one-person project. This book would not have been possible without the support of many wonderful people. First and foremost, I would like to thank my husband and our two incredible girls for their unwavering support and patience throughout this process.

I'm especially thankful to many friends who helped me along the way. My deepest gratitude to Carl Teichrib, Natasha Crain, Phoenix Hayes (my amazing chaos coordinator), Alisa Childers, Dr. Chris Berg, Dr. Frank Turek, Dr. Rob Bowman, Jen Storto, Marcia Montenegro, Kevin Smith, Jason Jimenez, Shanda Fulbright, Paul Carter, Holly Pivec, John Ferrer, Hillary Morgan Ferrer, and my professors at Southern Evangelical Seminary, Dr. Brian Huffling and Dr. Mel Winstead. Your peer reviews, feedback, and expertise were invaluable, and I truly appreciate your attention to detail and the insights you provided.

Thank you to Greg Koukl, my friend and mentor to many. You have always been my soundboard and cheerleader.

Thank you to Teasi Cannon. This book wouldn't be what it is without your hard work and raw talent. You told me the hard things that I didn't always want to hear, and it made all the difference.

Thank you to my ride or die, Kristi. You're the type of friend people pray for. Your humor, prayers, and friendship are the jackpot in the friendship lottery. I'm slightly concerned for how much you get me. You've been there since the beginning. Thank you for being my Bastian.

To Bill Jensen, my agent. You've been in the trenches with me and on top of the mountains. Thank you for being my Barnabas.

Thank you to my entire Zondervan team, regardless of the capacity in which we worked together. Paul Pastor, your insightful feedback made this book stronger. Your dedication to and belief in this project kept me motivated even on the toughest days. Kim Tanner, with your keen eye, you took what I did and made it better. My marketing squad, Katie, Matt, and Becca, you made this process more fun than it probably should be. Stay fresh, my cheese bags.

Lastly, thank you to the two nice Jehovah's Witnesses who knocked on my door in 2011. God used you in the most unsuspecting way that caused me to reexamine everything I believed. You are a testament to his goodness, sovereignty, providence, and grace. I think of you every day and pray for your salvation often.

Introduction

Why We're Here

> Nobody chooses evil because it is evil.
> They only mistake it for happiness.
>
> —**Mary Shelley**

The year was 2011. I had a sweet, energetic one-year-old girl, and I wanted to have spiritual answers ready for her when she grew up. When I became a Christian at sixteen, I struggled with finding answers to my spiritual questions. I had experienced salvation and was *very* hungry to learn. But I lacked discipleship and solid theology. I unfortunately also felt like intellect wasn't appreciated in the overall Christian culture. This was greatly discouraging. I yearned to have meaningful discussions about doctrine, philosophy, God, the Bible, and spirituality in general.

But there was a problem. What I saw on offer felt thin, and worse, many Christians just seemed so *cynical*. In my frustration, I started looking to popular (supposedly) Christian books, videos, and teachings for answers. What I found were "open-minded" and "positive" spiritual messages that at first glance seemed intellectual and spiritually superior to what I'd first encountered.

As I "grew" in this direction, so did my practices as I applied what I was being taught. I practiced visualization and manifestation. I began to believe that I could speak things into existence. My mind had creative power, or at least that's what I was told, and so I could make my reality just with the power of some positive thinking and speaking it out into the universe.

Along with these new practices, my Christianity took on some interesting theological distinctives, such as all religions basically believed in the same God, just in different ways. People were basically good. Being a Christian worked for *me*, but we need to be tolerant. There were many paths to God, and we worship him in the way that seems right for *us*. We were living our truths. All religions taught the same basic thing: to love and be a good person. Jesus was the "Way-shower" who came to show us the divine power inside us all and how to love others. We just needed to awaken to this realization. The Bible had many mistakes and was just one of many spiritual books God had spoken through. Because of this belief, it was understood that God communicated directly to us in our hearts, and our spiritual maturity was gauged by how well we accepted this personal, direct communication from God.

Although I was a Christian, over time I was influenced by these unconventional spiritual teachings. While I didn't agree with or fully understand everything at the time, I appreciated their inclusive and tolerant principles. My beliefs were based more on experience and what was culturally popular than what the Bible taught. (It didn't help that I had an unhealthy fixation on and yearning for power and supernatural experiences.)

I was a walking coexist sticker, the epitome of "spiritual but not religious." When I looked in the mirror, I saw a god looking back at me. I believed that discovering this inner power was a deeper, more *authentic* Christianity. How was this possible? It was as if I believed everyone else was poisoned, but in reality, I was the one who needed the cure. Little did I know that what I was believing were spiritual lies. They went against historic, biblical Christian teaching. They were also usually illogical and out of keeping with the way God's world works.

In a surprising twist, when I was trying to find more spiritual answers after having my daughter, it was the visit of two friendly Jehovah's Witnesses who knocked on my door that sparked a chain reaction of research into different religions. That's when I made my unexpected discovery. I loved God. I also loved truth. That was the annoying part. I found it incredibly inconvenient at this moment of realization. These "Christian" beliefs I had held dearly for so long were a facade. A caricature. A lie. God had finally answered my prayer to know truth. The question was: Did I really want it? I had two choices: answers or exits. I could look for exits and remain in happy denial. (Safe.) Or I could lean into my desire for truth and look for answers even if doing so made me uncomfortable. (Ugh.)

Option "ugh" it was. But I leaned in.

I've been leaning in ever since. Since that day, I have come to recognize a stealthy and attractive spirituality that has been right under our noses—a destructive and unbiblical code of beliefs that has been hiding in plain sight. It preaches messages of love, light, prosperity, thought power, health, tolerance, and positivity—which all sound happy and good. It also teaches the intrinsic goodness and wholeness of humanity, inner truth, and even self-divinity. It does this all while claiming to be Christian. These messages are found in some of the world's most popular books, TV shows, celebrities, and even some pulpits. Some *big* pulpits. This culture of ours is daily increasing in its "mirror" qualities, with looking inward and relying on ourselves as the ultimate source of authority and answers. The idea of the all-powerful self is taking over entertainment, morality, media, politics—you name it. And wherever it goes, its happy lies seem so good on the surface, but underneath contribute to confusion and ultimately despair. Just look at the numbers. In this self-obsessed culture, are we happy? Is all this endless positivity *good* for us? Where is all this coming from?

The lies overlap a lot, but they seem, at first, to be random.

But what if all these toxically positive messages from many different voices all came from the same place? What I uncovered as I searched for truth surprised me. Almost without exception, these "happy lies" of spiritually toxic positivity all came from a single source—a philosophy you've probably never heard of (I hadn't) called New Thought.

The results of my journey are detailed in the following pages. During my research, I visited several churches and spiritual centers, conducted dozens of conversational interviews, many of which are referenced in this book, with people who were kind, friendly, and welcoming (even when we didn't agree), and read extensively on the subject. This book contains thousands of hours of thought and research so that you can see these connections to New Thought. But this book is more than just an intellectual trip. It's also a call to a better way of living, an invitation to respond to Jesus's call to "love the Lord your God with all your heart and with all your soul and with all your mind" (Matt. 22:37) and to "love your neighbor as yourself" (Matt. 19:19). Love and truth go hand in hand. To love Jesus is to love truth. He testifies in John 18:37 that this is why he was born: "to testify to the truth. Everyone on the side of truth listens to me" (NIV). Each chapter has a section called "Unlearning the Lies" that helps you dig a little deeper and provides practical tools to navigate any spiritual throat punches you might have received.

What's at stake here? *So* much. You'll see as we go, but the key beliefs of New Thought lead not to worship of God but to self-obsession, not to true spiritual health but to a toxic false-positivity, and not to the truth but to the same old lie that has been told from the beginning: *You can be like God.* My purpose here is to help you connect the dots between the "harmless" messages that surround us and the sinister—and despair-inducing—"happy lies" that undergird them, and teach you how to lovingly help those who might have fallen for these deceptive ideas. Along the way, I hope you'll see just how important this is to our culture and neighbors, who are desperately looking for hope in a world that feels so hopeless.

My desire is for everyone to truly listen to Jesus rather than the lies that only masquerade as his message. Ultimately, this book is about helping us learn to *love*, to truly love. To love God, our neighbors, and, yes, even ourselves.

Maybe you've talked to someone at church or the grocery store, and they said they're a Christian and believe in Jesus. But what they said didn't sound quite right, and you couldn't quite put your finger on it. Maybe you are in a position similar to what mine was, where you're frustrated with the lack of theological dialogue and discipleship. Perhaps you've been hurt by other Christians or by the church. Maybe in the healing process, some questionable theology has offered comfort. Maybe you're watching troubling cultural shifts and wondering how we got here.

At times, this book might feel like drinking from a fire hose. I've done my best to organize a *lot* of material in a way that helps you connect the dots. If you get bogged down, step back for a moment and take a little time to process. Digesting all this might take some time, especially since the implications are often disturbing to the well-meaning people who have been deceived. (Most of us have been at one time or another.)

You see, no matter who you are, the happy lies rooted in New Thought likely have significantly impacted you. Maybe they've shaped how you think. Maybe they've influenced major life decisions. Maybe *right now*, they are distracting you from growing deeper in a rich, real relationship with Jesus based on the Bible's eternal truth. My most heartfelt prayer for you is by the time you finish this book, you'll be able to clearly identify what this stealthy spirituality is, why it's dangerous, and what to do about it.

I pray the following pages will help you find clarity, confidence, solid ground, and discernment to move away from our culture's happy lies and into Christ's joyous truth.

CHAPTER 1

What You Don't Know *Can* Hurt You

How New Thought Hides in Plain Sight

> Go into all the world and tell everyone
> that they're perfectly fine the way they
> are, and to do what makes them happy.
>
> **—something Jesus never said**

Imagine waking up for the day, pouring your hug in a mug (coffee), getting comfy on the couch, and grabbing your phone to do a quick scan of your socials before facing the day. You open the first app and almost spill your coffee (the horror!). You rub your eyes to be sure you're truly awake. You are, but what you're watching seems more like a bizarre fever dream. A woman who identifies as a transgender dog is being walked on a leash by her partner.

"This must be satire," you think. It's not. This person apparently identifies as a "human pup," adopting both the appearance and behavior of a dog, and even participates in "doggie" playdates. You notice the video has millions of views, and the comments are flooded with a mixture of praise and confusion. Some applaud this person for being authentic and demand tolerance, while others are skeptical.[1]

Next, you click on some celebrity news where you discover Gwyneth Paltrow promoting goop, her well-known business, which has a section for spiritual healing placed right next to the sex toys section. Classy.

Up pops a promotion for a blog entitled "10 Books That Can Help You Develop Your Intuition." It highlights the following quote: "Tapping into the science behind the law of attraction, neuroscientist Tara Swart explores the possibility that how we think influences how we live and that trusting your intuition begins by unblocking the mind. Her helpful book teaches us how to retrain our brains to manifest and visualize, with specific exercises for a clearer pathway to achieving goals." This is just one of ten self-help books promoted to "develop your intuition."[2]

You take a big sip of lukewarm coffee and rub your eyes. You then open a different app where you're met by a popular neuroscientist who posts, "Negative thoughts can make your food less nutritious," and adds, you will "lose up to 80% of nutrition if you're in a bad mood."[3]

Huh? Kale tastes like soapy dirt, and now I can't even benefit from its nutrients if I'm having negative thoughts?

Scrolling further, you're faced with a colorful image quote saying, "Let me be their authentic self!" You read it five times because you're sure this is a grammatical error, but the comments reveal the opposite. Sentiments like, "Yes!!! Everyone should be able to live their truth!" and "Do what's right for yourself!" and "Who are we to judge!?" assure you the quote says exactly what was intended.

You decide to switch gears and venture into Christian social media.

You see a queer Christian pastor talking about how Jesus loved men and how this mirrors his own life as a queer man.[4] He says Jesus just wants us to love and live our truth. In the comments, the pastor is applauded for his acceptance and tolerance. He's not like those fundamentalist Christians who aren't with the times.

Cautiously scrolling further, you see a man talking about something called "Christ Consciousness" and how this is what Jesus was really trying to teach.[5] *Wait . . . Christ? Is this person a Christian?* A quick Google check informs you that "Christ Consciousness" unlocks your inner divine spark through visualization, affirmations, the power of the mind, and positive thinking. You are the Christ. You have the same divinity Jesus did. Just awaken to it!

Next is a post about the teachings of Joe Dispenza, whose face and name you recognize because many of your Christian friends read his work. You click on the article. It explains Dispenza's teaching on the power of the mind and quotes him saying, "There are different levels of energy. The highest vibration (which [we] can't see with our eyes) being source, down to the slowest frequency (which we can see), matter. But it's still all just energy."[6] "I have no idea what this means," you think. "It's not entirely New Age, but then again, it's also not Christian . . . or is it?" It sounds like physics as a religion with Christian words.

You watch a couple of seconds of a slick megachurch pastor giving a biblically shallow motivational speech to a cheering crowd.

You scroll on to find a popular hypercharismatic church making the news again with sensationalistic claims about manifestations of the miraculous. They say Christians have the authority to channel dead spirits, summon angels, and see people's auras. They've apparently assembled a team of Christian seers who share their insights into how God is using sound, light, energy, vibrations, and the discoveries of quantum physics.[7]

Then comes a post from an idolized yet controversial prosperity preacher. He teaches that God *must* heed our will through the power of our faith and words. We have the same power and authority as Jesus. Therefore, we should never be poor or sick.

Just when your brain is about to wave the white flag, and your coffee has now become cold brew, one more post vies for your attention. It's a sharply dressed, flashy-smiled pastor with a thick accent and a lot of gusto assuring you (and the masses) that by simply using the biblical words "I am," you can speak and manifest your thoughts into existence. In one sermon called "A Magnet for Blessings," he says, "Divine connections are tracking me down. They're already in my future. Like a magnet, I'm drawing them in!"[8]

Okay. That's enough internet for today.

What's Going On?

If you're anything like me, you could be feeling discouraged, overwhelmed, or sad about the state of our world. (And disturbed.) You might be struggling with doubts or feelings of isolation. Everything is so *confusing*.

Suicide rates are soaring even though positive thinking and tolerance dominate our culture. People are allowed more sexual freedom and "lived authenticity" but seem emptier than ever. Believing in the Bible and reading it with proper historical context and hermeneutics can be seen as hateful, homophobic, closed-minded, and bigoted. Many churches seem to make customers, not disciples. Nobody can even agree on what a woman is anymore. Self-help is the best help. Mind over matter. Reality is based on our feelings. You can speak magic words. The Bible is a self-help book. Prosperity is the gospel. We reflect Jesus's divinity. Thoughts are things. Gender is subjective. Your *species* is subjective. Subjective morality. Entitlement. Selfishness.

I'm God?

This is madness. What's going on?

• • •

"How many here have heard of the term *New Age* before?"

Hands shot up all over the room. I wasn't shocked. The group

I was speaking to wasn't just a group of nominal Christians. I was speaking at a church to an audience of well-read, well-respected, theologically mature believers. Not only had they heard of New Age, but they shared several trendy examples of that catch-all spirituality, such as chakras, spirit-channeling, crystal energy, tarot cards, and more.

But then I threw out the curve ball: "How many here have heard of New Thought?"

For a few moments, there was silence. Then a hand raised, followed by a well-meaning but failed attempt to define it.

This was the perfect setup for my talk. Most Christians are cautious of anything appearing to be New Age. But New Thought doesn't come as a red dude with a pitchfork and a pointy tail and a megaphone, yelling, "Hey, look! Weird stuff the Bible clearly teaches against!" Quite the opposite. As I mentioned in the introduction, New Thought is far stealthier and has already infiltrated our churches. The worst part? New Thought ideas can deceive Christians before New Age ideas ever will.

I continued with my presentation, telling them what I'll tell you and need you to understand: *New Thought is much trickier, stealthier, and deceptive than New Age, particularly for Christians. And most Christians have never even heard of it before.*

You're not the only one wondering if the world has gone mad. I hear from people all over the country who are trying to figure out what's happening in our culture and in the church. It's disheartening to see so much despair. But something links all of this together. From the self-help movement, affirmations, and fancy prosperity teachings to the promotion of relativistic social causes, positive thinking, and more, all of these have a common philosophy as their "ancestor." They all are part of a toxic infection called New Thought. (If you've never heard of this term before, you're not alone. It has more influence than it has recognition.)[9]

Born out of the science and reason of the eighteenth-century

Enlightenment, New Thought was a way for people to combine science with their spirituality—a sort of spirit science. If you could open your mind and change your thinking, you could do anything. Heal yourself. Become rich. Manifest a BMW. Find your soulmate. The possibilities were pretty much endless. New Thought was the "spiritual but not religious" approach of the day. In many ways, it was a protest against biblical Christianity and the moral and spiritual limitations it imposed on people.

Sherry Evans, a New Thought author, describes it this way:

New Thought is a system of thinking that virtually everyone is familiar with; They just don't know it. Numerous authors and speakers, even composers and movie producers use New Thought in their works; they just don't call it by that name. To put it simply, New Thought is about right thinking, thinking that leads to positive results—to health, wealth, peace and happiness.... New Thought is a lifestyle, a metaphysic, and a religion.... [New Thought] practices what Jesus taught: healing, unity, cooperation, seeing the good in others, and trusting God for all our needs.[10]

New Thought is the echo that started the US's cultural avalanche of the positive thinking movement. It's the one big happy lie that, in this place and in our times, has spawned many, many others.

You're Probably a Carrier

Now, don't freak out, but if New Thought were a virus, chances are you would be infected. New Thought has so deeply permeated our culture and churches, you've probably adopted some of its teachings without even realizing it. It's in some of the books on your shelves. It's in some of your favorite films and songs. Think of a cell within your body going rogue. It turns cancerous. But it doesn't realize it's cancerous. It thinks it's healthy. After all, it's *growing*, right? It starts spreading, turning other cells into cancer. Over time, it creates a deadly and destructive mass.

It's incredibly hard to avoid exposure to the New Thought virus partly because it's not just a cultural message. It's also a spiritual one. This sinister ideology has successfully blended itself into the fabric of American society and the pews of many unsuspecting Christian churches. The main reason Christians are fooled is because New Thought often *looks and sounds Christian*. New Thought teachings are dangerous not because they look scary or dangerous but because they don't. Deception isn't supposed to be obvious. It's supposed to be *beautiful*.

New Thought is incredibly adaptable to its "hosts." It looks enticing, feels good, and tricks people into pursuing their own glory, thinking it's God's will. It is a stealthy message of encouragement to live your truth, seek happiness, find your identity through sexual freedom, and think your desires into existence. Often with the name of Jesus attached as an endorsement.

Theologically, it's spiritual chaos. People think it's spiritual freedom, but it's a false, toxic freedom. Sadly, after a steady diet of this watered-down, feelings-based counterfeit, even a small taste of the true gospel can taste bitter, like bondage and hate. This is the purpose of false gospels: make evil look good and good look evil. We should wholeheartedly *oppose* these false gospels. Unfortunately, for some Christians this isn't the case. Some have a hard time seeing what the problem is, and others unknowingly believe New Thought teachings.

One prominent example of New Thought in the church involves several books and teachings from various leaders of Bethel Church in Redding, California. One book called *The Physics of Heaven* created a firestorm of controversy due to its outright embrace of New Age and New Thought teachings.[11] This isn't the only book Bethel leaders have endorsed that misuses quantum mechanics and theology to try to show that Christians can have the same power Jesus did.[12] A particularly startling example is from Patricia King, who claims to be a prophetic and apostolic minister. In her book *God's Law of Attraction: Revealing the Mystery and Benefits of Your Soul's Prosperity*, she argues that there is a counterfeit version of the law of attraction and an authentic Christian version, particularly when it comes to health and wealth.

Many Christians are attracted to the thought of "redeeming" forbidden supernatural power. But Scripture teaches the exact opposite. God repeatedly tells his followers *not* to worship him in the way the other nations do because he hates it (Deut. 12:29–32). In other words, he commands, *Do not get your spiritual practices from religions that are against me.*

In Acts 19, we read about a large group of new believers who came forward with their books of magic. They didn't sit down together to figure out how they could redeem those demonic teachings, making them somehow Christian. No, they *burned* those books.

There is no way to redeem what is, by definition, against God's way. If you're married, picture your spouse coming home with someone else and telling you, "Guess what? I found a redeemable version of adultery. It's called 'open marriage'! God wouldn't allow us to be deceived, so let's go for it!"

Jesus didn't die to redeem what he commanded us to repent from. He didn't die to give us another spiritual idol to pursue. When you see a New Thought practice, it's not a counterfeit to redeem. It's a sin to flee from.

New Thought doesn't always look like eerie mysticism and pop culture wellness mantras. It can come looking, talking, and acting like Jesus, quoting Bible verses to go along with it. Many Christians I meet are stunned to discover they've adopted some of these New Thought beliefs themselves, thinking it is what Jesus actually taught because it all sounds like "love and light."

The Remedy

Charles Spurgeon is often attributed with saying, "Discernment is not knowing the difference between right and wrong. It is knowing the difference between right and almost right." If we are going to avoid the New Thought virus and help others do the same, we need discernment. The good news for all of us is that we can grow in our ability to discern. The author of Hebrews tells us exactly how to do it: "For though by this time you ought to be teachers, you need someone to teach you again the basic principles of the oracles of God. You need milk, not solid food, for everyone who lives on milk is unskilled in the word of righteousness, since he is a child. But solid food is for the mature, for those who have their powers of discernment trained by constant practice to distinguish good from evil" (5:12–14 ESV).

If we want to grow in our ability to spot counterfeits and lies, we need to read God's Word regularly so we can develop a solid theological and biblical foundation. We need to know what Jesus really taught so we don't inadvertently adopt feel-good ideas or fall for ideas that directly contradict him. (Pro tip: Check your Bible instead of your socials first thing in the morning.)

We don't want the virus of spiritual syncretism. It has infected and devastated many lives. It has caused deep division and spiritual confusion within the church for one clear reason: it has made us the ultimate spiritual authorities, promising to give us all we desire. But the promises are really pitfalls leading to our eventual demise.

New Thought's ultimate destination reminds me of Pleasure Island in the story of Pinocchio. Naughty boys were lured there by the promise of being able to do anything they wanted—to be their own boss. For a while, it was all fun and games. But once they were gluttonously numb, an evil transformation would begin. The boys would turn into donkeys and were then used as slaves to work the salt mines. The ones who retained the ability to speak were locked in cages. Eventually, they, too, turned into donkeys. By the time they realized what was happening to them, it was too late. Pinocchio himself barely escaped the island after growing a tail and ears.

This is a great metaphor for the pleasure and even moral relief that New Thought and its peripheral beliefs can bring. It all looks and feels good, and everyone is doing it. But eventually, many who consume what it offers become broken and bruised slaves desperate to escape.

We will talk quite a bit more about it in the following chapters. But first we need to know what we're dealing with here. Where did this spirituality come from? How did it become hidden in plain sight? And why have many Christians never heard of this even though they subscribe to some of its beliefs? To answer this and more, we need to look at the surprising origins of New Thought.

CHAPTER 2

New Thought, Old Lies

The Roots of Today's Toxic Positivity

> And then she understood the devilish cunning of the enemies' plan. By mixing a little truth with it they had made their lie far stronger.
>
> —C. S. Lewis in *The Last Battle*

Though I didn't know it at the time, my first introduction to New Thought ideas happened during my childhood visits to my grandma's house, specifically, to her bookshelves. She had *so* many books—many belonged to my great-grandmother—and I loved everything about them: the tattered covers, the messy stacks. Plus, as an eleven-year-old book sniffer, I didn't think they smelled half bad. I was thrilled when I eventually inherited them.

As a child, I'd never given much thought to the contents of these books. The titles seemed so mystical and over my head. I thought only super-mature and spiritual people could understand them, and it wasn't until they were on my own bookshelf that I took a closer look. They taught about things like the power of our minds, health, prosperity, who Jesus "really" was, and the spiritual laws of the universe, like tapping into the power of your mind and your hidden inner divinity to manifest the good life.

Some books were about Jesus, salvation, the Bible, and much more. There was a little fifty-eight-page booklet called *The Seven Days of Creation: The Ground Plan of the Bible*. Next to it was *The Ten Commandments*. Both were written by a man named Emmet Fox. My grandmother's name was written in her handwriting at the top. Then there was *The Contemplation of Christ* written by Ernest C. Wilson; "Self-Reliance," an essay written by Ralph Waldo Emerson; and other more well-known books like *A Course in Miracles* by Helen Schucman and *The Power of Your Subconscious Mind* by Dr. Joseph Murphy. Quite a variety.

I remember reading some of those old books as a naive new Christian, assuming they all taught the same Christianity, same Jesus, and same message I heard from church, only at a more mystical level.

Little did I know, my treasured "Christian" library, filled with spiritual teachings that made me feel powerful, important, and inclusive, was not what it appeared to be.

Older than Grandma

As I matured in my faith and learned the Bible better, my ability to distinguish scriptural teachings from the sort of material I found in grandma's books improved. Over time, my observations led to a radical life change for the better. This is a primary reason I'm passionate about helping others recognize this New Thought lie.

In my research on this topic, I learned that New Thought isn't new at all. Even though few Christians have heard of it, the messaging has been around for a long time. New Thought makes itself look like the more open-minded, tolerant, loving, and true way to view Jesus, the gospel, and the Bible. At the turn of the twentieth century, New Thought was an attractive alternative to "dogmatic"

Christianity and accommodating to the ebb and flow of the culture. Many people were disillusioned with the Christian concept of hell, sin, a God who controlled them, and what they saw as rigid restrictions on them. They wanted a new way of thinking, a "new thought" about spirituality and God that allowed for autonomy.

Now is a good point to pause and say this: You'll notice that throughout the book I make generalizations about what New Thought is or is not. These generalizations are solid summaries of the movement, but that doesn't mean there's not an exception to them here or there. New Thought is a loose set of philosophies and contains frequent contradictions among its adherents.

The core teachings revolve around the recognition, realization, and manifestation of God in humanity. If I were to describe New Thought in one word, it would be *metaphysics*.[1] My philosopher friends get a twitch in their eye when they hear this. In philosophical and theological circles, metaphysics is the study of the nature and knowability of reality. But in New Thought, it's used more esoterically, relating to hidden or spiritual knowledge in humanity's connection to God. "Metaphysical" becomes a way of describing a feeling or a "vibe" of hidden or untapped spirituality rather than the created order of the unseen universe.

New Thought is not an organized religion. It's a philosophy and a spiritual movement. It is the background for many beliefs and philosophies accepted in American culture. From the power of mind over matter, positive thinking, and visualizing your way to health and prosperity, it's everywhere. New Thought ranks emotions, experience, and intuition as equal to reason.[2] It emphasizes the individual self as being authoritative, often while claiming Jesus taught these concepts. Jesus was a model—a universal principle—for self-realized human potential, and together, we progress to become co-divine with him. It's God made in the image of *us*. It's Jesus without the dogma. Your inner voice is the source of inspiration, health, power, and prosperity.[3]

Understanding the past is key to navigating the present. It's like the saying goes, "Know thy enemy"—or in this case, "Know thy spiritual frenemy." If you were a Christian in the seventeenth or eighteenth century during the Enlightenment, you might have been disillusioned with biblical Christianity. Reading that old religious book on your shelf (a.k.a. the Bible) was as exciting as watching paint dry. You might have been searching for a new way to think about God. Something with a less (supposedly) oppressive perspective on humanity's nature, spiritual progression, and human empowerment. You might have been looking for more control over your own healing and destiny. And you'd be in luck because this—and more—is what New Thought authors and teachers were promising. And it all starts in the same place many of these empty promises start: the occult.

Emanuel Swedenborg (1688–1772)

One of the many pioneer influencers of the New Thought movement and a pivotal figure in American spirituality today was Emanuel Swedenborg. Some have argued that an entire library could exist on how Swedenborg has affected American society and spirituality, yet most people have never heard of him.

Swedenborg was a highly respected inventor, writer, philosopher, and scientist who lived at the peak of the Enlightenment. Raised Lutheran, over time he became disillusioned with orthodox Christianity. This was a time when reason and science were much more appealing than dogmatic religion. Like many in his day, he had a spiritual crisis.[4]

But in 1743 Swedenborg had a series of intense spiritual episodes that changed the trajectory of his life. He claimed to have had vivid dreams, out-of-body experiences, numerous visions, and conversations with what he considered to be angels.[5] These encounters convinced him he was chosen by God to share this information with the world.

He believed his experiences gave him secret, elevated insight into the spirit realm, which scientists of the Enlightenment neglected. Swedenborg openly denied the Trinity, the deity of Jesus, the authority of the Bible, and all other Christian essentials. But he didn't stop at merely denying them. He *redefined* them. (In the next chapter, we'll see how New Thought has perpetuated these redefinitions in today's society.)

Swedenborg wrote numerous books about his encounters and the new spiritual information he received. His beliefs had a supernatural allure that even the most skeptical minds couldn't resist. His ideas about heaven and hell and stories of his conversations with beings from the spirit realm set the stage for America's journey into spiritualism and gave curious souls the green light to dabble in the occult.[6] Swedenborg's influence on society was rather spellbinding. Pun intended.

A significant teaching from Swedenborg is called the law of correspondence. This law says that everything in the material world has a correspondence with something in the spiritual world.[7] In other words, how someone thinks, speaks, feels, and acts connects directly to something in the spiritual world—a belief like gnosticism. This greatly influenced how Swedenborg and his followers interpreted the Bible. This framed Scripture as one long parable of spiritual revelation.[8]

In this view, every physical object is a mere shadow of something real in the spiritual realm. What we experience in the natural world with five senses is a limited version of the ultimate truth or reality of a thing—including *words*. The words we speak and read are part of the natural world. They only find their true meaning and application in the spirit realm. This extends to words written in books, like the Bible. Smell what I'm stepping in yet? According to the law of correspondence, the Bible must be *allegorical*. Its teachings are shadows of what they truly mean in the spiritual realm. Only the spiritually enlightened, like Swedenborg, can understand what's being said. These are the types of messages he would receive from his "angels."[9]

Swedenborg's view of words seemingly diminishes their meaning. Yet, ironically, because Swedenborg's theological writings were so widely read and studied, the idea of "words having power" demonstrably influenced the positive speaking and thinking phenomenon in culture and the church. This says that our success or failure in life depends on what we're thinking, feeling, and especially speaking. Therefore, words have real power. This is especially true when it comes to sickness and wealth. When somebody is sick or poor, that corresponds with something in the spiritual realm. If something isn't right in the physical realm, that means something isn't right in the spiritual realm. This is corrected through right thinking, positive confessions, and affirmations.

No discussion on Swedenborg would be complete without discussing his views on love. To him, love was the highest and most divine force and was harnessed through desire. All truth proceeds from love, not the other way around.[10] (This is a key teaching I'll cover more in later chapters.) He claimed this is what Jesus himself taught. When Jesus and his disciples healed, for example, they were exercising this transcendent virtue of love by using the power of their words. These were acts of love carried out according to the spiritual laws of the universe.[11]

Swedenborg's occult influence is mainstream today. People don't call "talking with angels" occultic. They don't call "manifesting" occultic. Yet ideas like this are your basic TikTok "theology" today. His teachings have influenced every New Thought author. In turn, they have shaped millions of people. His influence is profound.

Franz Anton Mesmer (1734–1815)

If the name Franz Anton Mesmer sounds familiar, then you might already know what this man is known for. Does that thought *mesmerize* you? Yeah, Franz Anton Mesmer is the guy known for hypnosis and hypnotherapy.

Mesmer was known for his captivating secular teachings on what he called "animal magnetism." Today, this definition might sound odd. Someone might see this as a figurative way to describe someone's charisma or their power to attract others. But Mesmer's "animal magnetism" was a pseudoscientific theory claiming that all living things, including humans, animals, and even vegetables, possess an invisible magnetic force that can be used for healing purposes.[12] He taught that people could learn to manipulate this energy according to their will. You could say Mesmer had a *hypnotic* personality.

His teachings were popular. They brought practices such as trances and hypnosis into the mainstream. People no longer associated them with the occult but saw them as a scientific marvel, especially his focus on healing with forces instead of modern medicine.

Mesmer's healing performances drew much attention. He would put people into a hypnotic trance as he performed his healings. In his early stages, Mesmer used magnets, thinking their energy had something to do with the healing process. But it didn't take long for his views to change. He concluded it wasn't the magnets that had the energy to heal but, rather, it was *him*, and he could heal his patients just by touching them.[13] This idea was adopted into popular thought. You could say he had a *magnetic* effect on people. (Okay, I'll stop.)

We see his influence in pop culture even today. When you see anyone claiming that our own mental power can move spiritual forces, you can give some credit to Mesmer for this. People were fascinated with the idea of being able to produce results by their own invisible energy. We also clearly see Mesmer's influence in past-life hypnotic therapy practices and altered states of consciousness.

Some of Mesmer's methods were a bit odd but might be familiar to some. Mesmer's healings include stories of patients becoming hysterical during the process. Some would break down in uncontrollable laughter, nausea, tears, and convulsions, with some even losing consciousness, just to name a few.[14] These odd behaviors, which could occur at random, meant the healing was "working." Interestingly, in many religious settings, including some hyper-charismatic Christian churches, we see this same reaction when people claim to have an authentic spiritual experience. They roll on the floor, get nauseous (sometimes throwing up), convulse, and break out in uncontrollable laughter. The correlation is hard to ignore. Are they having an authentic spiritual experience, or are they being mesmerized? Mesmer shows us the power of psychosomatic effects when we might be desperate for an experience or healing.

Many claimed to have been healed by Mesmer, but it was difficult to confirm healings that couldn't be objectively validated. Skeptics concluded it was imagination—not magnetism—that caused results.[15]

Ralph Waldo Emerson (1803-1882)

Ralph Waldo Emerson was a key figure of the New Thought movement and probably the most important popularizer of the philosophy. He was also a big player in transcendentalism, a philosophical and literary movement in the United States during the nineteenth century.[16] His significant popularity meant he was a formidable promoter of his ideas, which found rapid traction in America.

Transcendentalism emphasized individualism, self-reliance, the inherent goodness of people and nature, and "transcendence" over materialism and reason. In this context, transcendence means people rely on their intuitive spiritual thinking rather than on science and what they can see and feel. Adherents believed logic and reason couldn't explain the most important questions about human existence, especially spirituality. So it's from *within* each person, through their own feelings and instincts, that truth is found. (Ironically, they were using reason to come to that conclusion.) This is what Emerson called "intuition," which is the spark of Divine with us all.[17] In other words, your mind isn't the source of truth. Your feelings are. Be spiritual, not religious, and follow your heart.

Above everything, Emerson championed the expression of one's unique, authentic self. He firmly believed that what's true for you is true for all. This is what he called "genius."[18] (Not like Einstein.) He argued that conformity and dependence on the opinions of others stifled this inner "genius." According to Emerson, people should trust their intuition, follow their own path, and not be afraid to express their original ideas and insights.[19]

Emerson was a former Unitarian minister, and some would call him an American prophet, philosopher, and possibly one of the biggest proponents of "self-worth" and individualism. He wrote numerous essays, turning a lot of heads in the nineteenth century.[20] Some consider one of his most famous essays, "Self-Reliance," one of the most important pieces of written advice ever published. Trusting your *self* is the overriding message of the essay. He believed self-reliance was God-reliance operating through intuition.[21]

Emerson was one of the first people to make "following your truth" cool, paving the path for the self-help movement and your "inner authentic self" being the true you. According to Emerson, feelings and intuition should be our ultimate guide. He viewed feelings on equal ground with facts and believed we could follow the divine presence within ourselves. This is literally the thesis of most self-help books: true power is within you, not outside you. Emerson in his "Self-Reliance" essay said, "Trust thyself: Every heart vibrates to that iron string."[22]

There is some truth to what Emerson says. There's virtue in knowing who we are on the inside and not conforming to certain things in society that are popular but aren't necessarily good. But his worldview was based on the individual *self*, not the Bible or what it says about humanity and God. In his view, you're the most authentic version of yourself when you are freed from all traditions, authority, and claims to truth.[23] (Yet ironically, he has to claim truth to believe this.)

It's no surprise he wasn't a fan of organized religion. To him, all religions were ultimately a part of one great religion. The biggest obstacle to recognizing your inner divinity was Christianity or any form of organized religion.[24] Jesus was seen as a normal human who was just like us but was able to tap into his inner divine potential.[25] Emerson taught that this is something everyone can do, consequently putting God on the same level as humanity.[26]

Emerson's transcendental philosophies have much in common with New Thought, but he wouldn't have seen Jesus as more than a great moral teacher, comparable to someone like Socrates.[27] In one famous and stunning speech, Emerson scolded the Christian church for making Jesus into an object of worship.[28] He believed it was shameful that Christians look to Jesus as their authority when they should be looking within themselves. Nothing can bring you peace but yourself.[29] He taught that direct personal experience should be the litmus test of what's true, not Scripture.[30]

If that's not the battle cry of the day, I don't know what is.

Phineas Quimby (1802–1866)

No other figure in New Thought history is referred to as the father of New Thought and the mental healing movement in America more than Phineas Quimby. If Emerson and Swedenborg were the spearheads, then Quimby held the spear.

An inquisitive clockmaker from Maine, Quimby became disillusioned with the doctors of his day because he struggled with tuberculosis but received no comfort from their treatments. Eventually, Quimby claimed to have healed himself through his mind. This led him to an unusual verdict: people are only sick because they or their doctors *think* they're sick. He concluded that if you can change your thinking, you can receive healing.[31] In other words, what you believe, you create.

Quimby's belief in healing through inner faith aligned with Swedenborg's law of correspondence, linking the physical to the spiritual. Sickness is in the physical realm, but something in the spiritual domain is what needs fixing. If you have a physical body, that means you have a spiritual body. Therefore, if something's wrong with the physical body, you must fix the spiritual body so it manifests in the physical realm. How is this done? Through correct thinking. Prosperity and health are products of the mind.

Quimby was the first to really bring Jesus into the equation. He believed Jesus was the founder of what he called "spiritual science."[32] He believed his own healing methods were consistent with what Jesus and his disciples taught. He believed Jesus's true mission and purpose was to treat and heal the sick and convince us of our inner power to heal.[33]

(Forget all that save us from sin and hell stuff. *Yuck*.)

Today, we see the influence of Quimby's teachings everywhere from TikTok trends to certain church teachings claiming we all have the power to do what Jesus did, *especially* to heal and manifest prosperity. All we need is faith and an understanding of our inner power to create reality.

Many people today may not be familiar with Quimby, possibly because his teachings gained more attention than he did personally. While men like Swedenborg and Emerson were known for their charismatic personalities, network connections, and compelling public presence, Quimby had limited networking, was more focused on his teachings, and had less personal charisma. But his ideas clearly have had a ripple effect that we see today.

Mary Baker Eddy (1821–1910) and Emma Curtis Hopkins (1849–1925)

It's difficult to bring up Quimby without mentioning Mary Baker Eddy, the founder of Christian Science. (But don't let the name fool you. It's neither Christian nor science.[34]) Eddy was one of Quimby's patients who claimed to have been healed by him. But their relationship grew contentious in later years, and Eddy took Quimby's teachings and built on them.

What she created, however, made her an overbearing leader. New Thought was supposed to be a progressive and pluralistic spirituality, but Eddy moved in an entirely opposite direction, building something dogmatic and cultlike.[35] One of her students, Emma Curtis Hopkins, had strong disagreements with Eddy, and they had a falling out. After this, three sects emerged:

- **Unity Church:** Founded by Charles (1854–1948) and Myrtle Fillmore (1845–1931). This is probably the most well-known sect of New Thought. Their enormous headquarters are in Unity Village, which is right outside Kansas City, Missouri. Some notable people affiliated with Unity have been Betty White, Marianne Williamson, and Maya Angelou.
- **Church of Divine Science:** Founded by Malinda Cramer (1844–1906) and Nona Brooks (1861–1945).
- **Religious Science:** This now goes by the name Center for Spiritual Living (CFSL) and was founded by Ernest Holmes (1887–1960). Holmes was deeply influenced by theosophy and Ralph Waldo Emerson and his transcendental beliefs. Holmes's biggest contribution to the New Thought movement was "affirmations," which are positive statements or declarations that people repeat to themselves to encourage a positive mindset and personal growth (more on this in chapter 6). In fact, Louise Hay, a notable member of CFSL

and one of the biggest contributors to the popularization of affirmations today, was also the founder of the popular New Age publishing company Hay House.[36] Another significant person Holmes heavily influenced was Norman Vincent Peale, a minister and author of *The Power of Positive Thinking*.[37] Peale was also cofounder with his wife of the popular *Guideposts* devotionals marketed toward Christians.

All are still around today. These religious denominations are relatively small, but their ideas are extremely popular and permeate society.[38] Although I only briefly mentioned Emma Curtis Hopkins, keep her in mind because her influence, particularly in the origins of the prosperity gospel, plays an integral part in later chapters.

It's at this historical crossroads where we see an ardent feminist focus in New Thought. Many women found New Thought teachings to be a spiritual alternative to what they considered the harsh, patriarchal Christianity of the day. This held women back, and the Bible's emphasis on male leadership was oppressive and insulting. New Thought undergirded a spiritual social justice feminist movement. In fact, Emma Curtis Hopkins created the first national network of New Thought organizations while establishing the first seminary to ordain women in large numbers.[39]

Warren Felt Evans (1817–1889)

Warren Felt Evans was an American Methodist minister who drank deeply from the well of Swedenborgian thought. He was a former patient of Quimby's who took his system of mental healing to the next level.

Evans became the first published author in the mind-cure movement, which later became New Thought. Adopting many of Quimby's beliefs, Evans wanted to help people discover the "Universal Christ within" and unleash their true selves.[40] Like other New Thought gurus, Evans believed every religion and philosophy has something to teach us. By sampling from each, we can unlock the secrets of the universe and our inner potential.[41]

We see the fruit of this today in claims such as, "There are many roads to truth! There are different truths to find! Quit judging! You're a closed-minded fundamentalist!"

According to Evans, receiving healing is based on how mentally open people are to it and their connection with the Divine Mind (New Thought's name for God). In other words, fix the mind, and you'll fix the body.[42] Want health, wealth, and prosperity? Check your connection with the Divine Mind, then believe with *no* doubt you already have it. Speak as if it's true. Believe, and you will receive.[43] Visualize and manifest. After all, doesn't Jesus affirm this in Matthew 7:7–12 and Mark 11:24? Jesus says to ask the universe for anything we want and expect to receive it—if we have no doubt. (Can we say faulty interpretive skills?) To Evans, Jesus was just a regular dude living in perfect vibrational harmony with perfect faith. This empowered him to impart healing to others and show us how to do the same.[44]

Evans played a key role in laying the foundation for a core concept in New Thought: "Thoughts are things."[45] (I hope you'll continue to spot this "thoughts are things" concept throughout this book, especially when we discuss the law of attraction.)

We can thank Evans for changing the spiritual fabric of American society. Because his teachings were attractive to both religious and secular audiences, his influence can be seen far and wide. Teachers and gurus of nearly every flavor have taken the New Thought baton and run with it. They promise the good life through positive thinking, positive affirmations, prosperity, self-expression, inner identity, and mental harmony rather than through Christian values and scriptural integrity.[46]

Napoleon Hill (1883–1970) and *A Course in Miracles*

Napoleon Hill is one of the more well-known New Thought authors. His books have sold millions of copies and are still in print. His New Thought teachings have been ingrained into the minds of millions of people. I'm stunned by how many Christians read Napoleon Hill but don't realize how deep into the occult he was.

For example, in his insanely popular book *Think and Grow Rich*, in his chapter on "The Sixth Sense," Hill claims to have regular meetings with several historical figures so he can learn from them. Some of these figures include Thomas Edison, Charles Darwin, Abraham Lincoln, Henry Ford, the apostle Paul, Plato, and even Jesus himself. He says, "These meetings became so realistic that I started to be fearful of their consequences and discontinued them for several months. The experiences were so uncanny, I was afraid if I continued them, I would lose sight of the fact that the meetings were purely experiences of my imagination."[47] He said what got him back in the game was Abraham Lincoln. Hill was awakened one night and saw Lincoln at his bedside. Apparently, Lincoln convinced Hill to continue these meetings.[48]

But that's not all. He also wrote a book called *Outwitting the Devil*. The entire book is an interview—with Satan.

This isn't the only example of spirit contact in a popular book. Another example comes from *A Course in Miracles* (*ACIM*) written in 1976 by Helen Schucman. She claimed she heard a voice that identified itself as Jesus. It told her to write down these new revelations.[49] Ironically, Schucman didn't endorse her own book. She was always unsettled about the whole project, even from the beginning.[50]

ACIM describes God as one with all creation, and the world around us as an illusion created by our false selves. Our true selves are perfect and whole. It's only by awakening to Christ Consciousness that we achieve a return to our true selves.[51] (More on Christ Consciousness in the next chapter).

ACIM could be considered New Thought that's been cross-pollinated with New Age, mysticism, psychology, gnosticism, and outright nonsense. It's similar to New Thought posing as Christian and using Christian terms, but it teaches the opposite of the Bible.[52] Many Christians—the ones sitting beside you in the pews and volunteering with you at bake sales—quote *ACIM*, thinking it's Scripture. I've personally had this happen.

Marianne Williamson, a Unity minister from 1998–2002,[53] helped *ACIM* blow up in the early 1990s with her book *A Return to Love: Reflections on the Principles of a Course in Miracles*, endorsed by Oprah. Oprah has also endorsed *The Secret*, another incredibly popular New Thought book that propelled the law of attraction into widespread recognition. What *The Secret* did for the law of attraction, Marianne Williamson did for *A Course in Miracles*.[54]

Much, Much Older than Grandma

We've only briefly explored some eighteenth and nineteenth-century New Thought figures and their lasting impact on culture and the church. Although their methods and terms aren't ancient, the lies lurking behind them are. Humanity being divine, whether in ancient paganism or revived gnosticism, is a recycled deception from Satan.

Demoting God and elevating humanity diminishes truth and morality while elevating pride and entitlement. That was Satan's plan all along. He knows we can't carry the burden of being our own God for long. He knows we flourish only when we're in a right relationship with our Creator, living as he alone knows is best. What better way to destroy God's beloved image bearers than to turn them inward rather than upward? New Thought is a spirituality Satan loves. It turns truth on its head, elevating error as something positive, beautiful, and self-affirming.

Staying Power

New Thought teachings wouldn't stand the test of time if they failed every test for truth or goodness. Every successful counterfeit has the appearance of the real. The same is true for New Thought. These teachings do contain some truth. They're practical and not *all* bad or wrong. That's what makes these ideas so spiritually dangerous and enticing. They're attractive to human nature. And sometimes the practices seem to *work*.

New Thought teachings continue to sell books and programs because people claim to have experienced results. People report they've been healed or have gained prosperity through these methods, changing their lives for the better. Of course, some of these correlations could be mere coincidence, psychosomatic, or even fake. But reports of powerful personal experiences and a general trust in pragmatism—"it worked for me"—have contributed to New Thought's staying power. If it feels good and it yields results, then it "works" and must be true. Furthermore, if it feels good and works for me, it must be *morally good*. This concept is discussed further in chapter 7.

New Thought stands the test of time because it changes with the times. It's like a spiritual and cultural chameleon changing with anything and everything. It's not restrictive but progressive. It's the ultimate spiritual shape-shifter.

Bait and Switch

Hurting people are drawn to New Thought. People who struggle with anxiety, depression, self-image difficulties, and a host of other issues are drawn to its ideas, which seem spiritually enriching and look like love. New Thought opens its arms wide at first but then leaves people more broken than they were to begin with. It baits you in, then leaves you wondering how you got hooked. This is a perfect setup.

It reminds me of Mother Gothel from the movie *Tangled*. Mother Gothel kidnaps Rapunzel and masquerades as her mom. Over time, she mentally and emotionally abuses Rapunzel, creating a toxic relationship. Rapunzel begins to wise up and runs away. She gets close to freedom, but Gothel is one step ahead. She hires a gang of bad guys to kidnap Rapunzel so she can swoop in and play rescuer. Did you catch that? Gothel manipulated a problem (bait) so she could be that hero (switch). Rapunzel's salvation was an illusion.

This is what New Thought ideas do to the unsuspecting. They attune to our struggles, charm our pride, create a mess of things, and then masquerade as the solution. Challenging the assumptions and apparent solutions offered by New Thought labels *you* an enemy of God and progress—and in need of more New Thought healing, of course. This isn't salvation. This is slavery.

New Thought is like an online predator. It spiritually baits, grooms, and woos you with positivity, coexist stickers, good feelings, an inclusive love, and promises of power, often under the "Christian" label. It hijacks Christian doctrines and words, redefining them, putting the unsuspecting in theological choke holds.

So let's build up our defenses. Let's define some of those terms.

CHAPTER 3

The Teachings

Some Terminology and Beliefs of New Thought

> The motto of the old crusaders was "God with us." The motto of the New Thought is "God in us."
>
> —Horatio Dresser

Christic. **Christian, what** do you think of when you hear this term? With confidence, I can assume most of you naturally think this refers to Jesus. You might be thinking, "Um, of course, it's Jesus, Mel. He's the Messiah, the Anointed One. What else could this possibly mean?"

I'll tell you. When someone with New Thought beliefs says "Christ," you might find yourself agreeing with them without realizing the consequences of this.

"Christ is in me!" they say.

"Amen!" you heartily respond. It's in the Bible, right? This sounds good. This sounds *scriptural*. But in New Thought, familiar words like *Christ* can mean something altogether different. Before we know it, our blind agreement with one word can lead to acceptance of an entirely unbiblical teaching. No matter how much we might love Jesus, we could find ourselves involved in spiritual practices he forbids. Ain't that a real wild card? If you discover— much to your dismay—that some of your beliefs line up with New Thought ideas, the culprit is likely undefined terms.

Get this. New Thought teachings do not *deny* God, salvation, sin, or Jesus. Followers will say they affirm Christian doctrines like justification, grace, and even the atonement. But they *redefine* them. Their definitions look nothing like biblical ones.

Imagine a vegan who loves meat. They're tired of the limitations of fundamental veganism. Blech. So they decide to keep the "vegan" name and some behaviors they resonate with but have opposite beliefs. Are they really vegan then? This is how it works in New Thought. Same words, different definitions. But with the "Christian" label.

How can this be? Because, as noted in chapter 2, New Thought is a *metaphysical* spin on Christianity. This means they look *beyond* the literal historical account of Christianity to what they consider a more awakened spiritual perspective. Add to that ideas like the one I heard from a New Thought reverend who claims that following God isn't about your beliefs and definitions but your *values*—the way you live your life. In other words, he teaches that people can define Jesus and the Bible however they like as long as they're a good person (with "good person" defined subjectively, of course).

There's a lot of confusion here, so let's take some time to sort through some core terms and teachings.

The Occult

Imagine a big bowl with ingredients. Inside are tarot cards, parapsychology, fortune-telling, astrology, witchcraft, divination, spirit guides, mysticism, gnosticism, law of attraction, satanism, magic, and self-worship—maybe with a dash of salt—then stir it all up. What do you get? Besides a lot of heartburn, the occult.

The dictionary defines *occult* as "supernatural, mystical, or magical beliefs, practices, or phenomena." Occult practices and beliefs have been around since the beginning of time, tempting, deceiving, and wounding people around the globe. Its tentacles wrap around people of all ages, starting with the young and naive (Ouija board anyone?)

The Bible is filled with warnings against participating in occult beliefs and practices. From cover to cover, God warns his children to avoid having anything to do with the occult practices of pagan nations. The Israelites were repeatedly warned and judged for adopting practices such as human sacrifice, speaking to the dead, and worshiping pagan (demonic) gods. But before we snub our noses at them, thinking how foolish they were, let's remember that the rise of the occult in our day and beyond is one of the signs of the end times (1 Timothy 4:1). We can be just as ignorant if we're not prepared.

You might be thinking, "Not me! I have nothing to do with the occult." But I'm going to go out on a limb and say, "Don't be so sure." Why would I say that? Because throughout the rest of this book, I hope to demonstrate how New Thought ideas have infiltrated Christian settings. Whether we like it or not, New Thought (and its close cousin, New Age) is one of the ingredients in the occult soup. New Thought aligns far more with the occult than it does with the Bible.

Close Cousins

I have always described myself as an "ex–New Ager," a term most people recognize and understand. To be accurate, however, I'm mostly an "ex–New Thoughter." (It's not as smooth as "ex–New Ager" though, is it?) But something needs to be cleared up about this.

When people might hear "New Thought," because they are

unfamiliar with it, they might think it's the same as New Age. *It's not.* Both are distinct. New Age and New Thought share a fundamental belief that humanity is ultimately divine. Both are syncretistic in nature, merging many beliefs and blending with whatever is popular in the culture. They freely cherry-pick beliefs and accept more than they reject. Because they're so broad in what they'll accept into their worldview, their filter for what's true is simply whatever works for them, serves them, and feels good.[1] But New Age is rooted in more Eastern mysticism, Buddhism, and Hinduism and doesn't identify as a Christian movement, whereas New Thought is more gnostic in origin and claims to be Christian.

Personally, when I was in New Thought, I created a patchwork quilt of ideas. I believed in a form of reincarnation and crystal energies and wanted to astral project and get a spirit guide. But most of my beliefs were grounded in what I erroneously thought were Christian teachings. I believed people were free to choose their own spiritual path.

Yes, New Age and New Thought share commonalities. But let's briefly look at some distinctly New Age teachings and practices so we can more readily spot some key differences. This isn't an exhaustive list, but New Agers engage in the following:

- crystal energies
- essential oils (Oils and crystals aren't New Age in *origin* but New Agers consider them power objects. Many people believe oils and crystals can have vibrational frequencies attracting desirable outcomes or provide healing.)
- astrology
- numerology
- tarot
- chakra balancing
- spirit animals
- sacred geometry

- feng shui
- tai chi
- yoga
- reincarnation, past lives, and karma (Some in New Thought might have believed in a form of this too.)
- ancient aliens / ufology (This is a dense topic, but many New Agers are fixated on extraterrestrials who were once on earth and how they shaped human civilization.)
- starseeds
- lightwork
- spirit guides (Though as we've seen with people like Swedenborg, there is some crossover to New Thought here.)
- occasional reliance on psychedelic drugs for a spiritual experience
- astral projection
- ascended masters, as well as Jesus as an ascended master who can be channeled (Both New Age and New Thought can focus on the mystic teachings of the Bible and Jesus, but most New Agers wouldn't say they're Christian like New Thoughters could.)
- a goal to bring a New Age of enlightenment to the earth, a spiritual utopia
- Mother Earth worship
- transcendental meditation
- the zodiac
- tapping and EFT (emotional freedom techniques)
- Reiki (New Thought has its own type of energy healing through different means.)
- Akashic Records

Most people lump in every strange teaching under the umbrella of "New Age." However, this would be incorrect. In my case, in 2011, when I started reforming my beliefs back to the Bible,

I noticed a distinction in what I had believed compared with what other ex–New Agers believed. Former New Agers would come to me for counsel or advice about these beliefs. But I simply wouldn't know how to answer most of them since I was unfamiliar with many New Age beliefs.

I would argue that it's *New Thought* that has informed many New Age teachings, not the other way around. This explains why we see such an overlap between the two and why New Agers have adopted many New Thought beliefs.

Not Even Close

While New Thought can overlap with New Age beliefs because they are syncretistic, the same cannot be said of historical, biblical Christianity. What I mean is that Christian teachings result from a systematic study of the entire Bible using sound interpretive methods (hermeneutics), which involve a plain reading of Scripture. This ensures a comprehensive understanding of biblical messages that doesn't change with the times but is preserved through the times.

With this in mind, let's compare how Christianity and New Thought define key teachings and terms, which can help clarify things for those who may not see the differences.

God

According to Christianity

Christians are monotheists who believe in one personal, holy God *who is separate from them*—another being altogether. He is not absorbed in the fabric of creation, as pantheism suggests (Isa. 55:8–9; Ps. 97:9; Rom. 1:18–22). Our sin has separated us from God because he is holy, and humanity is not (Isa. 59:2). Christians look outside themselves for true divinity, not within. God is omnipresent (everywhere present) but not within creation (Jer. 23:23–24, Acts 17:24–25). God is spirit (John 4:24). God is infinite and immeasurable, matchless, incomparable, and immutable or unchanging (Ps. 86:8–10; Jer. 10:6; Mal. 3:6; Dan. 7:14). He is all-knowing, with complete power and authority (Ps. 44:21; Ps. 115:3; Rom. 11:33–36). God is just, loving, and truthful (Isa. 30:18; 1 John 4:7–12; John 14:6). God judges sin but also offers forgiveness (Rom. 6:23). A Christian's identity and ultimate purpose as God's image bearers is inextricably linked to God's attributes and nature (2 Cor. 5:17–21).

God reveals himself as the Great I Am (Ex. 3:14), not made like us or to please us, but to bring glory to him. He prioritizes our holiness over our happiness (1 Pet. 1:16). This is because he is the epitome of goodness (Ps. 25:8–9), but that doesn't mean he always keeps us from danger.

Get the identity of God wrong, and everything is wrong.

According to New Thought

New Thought claims a more enlightened "metaphysical" view of God, saying God is not a "he" (or personal being) but a universal or Divine Mind. God is an "it."[2] An example of this is the late Bishop Carlton Pearson, a New Thought minister of New Dimensions Church in Tulsa, Oklahoma. He said, "God Dwells with Us, in Us, Around Us, as Us."[3] Pearson described God as an "it," a collective consciousness who spoke to him and told him the Bible was wrong.[4] In this panentheistic view (which is a contradicting combination of theism and pantheism), New Thought makes God an indifferent creative force, energy, the universe, or a spiritual source. New Thought also equates "God" with "love." Consider the following verses:

> I am God, and there is none else.
>
> **—Isaiah 45:22 KJV**

> In the beginning was the Word, and the Word
> was with God, and the Word was God.
>
> **—John 1:1**

> In the beginning, God created the heavens and
> the earth.
>
> **—Genesis 1:1**

Here's how someone with New Thought goggles on would read them:

> I am Love, and there is none else.
>
> **—Isaiah 45:22**

> In the beginning was the Word, and the Word
> was with Love, and the Word was Love.
>
> **—John 1:1**

> In the beginning, Love created the heavens and
> the earth.
>
> **—Genesis 1:1**

"God is love" (1 John 4:8) is taken quite literally.

New Thought teaches that biblical Christians incorrectly attribute human characteristics to God to make him seem more personal. They say as humans, to make sense of God, we call God "he" and assign certain names and identities such as Jesus, I AM, Father, King, etc.[5] We needlessly give humanlike qualities to something impersonal.

In New Thought, God is sometimes viewed as a cosmic genie granting happiness and prosperity. They reason that because God is *only* good, love, and light, then God must want to give only goodness to us. New Thought author Emmet Fox wrote in his essay

The Presence that "God never sends sickness, trouble, accident, temptation, nor death itself; nor does He authorize these things. We bring them upon ourselves by our own wrong thinking. God, Good, can cause only good."[6] This view merges theism and pantheism, creating a god that is both personal and impersonal. This is contradictory.

New Thought teaches that God is within all of *us*, waiting to be awakened. The goal is recognizing our spiritual birthright as humans. Through techniques like affirmation, visualization, and meditation, everyone can access and harness the power of God. In New Thought, God progresses and changes over time with humanity.

Jesus Christ

According to Christianity

According to Christianity, Jesus was and is the unique Son of God, the image of the invisible God (Col. 1:15). To know who God is, we look at Jesus.

In the person of the Son, God became incarnate (John 1:14). Jesus was *not* just an enlightened human comparable to someone like Buddha. He is Buddha's king, his Creator. The title "Son of God" indicates that Jesus is literally "of God," which means he was human, but he also shared in God's very nature, making him divine. In Colossians 2:9, it says, "In Christ all the fullness of the Deity lives in bodily form" (NIV). Jesus is truly God and truly human.

The Son of God became the Son of Man and is, therefore, the "bridge" between God and humanity (John 14:6; 1 Tim. 2:5). Jesus was the *unique* Son of God who died on the cross for our sins. He then rose again from the dead, proving he was God and conquering death (John 3:16; 1 Pet. 2:24; 1 Cor. 15:3–4). Jesus is the only one to be raised from the dead, never to die again. The resurrection of Jesus was an isolated event occurring once in the history of the world. It is through Jesus alone we can have forgiveness of sins, reconciliation with God, and eternal salvation (Acts 4:12, Rom. 6:23).

Jesus *exclusively* claims the label "Christ." This isn't his last name. It's a unique title meaning "anointed one," who's prophesied throughout the Old Testament as the long-awaited Messiah to whom the Jewish people looked for their salvation and redemption (Matt. 16:15–16). *Christ* is synonymous with Jesus himself. He is the Messiah—the only one who fulfilled prophecy and demonstrated through many signs and miracles that he is *Lord of all*. God of all. This means if Jesus is your Lord, he sets the rules. He calls the shots. And he says those who love him will obey him (Acts 10:36, John 14:15).

According to New Thought

According to New Thought, Jesus is a great human teacher who awakened his inner divinity. He's comparable to Buddha or Gandhi. Jesus was the embodiment of a coexist sticker. He taught love, acceptance, and tolerance—the perfect social example for us.

The resurrection of Jesus is not taken literally. It's a metaphor for the constant spiritual process within us. Resurrection symbolizes triumphs and victories over life's challenges. One New Thought book puts it this way:

> Once we have gleaned, even a rudimentary understanding of what [metaphysical Christianity] means, we begin to view the crucifixion of Jesus not as an experience of helpless martyrdom, nor the cross of Calvary as the ultimate symbol of suffering, humiliation, and sacrifice, but rather as supreme symbols of *victory*. We learn to approach personal times of severe testing—crucifixion experiences—with a growing awareness of the ever-present and victorious Christ Spirit within. . . . In order for the life-transforming power of the

Christ principle to work on our behalf, however, it must be *activated*, called forth from the realm of Divine potential to be utilized in the practical dilemmas of our daily lives.[7]

Crucifixion is redefined to represent the overwhelming obstacles we face during our lives, whether it's a medical diagnosis, the loss of your job, a bad breakup, or any challenge you can think of. In other words, "resurrection" is you conquering your Goliaths. Just find the David in you.

One woman I interviewed in a New Thought church said she believed Jesus was murdered because he taught a suppressed truth: that humans are actually gods. She said this truth was forbidden by the fundamentalists of Jesus's day and is still being suppressed today. According to her, Jesus spoke truth to power, and they killed him for it.

Then there's the term *Christ*.

To understand New Thought, it's essential you understand this: In New Thought, *Jesus* and *Christ* are *not* identical. They are *not* used interchangeably.

Remember, New Thought is *metaphysical* Christianity. *Christ* has a secret metaphysical meaning that is a *separate entity* from Jesus the man. *Christ* is the dormant inner divine spark within all humanity. It's God in us. In New Thought, what made Jesus divine was his becoming conscious of "Christ" within. He demonstrated that when we're properly attuned, "Christ" is a channel for humans to connect to health, prosperity, abundance, and happiness.[8] I mentioned Phineas Quimby in chapter 2. He popularized this teaching saying that "Jesus" was the historical figure from ancient times, while "Christ" was more about a deeper, metaphysical truth. He believed that this "Christ" referred to a universal divine mind or intelligence that anyone could tap into for healing and insight. To Quimby, "Christ" wasn't exclusive to Jesus—it was a divine consciousness that everyone could access.[9]

In other words, Jesus, a historical figure from Nazareth, was just a man who obtained the Christ Consciousness, an enlightened state for all humanity to achieve, including you. New Thought has a name for this: the "Christ principle." Jesus was *the* example of this divinity. You have the potential to be just as much the I Am, the Christ, as Jesus was. In the Christ Consciousness, you can do everything he did.

New Thought says humanity's true nature is divine and celebrates this untapped divine potential. This is why "I am" statements are crucial in New Thought. They shape your reality and declare your divine identity. In this context, "I am" is not just a statement about your egoic self but a recognition of the divine self within. We are "gods in embryo," as we progress in awakening to our divine development toward the Christ principle.[10]

The Christ Consciousness informs another popular New Thought teaching: the true self and the false self. Your true self is divine and is the real you. It's the "Christ" within. You must overcome your false self, or ego, to awaken the "Christ."

Thomas Merton, a Trappist monk and mystic, is highly respected and is often quoted in New Thought circles. He says about the true self that "at the center of our being is a point of nothingness which is untouched by sin and by illusion, a point of pure truth, a point or spark which belongs entirely to God." This spark within us is "like a pure diamond, blazing with the invisible light of heaven" and is "in everybody."[11] Biblically, there is no false self. There is no true self. There are only two kinds of selves: the old self and the new self.[12]

According to New Thought, when Jesus performed miracles or healed, he was merely using his Divine Mind to its full potential, modeling something we can all achieve. I grew up being taught he was the Wayshower, the example of our potential. Whatever Jesus did, we could do—literally. This includes walking on water and even overcoming death. (Yet *nobody* has been able to achieve this.) He excelled at mind over matter and was our teacher, not our savior.

It's not a problem for New Thoughters when a Christian says Jesus is God. But they would *not* agree he's *uniquely* God. He's only the savior in the sense that he showed humanity their divine potential, not because he saved sinners from punishment. Let me give you a brief example of how "Christ" can be redefined. Let's use a famous verse that most Christians go to when they want to show that Jesus is the only way to the Father: John 14:6. It says, "Jesus answered, 'I am the way and the truth and the life. No one comes to the Father except through me'" (NIV). A New Thoughter would *heartily* agree with you! Of course "Christ" is the way, truth, and life!

See what happened there? Because "Jesus" and "Christ" have two different meanings, they interpret this verse to mean that Jesus was speaking from the posture of *the Christ Consciousness*. In this interpretation, *anyone* can be the way, truth, and life.

Jesus was a normal human being with flaws, just like any of us. He gradually grew into his full divine nature through living a good life, loving others, and through his own personal struggles and temptations.[13] And so can we.

Prayer

I'm going to put a pin in this one. You'll have to wait until chapter 7 to learn more about how New Thought defines prayer.

The Trinity

According to Christianity

According to Christianity, although he is one being, God exists as three distinct persons: the Father, the Son, and the Holy Spirit (Matt. 3:16–17). One way to say it is God is one *what* with three *whos*. Each is called God and has different tasks (John 6:27; John 1:1; Acts 5:3–4). It's not tritheism with three separate gods, but monotheism with a God that is not completely understandable on human terms. The God of Abraham, Isaac, and Jacob was not created by human minds or human hands (John 1:1–3; Acts 17:24–28).

According to New Thought

In New Thought, the Trinity is a radically different concept. It's a symbolic metaphysical representation of the divine trichotomous nature of human beings as spirit, mind (or soul), and body. According to New Thought author Emmet Fox, it's also the principal aspects of God, which are life, truth, and love.[14]

The historic Christian view of the Trinity is limited. New Thought has the true, yet hidden, meaning. The New Thought Trinity consists of three phases of mind—Father, Son, and Holy Spirit—each representing a spiritual level of mental, emotional, and physical existence.[15]

Satan / Evil / Heaven and Hell

According to Christianity

In Christianity, heaven and hell are all literal places, evil is not metaphorical but objectively real, and Satan is a literal spiritual being who is our enemy (1 John 3:8; 2 Cor. 11:3; Mark 9:43). Evil comes from both humanity and Satan because humans are depraved (Rom. 3:10, 23; Eccl. 7:20; Ps. 143:2). Heaven is where God resides, and hell is reserved for Satan and his demons. It's a quarantine for evil and depicts the justice and wrath of God (Ps. 103:11; 2 Cor. 5:1–4; Matt. 25:41).

According to New Thought

According to New Thought, heaven and hell are states of mind, not literal places. Satan is not a literal being but a representation of the false self.[16] Evil is the unawakened self. In other words, according to New Thought, anything labeled as "evil," such as someone flying into the Twin Towers or a parent abandoning their child, is a result of someone acting in their false self. The reason for pain, suffering, and evil is humanity's ignorance of their inner divinity. They are asleep to their true self and have created their own personal hell, which is a false state of consciousness.[17]

New Thought affirms Universalism, the belief that everyone will eventually be saved or ascend into an ambiguous enlightened state after death. Heaven is within, meant for you to find here and now. As a Christian influenced by New Thought, I also believed in Universalism. I saw Jesus as dying for the whole world, whether they knew about him or not. I reasoned that as long as you believed in God, and loved him in your own way, then that was sufficient.

The Gospel / Salvation / Born Again

According to Christianity

The core of Christianity is the gospel, centered on the person and work of Jesus. According to the Bible, Jesus is the Son of God who came to earth in human form to offer himself as a sacrifice for the sins of humanity. He lived a perfect and sinless life, died on the cross, and rose again from the dead on the third day. The gospel message is considered "good news" because it offers a way for humanity to be saved from the consequences of sin and death (Heb. 9:26; 2 Cor. 5:21; Col. 1:20; Rom. 1:16).

The Bible teaches that all human beings have sinned and continually fall short of God's standard of righteousness (Rom. 3:23). The consequence of sin is death, both physical and spiritual, which means eternal separation from God (Rom. 6:23). Jesus bore our sin on the cross as a substitute for sinners, which Christians know as the atonement (1 Pet. 2:24; 3:18; Isa. 53:5). Christians believe we can't save ourselves. We need someone to pay a price we can't even come close to paying (1 Pet. 1:18–19). This is why Jesus *alone* is the only one who can reconcile humanity to God. We recognize our sinfulness and bow to Jesus as our Lord and God. We then participate in the Great Commission, spreading the gospel to the world.

According to New Thought

New Thought has an all-inclusive definition of salvation. The "good news" is that all people have the potential for spiritual awakening. They have the power of God within themselves to create positive change in their lives. This is an ongoing process.[18] It teaches that by focusing on the positive, we can overcome challenges, manifest abundance, and live fulfilling lives. Salvation all starts in your mind. New Thought teaches that each person can produce salvation when they turn from negative thoughts to positive thoughts.[19]

Marianne Williamson put it this way on Facebook: "Salvation is not just a theological concept. It is metaphysical and psychological as well. The only thing to be saved from is our own fear-based thinking."[20]

In New Thought, to be "born again" means a deconstruction of your false self and awakening (being *born anew*) as your true self, the Christ Consciousness. It's a dismantling and restructuring of your consciousness.[21] The atonement is similar. One New Thought author describes it as a reestablishment of our conscious awareness of our true selves. It's realizing God not only lives in us but lives *as us*.[22] Atonement is separated into three parts: at-one-ment, which is our awakening from our false separation from the Divine Source (God within).[23]

The gospel of New Thought is ultimately a self-help message of hope, empowerment, and spiritual transformation—with *you* as the savior. Our only sin, and the only evil, is our ignorance of our true authentic selves. True salvation is achieved through "correct" thinking, altering or creating reality through your thoughts, and the realization of one's divine self.[24]

Love

According to Christianity

Love and truth are central principles deeply rooted in the Bible's teachings. Jesus emphasizes that the greatest commandments are to love God with all your heart, soul, and mind and to love your neighbor as yourself (Matt. 22:37–39). He warns about loving the things of this world. You can't love both God and the world (1 John 2:15–17).

First Corinthians 13, often referred to as the "Love Chapter," provides a detailed description of love. It delights in truth, not evil. God's ultimate act of love is by becoming human and atoning for the sins of humanity (John 1:1; 3:16; Heb. 9:12–14). God is love, and whoever loves has been born of God (1 John 4:7).

Unbelievers can display love. This is clear. We are all image bearers of God, and love is a human trait. However, according to the Bible, human love is shortchanged. It's *incomplete*. Through our obedience to God, his love is made *complete* in us as believers (1 John 4:7–12).

Love is only *one* attribute of God.[25] God's attributes do *not* mean he's a mix of parts of these things. For example, he's not part love or part holy. God is not *made up of* goodness, mercy, justice, and power. He *is* goodness, mercy, justice, and power. So we can't say love, for example, is more central to God than sovereignty or vice versa.

In the Christian faith, truth and the true meaning of love and compassion are found in Scripture personified in Jesus. The Bible emphasizes many times that truth and love go together.

According to New Thought

According to New Thought, love is a spiritual cosmic power. It's the ultimate spiritual virtue. God and love are synonymous, and fear is seen as the enemy and opposite of love. New Thought will take passages such as "God is love" in 1 John 4:8 and "there is no fear in love" in 1 John 4:18 and claim that these affirmations of love ultimately overshadow anything negative in the world or about God. Love is why there is no wrath, condemnation, hell, justice, or negativity in God's character. These ideas are fear-filled and are discarded.[26] Love is God, not the other way around.

New Thought also equates what's *true* with what's *loving*. The term *fundamentalist* is often used as a derogatory term referring to those who believe in what they would consider "negative" attributes of God mentioned previously. Many times, this perspective comes from a negative experience with Christians that informs their view of love and God. I admit there are theological ditches people fall into when it comes to what is "loving" according to God.

The following chart can help explain these ditches and show the biblical position.

New Thought	Ideal	Elitist / Legalistic
Love is God	God is love	Truth is God
Love is Truth	God is truth	Truth is Love

The ditches make the mistake of overemphasizing one attribute over the other and throws off the entire balance. New Thought puts love before God, but they do so at the cost of truth. I'll cover truth more in chapter 4.

Humanity

According to Christianity

According to Christianity, God loved and created humanity, but we all fall short of the glory of God. The Bible is clear: *nobody* is good; we've all sinned (Rom. 3:9–20). *Compared to God, humans are not good.*

We are made in the image of God, but this does *not* mean we are the *same* as God or divine as he is (Ps. 8:4–8). We rule creation on his behalf and are connected to him spiritually and to one another communally (Gen. 1:26–27; Ps. 8:5–6). We are made different from the rest of creation. We intuitively understand and follow a moral law of knowing right from wrong, but we are prisoners of sin (Rom. 2:14–15; Gal. 3:22).

Being made in his image means we represent him and are part of his spiritual family but are estranged from him. Being in his image has to do with our identity. We either submit to our identity in him, or we rebel against this and make *him* in *our* image. A root cause of sin is that humans aren't satisfied being human. They want to be God.

According to New Thought

According to New Thought, to be made in the image of God means having divine qualities, creative potential, and the ability to shape reality through thoughts and beliefs. Horatio Dresser, a key figure in the New Thought movement, says that "if man is made in the image of God, he partakes of the divine nature. God is Love, God is Health, God is Abundance, God is Joy, God is Peace, God is Illuminated Intelligence, God is from Everlasting to Everlasting, in the eternal Here and Now, and man, who is the child of God, made in His image, partakes of all these things. This is the New Thought—the New Thought of God."[27] This means people are inherently good.

This core belief makes it difficult for anyone immersed in New Thought to accept the true gospel. After all, if you're not sinful, why do you need a savior? When I was in New Thought, my reasoning went something like this: We're good because God is good. And if God dwells in us, then we are inherently good.[28]

It then follows that if humans are inherently good, then we're *God*. If humans are God, then we create our reality and morality. If we create our reality and morality, then truth is what we define it to be.

Bible

According to Christianity

The Bible is the divinely inspired Word of God given through the Holy Spirit. In Christianity, it is regarded as both a spiritual and a historical text, chronicling humanity's separation from God and his ultimate redemption of humanity and creation (Rom. 8:18–23; 2 Tim. 3:16–17; 2 Pet. 1:2–21).

The Bible is the spiritual authority to the Christian and is sufficient for living the Christian life as God instructs (2 Tim. 3:16–17). Christians take a historical, grammatical, and literary approach to understand what it is saying. We want to understand the Bible in the context the original writers meant for it to be understood.

Christians read the Bible literally, but this doesn't mean taking *everything* in it literally. The Bible uses many figures of speech, such as simile, hyperbole, or metaphor. It was written by a variety of authors. Some books fall into different genres, such as poetry, history, Law, or prophecy. When this is taken into consideration, the reader understands that reading "literally" means believing the Bible communicates literal truth, but not always in a literal way.[29]

The Bible does not have any secret knowledge for the spiritual elite. It reads plainly so the average person can know the simple truth about God and how he has revealed himself to humanity.

According to New Thought

In New Thought, the Bible is just one of many spiritual books containing truth. It's an esoteric book that has hidden codes in it to uncover special spiritual laws.[30] It's incomplete and full of errors, but it's a sacred text to be honored and applied in a metaphysical way.[31] This is why God has awakened spiritual leaders and inner wisdom to help guide us to the truth about what it says and who we truly are.[32] The Bible is to be understood through a modern, awakened interpretation—sometimes through spirit contact.

The Bible was written with the ancient, limited perspective of the original authors. We've grown and spiritually progressed, meaning we can understand the deeper significance of the Bible far better today.[33] But in what might seem a contradictory idea, Ernest Holmes, the founder of Religious Science, said in his book *Science of Mind*, "The full meaning of scripture and what Jesus said can never be clear to you until you have contained a consciousness equal to his."[34] We have all we need inside, but we might have to work to awaken it.

A core belief is that Christianity tries to suppress spiritual truths, especially about our divine potential. They keep people captive to only *one* perspective on Christianity and humanity and *one* proper way to interpret the Bible. Joel Goldsmith, a New Thought author, once said, "Scripture should not be interpreted merely as historical documents but as the spiritually revealed Truth of inspired sages and seers. In this light, there is but one Presence and one Power—and I AM that."[35] In other words, the Bible is not the authority. *You* are.

The New Thought approach to reading and applying Scripture is deeply metaphysical, mystical, and allegorical. The Bible is a highly subjective text not meant to be taken literally or at face value. I've coined my own term for this multifaceted approach: *metamystigorical*. (You heard it here first, folks—a term as multifaceted as New Thought's interpretive dance with biblical texts.) Questions like "What does this verse mean to *me*?" are encouraged. In one of my many interviews with New Thought proponents, one woman said, "Your *experience* is your Bible." This approach makes sense when we remember their belief that humans have ultimate inner authority as divine beings. This would give us the authority to subjectively interpret the Bible or any other religious text.

Charles Fillmore, the founder of Unity Church, created the *Metaphysical Bible Dictionary*. In the preface, he says "Our real aim is to assist in leading the student into the inner or spiritual interpretation of the Bible that he may apply it in the very best and most practical way in his own life. . . . We are always pleased when anyone learns to go within and get his inspiration, direct from his own indwelling Lord or Spirit of Truth."[36] This means Enoch represents repentance. Peter represents faith. The cross represents two currents of thought: The perpendicular bar symbolizes the inner current of divine life. The horizontal bar symbolizes the crosscurrent of human limitation.[37] Or simply look within and interpret it in a way that resonates with you.

This is not an exhaustive list of the differences in key teachings and terms. But here's a basic way to describe New Thought beliefs: Take every Christian definition you can think of. Then redefine it with a super spiritual metamystigorical definition. There. Now you have New Thought.

It's in the Bible . . . or Something

It's odd how New Thought leaders and adherents talk about Jesus yet reject the Bible as being literally true. I once heard a progressive reverend say he believed the Bible is trash. (Yes, he used that exact term.) I couldn't resist the urge to push back a little, so I asked him, "You teach a lot about what Jesus said and taught. Where do you learn this?"

"The Bible," he responded.

I was confused. Didn't he just say he believed the Bible was trash? "But you don't trust the Bible. So how do you come to the conclusion that what you're saying about Jesus is even true?"

He hesitated. "Well, if I'm honest . . . I don't really think about that. I teach what resonates with me."

That about sums it up.

In another eye-opening conversation, I was talking with a woman who worked *on staff at a Christian church*. I asked her simple questions about God, the gospel, and the Bible—Christianity

101 stuff. I readily agreed with many of her answers. But others astonished me.

First was her belief in spirit guides. This Christian woman, who is made in the image of God and is valuable in my eyes, told me she believed we could have spirit guides—which she called "angels"—who would give us guidance and show us how to live in light and love. Her guides gave her heavenly messages.

Then there was her belief in the Holy Spirit. To her, following the Holy Spirit is simply following our heart. Listening to our heart equals hearing the Holy Spirit. In her view, faith is experiential. It's through experience and listening to our heart that we truly know who God is.

What shocked me most was her belief in hell. I asked her if she thought hell was literal. She replied, "Oh, hell is literal, but it's not like how some people think."

"What do you mean?" I asked.

"It's more of a frame of mind. It's like heaven. It's something we can have here and now or not. So we bring hell or heaven here by what we say and do."

"So what happens after we die?" I wondered.

She looked up thoughtfully. "If I'm honest, I'm not sure."

"Jesus seemed sure," I challenged.

"Yeah, some of the Bible is metaphorical, you see," she replied. "We need to be spiritually attuned to know the *true* meaning of what we're reading. That's where the Holy Spirit comes in."

I could see what was happening. Some of her views were biblical, and others were built on what she *felt* was right. She was uncomfortable with the historic Christian view of hell. It didn't sit right in her heart. Therefore, it must mean something other than what Jesus plainly taught. Keep in mind this was a staff member at *a Christian church*. The pastor had hired her. Something is wrong here. Remember, in New Thought, hell is simply a frame of mind that's corrected by the right thinking. And Scripture is interpreted by what "resonates" with you. The biblical view of hell didn't "resonate" with her, so she redefined it to her liking. My new friend's beliefs don't align with Christianity, which teaches that hell is a real place of separation from God, and that the Bible should be interpreted based on its original meaning, not through personal feelings or opinions.

In the Christian worldview, God speaks differently. He is often more concerned with revealing himself to people as a whole, not just individually. Though he does speak to individuals on many occasions. God wants to reveal himself to people, and he has done this through a medium that is accessible to *everyone*, not just one individual claiming divine revelation.[38]

God made an objective way to test revelation: the Bible.

It's always a red flag when any group or person claiming to be a Christian downplays the Bible and uplifts personal experience. Take away the Bible—the most important way to verify and test someone's personal revelation—and anyone can make any audacious claim and say it was from God.

It's crucial we prioritize regular Bible reading and study or we will be vulnerable to these hidden New Thought ideas. *Those who don't read and study their Bible consistently are the easiest to deceive by those who misuse it.* One of Satan's best tactics is working to keep Christians ignorant of the one spiritual weapon we have in our battle against him: our Bibles, the Sword of the Spirit. If you know your Bible and are prepared to stand for what's true, you will be a snare to the devil's schemes instead of an unexpected accomplice.

Checking In: The Beauty of the Gospel

Understandably, this might be a lot to take in. I think of everyone reading this and the millions unknowingly influenced by New Thought teachings. As I write this, I'm taking a moment to think of *you*. No matter where you are mentally and emotionally with what we've covered, God knows exactly what you're thinking. It doesn't surprise him. His providence and sovereignty comforted me when I struggled with what to do to help Christians see what New Thought is.

I'll never forget my first year attending church as I was unlearning many New Thought beliefs. I heard songs like "The Great I Am" and "Christ Be Magnified" with humbled eyes and ears. They brought me to my knees. The meaning of these words matters. Similarly, the history of New Thought matters. Where New Thought came from can help us understand where we're going. Reflecting on why I had been so drawn to this positive form of "Christianity," I realized it wasn't just because I wasn't reading or studying my Bible. It was also because of my perspective on myself. New Thought beliefs place you at the center, making you feel like the chosen one, the special one who must recognize and awaken your spiritual potential, almost like discovering a hidden superpower. This distorts the gospel message, the very thing people truly need.

If New Thought were true, then that would mean Jesus didn't die to save us from sin and he didn't physically rise again. It would mean our God is dead, and everything we go through in life really does depend on us. It would mean repentance is not about turning away from sin and following Jesus, but rather about inner transformation and mental renewal. I *rejoice* because none of that is true! Jesus *did* rise again, he *did* take away our sins, and the gospel is alive. Jesus's death and resurrection is not an allegory or a metaphor. The God who created the world and became part of his own creation to save us is alive.

Jesus says to come to and follow *him* for rest. He never says to look within. Rather, Scripture *warns* us against doing so (Prov. 3:5–6; Jer. 17:9; Gal. 5:17; Matt. 15:18). All your pain, tears, burdens, doubts, and sins *become his* when you place your trust in him alone. Lay them on his shoulders, and he will carry them up the hill and nail them on the cross. There is no other way. Unlike New Thought spirituality, which emphasizes individual power, following your heart and desires, and self-realization, the gospel focuses on grace and redemption, offering peace and eternal hope, which is what people are truly seeking. He doesn't *fix* your heart. He gives you a *new* one. These lies are like a proverbial Instagram filter that distorts your soul. But the gospel *remakes* your soul. It provides the assurance of unconditional love, grace, and salvation through Jesus, offering a relationship with a personal and loving God. The beauty of the Christian message makes us look to the cross with awe and wonder. It brings comfort and assurance of a purposeful, eternal life rooted in truth.

New Thought might sound Christian, but it's a different Jesus, a different gospel, and even a different *truth*. It's always mutating and is not going anywhere anytime soon, which is why there's another element of New Thought we must cover next. It's the secret ingredient that brings everything into perspective. New Thought—and its effects—can't exist without a fluid view of truth.[39]

CHAPTER 4

True for Me

Relativism and New Thought

> We love truth when it enlightens us, but we hate it when it convicts us.
>
> **—Augustine**

> One of the most cowardly things ordinary people do is to shut their eyes to facts.
>
> **—C. S. Lewis**

"What is truth?"

I sat across from a friendly and gracious New Thought minister in a Unity Spiritual Center asking questions and taking notes.

"Truth—with a capital *T*—is whatever resonates with your heart. It's the God spark, the I Am within. This is our true self, the Christ, where we're perfect. Living our truth means following our hearts."

"What do you mean by living our truth? What if 'our truth' is not objectively true?"

"I'm not sure I follow," she said.

"I mean, if living your truth and following your heart doesn't align with reality—or morality, for that matter—wouldn't that be an unreliable compass to follow?"

She dodged the question. "Truth is within. Not everyone is interested in objective truth, especially if it makes us intolerant, judgmental, or unhappy. That's when I know it's wrong and not loving. If truth exists like how you're saying, then that means we *exclude* others. We want to *include everyone*."

I kindly posed another question to my new friend. "Can something be true and loving *and* exclude what's *not* true *or* loving? I mean, what if something is true but challenges our perception of what's loving or tolerant?"

She didn't skip a beat. "No. What's true is always loving and tolerant. We need to test truth by what resonates with what's in our hearts, from within! This is how we know what's loving or tolerant. Truth is constantly being revealed. When God speaks, it ends with a comma, not a period."

I pressed further. "What if what's true in someone's heart isn't moral? What if someone's truth tells them to abandon their wife and children, so they can live their dream as a traveling polygamist drag queen?"

She hesitated. "I can't say I can pass judgment on them. If that's *their* truth, who am I to stand in their way?"

A Moving Target

This is just one example of the types of conversations I've had with New Thoughters about truth. Whether my minister friend realized it or not, she was telling me she believed in *relativism*. Relativism is an interpretation of "truth." In his book *Street Smarts*, my friend Greg Koukl describes relativism this way: "The word *relativism* is used to communicate a particular understanding of what it means to say that a belief, statement, or point of view is true.... If the truth you have in mind can change simply by changing your mind, then that 'truth' is only in your mind. It's not in the world. It's on the inside, not the outside. That's relativism."[1]

Relativism says there isn't a single truth for everyone. What's true for one person might not be true for others. Simply put, relativism says, You do you.

When I was steeped in New Thought beliefs and practices, I basically had a black belt in relativism. I would have shared the same beliefs my minister friend did, thinking it was loving, tolerant, and what Jesus would do. Today's society would have applauded me. Our current culture champions inclusivity, tolerance, and open-mindedness. People are encouraged to "live their truth,"—unless, of course, their truth disagrees with relativism.

In New Thought, truth is entirely individual. *An individual person's* experience, beliefs, and feelings are the authority for *their* truth. If what resonates with you one day no longer serves you the next, discard it. Your inner divinity—your true, authentic self—guides you. Your divine spark within tells you what's true. Since you are divine, trusting yourself equals trusting God, and any attack on your truth is an attack on God. That's how they see it.

Wayne Dyer, a prominent New Thought self-help author and speaker, explained this concept in an affirmation: "When you trust in yourself, you are trusting in the wisdom that created you."[2]

Keeping in mind the New Thought terms and definitions we went over in the last chapter, note how this New Thought site describes truth: "Truth abides in fullness at the very core of man's being. As his consciousness (awareness) expands, he touches the everlasting Truth. What seems new is but the unveiling of that which always has been. The basic principle of Truth is that the mind of each individual may be consciously unified with Divine Mind through the indwelling Christ. By affirming at-one-ment with God-Mind, we eventually realize that perfect mind which was in Christ Jesus."[3]

Simply put, in New Thought, truth can progress and is based

on what is inside a person rather than on what is outside a person. Why? Because, according to them, we all have a perfect, inner divine spark to consult for wisdom and direction. In New Thought, then, truth is subjective, which is supposed to be freeing and inclusive. Yet as our culture becomes more relativistic, statistics measuring depression, suicide, and anxiety skyrocket. Ideas have consequences. *Your* truth and *the* truth are not necessarily the same thing.

Note how this New Thought source further confuses people by citing Jesus in support of their brand of relativism:

> As Truth students we follow a course of study that turns everything the world teaches upside down and shows us a path that actually frees us from the bondage of limited thinking and allows us to think from a Source of infinite love and wisdom. . . . We get our True guidance from within. Truth students always go within to where the real information resides when they want to know the Truth. . . . "And you shall know the Truth and the Truth will set you free." (John 8:32) . . . Begin to desire Truth more than you desire your illusions. Keep asking the Divine Voice within you to guide your mind to Truth.[4]

Mischaracterizing Jesus in this way creates a false sense of safety for New Thoughters—and even a sense of moral superiority. Ironically, when New Thoughters claim that true guidance—the truth that sets you free—comes from within, they are teaching exactly the *opposite* of what Jesus had in mind: "Jesus was saying to those Jews who had believed Him, 'If you continue in *My word*, then you are truly disciples of Mine; and you will know the truth, and the truth will make you free'" (John 8:31–32 NASB 1995, emphasis added).

New Thought tells us to embrace the truth of our own divinity. *We* are the way, truth, and life. Any other view is an illusion.

Sneaky, isn't it? Jesus says *he* is the truth (John 14:6), and only when we abide in the truth of *his* teachings will we be free from the sin that enslaves us (John 8:33–36).

New Thought did not invent relativism, of course, but it depends on it. No relativism, no New Thought. If everyone is their own god, then everyone is entitled to their own truth. A lady from the International New Thought Alliance once told me, "If I come across a Scripture that doesn't sit well with me, I throw it out. I discard what doesn't align with my Truth."

Clearly, this woman is her own spiritual authority. No need to submit to anything outside herself, especially the Bible. According to many, it's merely a book of memories from ancient people doing their best to make sense of things. For others, it's not worthy of any attention whatsoever. Apparently, this woman still reads her Bible, but why?

New Thought's relativism fits hand in glove with the cultural status quo and popular opinions about Jesus and the Bible. "You do you" is a great way to win friends and influence people. It's also a great way to deceive them. We're not living in a post-truth era. We're living in an anti-truth era.

The Death of Morality

Once you see the difference between objectivism—truth based on what's outside of us—and subjectivism—"truth" based on what's inside of us—you'll see how it affects nearly every aspect of culture. You'll also become more familiar with its dangerous consequences. If truth can't be known, then moral truth can't be known. Ethics become subjective. We lose a reliable measuring rod for what is right and wrong, good or evil, or even loving or unloving. When we abandon the idea that a higher law of moral truth applies to everyone, all that remains are *feelings*.

One writer put it this way:

When morality is reduced to personal tastes, people exchange the moral question, What *is* good? for the pleasure question, What *feels* good? They assert their desires and then attempt to rationalize their choices with moral language. In this case, the tail wags the dog. Instead of morality constraining pleasures ("I want to do that, but I really shouldn't") the pleasures define morality ("I want to do that, and I'm going to find a way to rationalize it"). This effort at ethical decision making is really nothing more than a thinly veiled self-interest— pleasure as ethics.[5]

If truth is fluid and based on opinions, there are no divine imperatives. Meaning if there are no objective moral laws binding on all people everywhere, then morality is relative to how someone feels. If objective moral truth doesn't exist, though, and pleasure becomes the ultimate action guide, then whose standard of pleasure do we follow? The one with the most power.

Clearly, the people in power don't always have our best interests in mind. Our fallen human nature, though, *loves* this idea because it appeals to our darkest impulse to lord over people. We tend to do what pleases *us*, not what is good or right for *others*—the opposite of the Bible's teaching.

When power is used to exploit the ignorant, people are prone to deny what's objectively true because of the influence of those in power. They aren't convinced by what's actually true. They are convinced because of *who* is saying it. The value of truth claims depends on who's making them.[6] Relativism is like a symphony with no composer or sheet music. It's just noise.

The idea of relativism raises an interesting question. If there's no objective truth, can anything be false? Can anything be a lie? I asked a New Thought cleric this question. He said, "Truth progresses. Truth is never settled. We can't know for sure what's moral or true because our definitions of it change."

This seemed like a self-defeating statement, so I asked him, "Is *that* truth settled? Or is *it* still progressing?"

"That's a good question. I don't know."

"Okay, do you believe lies exist?"

"Of course I do."

"How would you define a lie, then?"

"I would say that a lie is when someone's not being truthful."

"But you said truth progresses. By that same standard, doesn't that mean lies progress too?"

He didn't know what to say to this. Notice he wasn't doing backflips, saying, "This means I can never lie? Sweet!"

Here's the irony. Lies *prove* truth exists. Something evil or bad can only make sense against the backdrop of good. In the same way, there can be no lies without truth. Think of the theological implications. Jesus said Satan is the father of lies. But if there is no truth, there can be no lies. If there are no lies, then Jesus was wrong and Satan is off the hook. Checkmate!

There's a reason people deny truth on a massive scale. There's a *spiritual* payoff. If we do away with truth, especially moral truth, no one has to hold others accountable. The most we can do is disagree with them, which isn't appealing to most New Thought believers either. Most people I talked with while doing research for this book were hesitant to make any definitive claims about what they believed. I suspect this has a lot to do with their aversion to conflict. They don't want to upset what "resonates" with someone else.

One person I talked with said, "My feelings will *always* trump facts. If something contradicts my Truth, I quit thinking. I put it out there in the Universe and let it go. I do not wrestle with it to find truth. I wait for God to deliver a message, then I ask if it feels right to *me*." I couldn't help wondering if her claim that her feelings always trump facts was itself a fact. Notice how she had to abandon critical thinking to follow her "truth."

The point is that a person claiming there's no objective truth doesn't typically play the movie forward. They don't contemplate the ramifications of their relativism. A world where everyone is his own authority becomes a breeding ground for chaos and evil. Besides a toddler, who can live in a world where yes is the same as no?[7]

Truth You Can Count On

There's a popular story about blind men and an elephant that people use to illustrate how truth works. Six blind men encounter an elephant, but each one has a different "truth" of what an elephant is like:

> The first blind man put out his hand and touched the side of the elephant. "How smooth! An elephant is like a wall." The second blind man put out his hand and touched the trunk of the elephant. "How round! An elephant is like a snake." The third blind man put out his hand and touched the tusk of the elephant. "How sharp! An elephant is like a spear." The fourth blind man put out his hand and touched the leg of the elephant. "How tall! An elephant is like a tree." The fifth blind man reached out his hand and touched the ear of the elephant. "How wide! An elephant is like a fan." The sixth blind man put out his hand and touched the tail of the elephant. "How thin! An elephant is like a rope."
>
> The rajah calls out from the balcony. "The elephant is a big animal," the Rajah says from the balcony overlooking the square. "Each man touched only one part. You must put all the parts together to find out what an elephant is like."[8]

I heard this story more than once in my research. People would share it with me to illustrate how there's truth in all religions and all perspectives. If we combine them, we will have true understanding and world peace.

But something has always bothered me about this story. See, the blind men were mistaken. Only the one who wasn't blind, the rajah, was able to say *what an elephant was truly like*.

Some things are subjective, like how a piece of art makes us feel, or if we think chocolate tastes better than vanilla. That kind of "truth" does vary from person to person. Claims like "Insulin treats diabetes better than ice cream," though, are different. Objective truth tells us about reality. It tells us the way the world actually is. It corresponds to, or fits with, reality. If reality had a mirror, objective truth would be its reflection.

Subjective, relativistic "truth" just tells you about an individual's beliefs, tastes, or preferences. That's all.

Objective truth is truth you can count on, but it's helpful to know what objective truth is not:

1. Truth is not simply whatever works. This is the philosophy of pragmatism—a concept New Thought is in line with. Lies can appear to "work." Someone who is guilty of a crime can lie to get out of the consequences. Lying worked! It brought desired results, but they are still lies.
2. Truth is not simply what the majority believes. The majority of people can believe potatoes are secretly undercover aliens that are going to take over the world, but that doesn't make it true. In the past, just because the majority believed the sun revolved around the earth didn't make it true.
3. Truth is not what makes people feel good. Bad news can be true.
4. Truth is not what is comprehensive. A lengthy, detailed presentation can still result in a false conclusion.
5. Truth is not determined by intentions. Good or bad, it can still be wrong.
6. Truth is not simply a belief. A lie believed is still a lie.

Here are a few examples of biblical claims about truth:

- 2 Thessalonians 2:11–12 (NIV)—"For this reason God sends them a powerful delusion so that they will believe the lie and so that all will be condemned who have not believed the truth but have delighted in wickedness."
- Romans 1:18 (NIV)—"The wrath of God is being revealed from heaven against all the godlessness and wickedness of people, who suppress the truth by their wickedness."
- Romans 2:6–8 (NIV)—"God 'will repay each person according to what they have done.' To those who by persistence in doing good seek glory, honor and immortality, he will give eternal life. But for those who are self-seeking and who reject the truth and follow evil, there will be wrath and anger."
- 1 Corinthians 13:5–6 (NIV)—"[Love] does not dishonor others, it is not self-seeking, it is not easily angered, it keeps no record of wrongs. Love does not delight in evil but *rejoices with the truth*" (emphasis added).

According to Scripture, objective truth exists and can be known by those who seek it.

Relativism's Appeal

If relativism is contrary to what Jesus taught and its consequences can be devastating, why would anyone find this perspective appealing? There are several reasons, and it's important to understand them to help people find their way back to the security and hope of God's true Word.

To begin with, relativism is a way for humanity to embrace and justify its own sin and maintain its illusion of self-divinity. It justifies a life of pleasure and convenience and is conflict avoidant. Relativists see themselves as open-minded, nonjudgmental, and tolerant, which, of course, is popular today. And who doesn't want to make their own rules about what's right or wrong, good or bad? In other words, relativism is *relieving*.

Imagine you're a college student. You love admirable and important things like learning, reading, and hearing new ideas. You're in a world religions class with a good professor who walks students through each religion, detailing with intentional accuracy (no straw men) what each teaches and the differences between them. It doesn't take long to discover each religion contradicts the one before it.

Your pulse quickens. You become overwhelmed and anxious by the thought of trying to sift through each religion to discover which one might be true. You can't possibly handle the immensity of this task. You feel extremely small. You think of the vast amount of knowledge to know in the universe and compare it with the little anyone really knows. "Does anyone know what they're even talking about? Do *I* even know what I'm talking about? How can we really know what's true? I've been wrong many times in the past. How do I know I'm not wrong *now*?" You find yourself growing more uncomfortable by the minute.

In this overwhelming state, you inevitably default to relativism to relieve the discomfort. You immediately feel relieved. You feel liberated. You are totally okay with suspending judgment. You decide it's more tolerant and loving to believe that we all have the truth, just expressed in different ways. This is heralded as the popular high moral ground, making you more likeable, further incentivizing your position. Your uncertainty will be seen by many as enlightened spirituality. After all, the exclusivists are closed-minded and see the world through the lens of their false self.[9] What do they know?

Or maybe someone resorts to relativism to relieve their discomfort with authority. They don't like moral boundaries. They don't like someone being boss over them. But they don't want to be a full-on rebel, so "love" becomes their religion. Relativism allows them to be pragmatic. It works for them—at least at the moment—so it's true *for them*. They've successfully evaded critical thinking by embracing entitlement under the guise of virtue. Whew!

Another appeal to denying truth is that it seems to alleviate pain. This is one of the main themes in utopian novels like *The Giver* or *Brave New World*. The idea is to create a world of peace and happiness. But it's ultimately an illusion. In *Live Not by Lies*, Rod Dreher says that "truth cannot be separated from tears. To live in truth requires accepting suffering. . . . This is the cost of liberty. This is what it means to live in truth. There is no other way."[10]

This personal relief gained from relativism empowers you to live and let live. Conflicting ideas no longer trouble you. How convenient. How comfortable. But how deceptive.

Relativism is also a wonderful choice for people pleasers. This was true for me. I was always hesitant to claim absolute truth for my beliefs in case I turned out to be wrong. I always made sure to qualify my beliefs by being open to differing opinions, but it was less about finding truth and more about avoiding conflict and securing my "People Pleaser of the Year" trophy (made out of insecurity, anxiety, sweat, and eggshells). I looked tolerant while at the same time passing as a Christian.

People are exhausted from conflict coming from just about everywhere. To avoid division, it's easy to default to relativism to find neutral ground and "keep the peace." Truth becomes nothing more than convenient collective hunches because nobody should believe a truth that excludes others or offends them.[11] The problem is that truth is sacrificed on the altar of peace.

Sadly, many Christians have fallen prey to this temptation to use relativism to avoid conflict. In her book *Faithfully Different*, Natasha Crain describes the allure of relativism. She says relativism is so influential because it appeals directly to our fallen nature and reinforces our desire for autonomy. Ultimately, our self-authority is condensed into four statements: Feelings are the ultimate guide, happiness is the ultimate goal, judging is the ultimate sin, and God is the ultimate guess.[12]

Relativism speaks to people's felt needs and is key to understanding why New Thought ideas are so persuasive, even though the beliefs of New Thought are not always recognized. Relativism makes us our own experts on self-sufficiency and reality. It's the essence of "follow your heart."

The Truth Sets Us Free

Over two thousand years ago, Jesus stood before a powerful Roman leader named Pontius Pilate. Pilate asked Jesus if he was a king. Jesus said, "You say that I am a king. For this purpose I was born and for this purpose I have come into the world—to bear witness to the truth. Everyone who is of the truth listens to my voice" (John 18:37). Pilate said famously, "What is truth?"

Throughout the ages, people have asked this same question. Jesus has given us the answer. "I am the way, and the truth, and the life," he said. "No one comes to the Father except through me" (John 14:6). Jesus's purpose was to bear witness to the truth (John 18:37). He didn't come bearing witness to *a* truth, or *his* truth, but *the* truth.[13]

The problem is that relativism speaks out of both sides of its mouth. One side demands we shouldn't judge and should coexist, while the other side demands justice, makes judgment calls, and loudly disagrees with what they don't tolerate. It's madness.

Truth can't speak out of both sides of its mouth. Truth can't contradict itself. You can't say all truth is relative and then say it's true that you ought not judge.

Nobody can be a consistent relativist. Nobody can "live their truth" for long. Everyone knows this. Some people choose to suppress or deny it.

Second Timothy 4:3 is one of the best Scripture passages to explain why this happens: "The time will come when people will not put up with sound doctrine. Instead, to suit their own desires, they will gather around them a great number of teachers to say what their itching ears want to hear" (NIV).

Relativism is humanity's broken attempt to justify their sin and live as their own god. It's self-idolatry. This has a strong appeal because it makes us feel important and powerful. But it leaves us bound and broken. Truth, by contrast, corrects, informs, instructs, rebukes, and challenges. Without truth, we are in bondage to our depraved nature that, if followed without moral restraint, will eventually lead to addiction, brokenness, and death—both physical and spiritual.

God exists and, therefore, truth exists. This is foundational to everything in our lives. Our standards are set by the truth of who God is and what he says about reality, and therefore, we seek to know him and to obey him. He is the ultimate standard of what's true and good.

Now that we've built a strong understanding of what New Thought is, where it came from, and how it functions with a relativistic view of truth, it's time to dig deeper. Next, we're going to dive into the virtually unknown ways in how New Thought has played into the identity crisis we're seeing today. It might shock you.

Unlearning the Lies

Now that we've shed some light on New Thought's reliance on relativism and the false hope it brings, let's take some steps toward removing any of this spiritual poison we might have ingested along the way.

1. Focus on Truth

Here are some recommended Scripture passages to read and ponder. To understand the context, I highly recommend reading the whole chapter where these passages are found:

- 1 Corinthians 13:6-7 (NIV)—"Love does not delight in evil but rejoices with the truth. It always protects, always trusts, always hopes, always perseveres."
- John 8:31-34 (NIV)—"To the Jews who had believed him, Jesus said, 'If you hold to my teaching, you are really my disciples. Then you will know the truth, and the truth will set you free.' They answered him, 'We are Abraham's descendants and have never been slaves of anyone. How can you say that we shall be set free?' Jesus replied, 'Very truly I tell you, everyone who sins is a slave to sin.'"
- Ephesians 4:15 (NIV)—"Speaking the truth in love, we will grow to become in every respect the mature body of him who is the head, that is, Christ."
- Psalm 119:29-30 (NIV)—"Keep me from deceitful ways; be gracious to me and teach me your law. I have chosen the way of faithfulness; I have set my heart on your laws."

2. Stand Firm

There's an incentive for believing in relativism: you'll "fit in." But at the cost of truth. You must resist living by lies. Even if doing so seems to bring "happiness," it's an illusion. If you see the chaos too, know that *you are not alone.* Because God is truth, that means truth can never die. The Holy Spirit is at work and always has been.

Here are some recommended resources on this topic that have been immensely helpful for me in this area:

> *Relativism: Feet Firmly Planted in Mid-Air* by Francis J. Beckwith and Gregory Koukl
> *Faithfully Different: Regaining Biblical Clarity in a Secular Culture* by Natasha Crain
> *Live Not by Lies: A Manual for Christian Dissenters* by Rod Dreher
> *A Prolegomena to Evangelical Theology* by Norman L. Geisler and Douglas E. Potter

Also, investing in a logic or critical thinking class or book can be invaluable when confronting relativism. Here are some resources on critical thinking:

> *Tactics: A Game Plan for Discussing Your Christian Convictions* by Gregory Koukl
> *The Art of Argument* by Aaron Larsen, Dr. Christopher Perrin, and Joelle Hodge
> *The Discovery of Deduction* by Aaron Larsen, Shelly Johnson, and Joelle Hodge
> *Socratic Logic* by Peter Kreeft

3. Pray and Proclaim

Stand firm in the truth, no matter the challenges you may face. God's Word teaches us that truth is real and Jesus is the embodiment of everything true. Follow him faithfully. Here's a prayer for you:

Lord, in a world filled with distractions, doubts, and deceptions, help me to anchor my faith in your unchanging truth. Grant me discernment to recognize falsehood and the courage to reject it. In moments of doubt, remind me of the words of Jesus and your love for me. Strengthen my faith so that I may never waver but instead hold fast to the truth revealed in your Son, Jesus Christ. I ask for your protection against the lies and deceptions that try to lead me astray. Help me to be vigilant and steadfast, knowing that the truth you offer is the source of my hope and salvation. Empower me to share this truth with others, that they, too, may come to believe in you, the one true God.

4. What We All Really Crave

What people are ultimately searching for is truth and love. But they're looking in all the wrong places and therefore discovering a caricature of both. They seek happiness at the expense of truth—and also at the expense of *goodness*.

CHAPTER 5

Identity Crisis

What Do You Do When You Don't Feel Like You?

> To believe your own thought, to believe that what is true for you in your private heart is true for all—that is genius.
>
> —Ralph Waldo Emerson

If you're on social media, you've probably come across a post or two (or a thousand) like this one from @spicytweet (with over 712K likes) on TikTok:

This is just a reminder for all of you (including myself) that this is your life. This is not your boss' life. This is not your partner's life. This is not your parent's life. This is *your* life. Do what you want.

Just out here listening to my divine self and no one else:-) #healing #consciousness #innerchild #lesbian #lgbtq #wlw #fyp #foryourpage[1]

Or maybe you've seen video clips spreading wisdom such as

this encouraging word from TikTok's @MegEmikoArt (over 587K likes, trans nonbinary artist) answering this question:

"If you say you want to be your most authentic self, why did you get top surgery? Why did you change your body?" So, my first thought and response is to always think about the definition of authentic. What does it mean to be your most authentic self? Being my most authentic self is being my true self, and being my true self means looking inward and figuring out what I'm needing and wanting for *me*, what makes *me* feel good, what makes *me* feel like *me*? . . . When I chose to love myself and embrace my transness and my gender, I became the most authentic Meg that I had ever been in my entire life.[2]

You'd have to be living under a rock to miss the gender and sexuality wars we're witnessing all around us. From drag queen story hours to pronouns and Pride parades, the evidence of increasing personal and cultural confusion abounds.

Who or What Am I?

Imagine a thirteen-year-old girl looking in the mirror. She knows the reflection is just her face, her body. But she feels a fierce disconnect between what her body shows and what she desperately wants it to be. She doesn't quite understand all her feelings, but one thing is certain: she is *obsessed* with the thought of being a boy. She hates being a girl. In her mind, boys are funnier, smarter, and objectively more likable. Even their bodies seem effortless to live in.

"Life would be much easier if I were a boy," she thinks. "They're taken more seriously. People listen when they talk. No matter how hard I try, I feel like I don't fit in. Please, God, please make me a boy."

These are complex feelings. Her spiritual beliefs undergird and inform how she understands who she is. True identity is not based on outward appearances but on who she is on the *inside*.

For her, this is her true, authentic self. This is a core belief, giving her the fuel to know what she feels inside is her identity. This spiritual belief is the only relief she has. She believes that it's in the Mind reality is created. Spirit is more powerful than what we can see, touch, and feel. She even thinks perhaps she is a boy in another dimension somewhere.

She doesn't understand this at her young age. She seems to be constantly frustrated, blurring the lines between reality and imagination. She was taught we are powerful beings who aren't just limited to our bodies. Does this mean she is more spiritually advanced? Is this an inner evolution of spirituality? It must be. But how could she live out her reality? Could she ever actually *become* a boy?

She's not attracted to girls at all. She's attracted to boys and even has quite a few crushes. She's quite the tomboy too. She dresses pretty grungy—flannel shirts, ripped jeans, tees, and oversized sweaters, always trying to show the guys she is one of them, but she also has best friends who are girls. As a girl in middle school, she has no paradigm to understand any of this. She doesn't exactly hate herself. She just hates being a *she*.

She even tries passing as a boy for a short while, asking her friends to accept her. But she's met with swift judgment. She's crushed. But one thing brings an unexpected but relieving outlet: the internet. She creates an entire male persona online. Here, she becomes a boy with a different name and even a different look. "He" is thirteen with blond hair and blue eyes. He is edgy, funny, and attractive. Through this male persona, she lives an entirely different life online. "He" even gets crushes on girls online. There is something deeply seductive about living this fantasy where she takes on a male persona. It's thrilling.

Every day after school, she sneaks to the computer to check her email and see who's written her, and she joins many chat rooms in search of friends with whom she can live this complicated side of herself. Who knows how many people are like her, living their truth online?

Every night, she goes to bed but doesn't feel fulfilled outside the virtual world she has created. She knows it's a fantasy and it will never be real. This causes excruciating dissonance to the point of making her hide in the closet and weep. She *grieves* over being a girl. What is wrong with her?

This girl doesn't need validation. She needs clarity. She doesn't need a new identity. She needs to be made new. She doesn't need to accept the lie that being a girl is terrible. She needs to know she is wonderfully and beautifully made. This girl doesn't need affirmation. She needs healthy confidence.

I know. Because this girl was me.

Identity Crisis

This information might be surprising to some of you who follow me on social media because this is the first time I've ever shared this. But yep, that's right. I was on the LGBTQIA2S+ ride *before* it was trendy and cool.

What we're seeing in our world today is not only what I consider the biggest cultural identity crisis in our history; it's also personal. Before common parlance included phrases like breast binding, gender spectrums, gender unicorns, personal pronouns, puberty blockers, and before anybody knew there would be an ever-lengthening future for the LGB acronym, I struggled with my gender identity. But I had *no idea* what this even was. Picture my astonishment as I grew older, observing something I had previously deemed unimaginable during my teenage years now rapidly evolving into an overwhelmingly popular trend, influencing every facet of our lives. There's a reason why I'm so vocal about this topic on social media. I also have genuine care and love for the people struggling with their gender identity. I want them to know they are deeply loved but also deeply deceived. There's a better way. When people believe their inner self is divine and they're letting that guide *their identity*, it sounds all too familiar to me.

The worst part? If I had grown up in today's cultural climate, I might have been on my way to puberty blockers or worse—permanent, irreversible surgery.

Today, society says our identity is defined by our feelings. Everything else on the outside must conform to this. When I was a child, this ideology wasn't being promoted culturally, but it was present in my life via the spirituality I was taught (not realizing it was New Thought). For example, I remember seeing an affirmation on a piece of paper on a family member's wall that said, "You are what you think. Your mind is your world. All power is yours. So Trust Thyself." Many years later, I realized this was a mix of Ralph Waldo Emerson and New Thought literature. The "Trust Thyself" was from Emerson's essay "Self-Reliance," and the rest of the saying was from a New Thought book called *What Are You*. I figured this out some twenty years later when I spotted the saying in the chapter titles of a book I was reading.

I recently picked up the same book and noticed this from a chapter on "Your Identity": "In your true mental identity, you are the mind of God. That mind must be permitted to act in you. It knows all things; it makes no mistakes. . . . The mental you is born of the spiritual you, and the physical you is your mind's outer translation of God's idea."[3]

Did you catch that significant progression? Your true mental identity is the mind of *God*. The physical you is your mind's outer translation of God's idea. So, naturally, if the mental and physical aren't in agreement? The inner self is what you should trust. Because God must be obeyed.

Transcendent Connections

The idea that our inner self is divine or God isn't just a flippant observation. This has been brewing for decades. There are striking similarities between the culture's "authentic self" and New Thought. But why?

As discussed in prior chapters, New Thought's teachings on the "true authentic self" align with Ralph Waldo Emerson's transcendental ideas. And the transcendental movement is another key part of how these spiritual ideas became embedded in the culture.[4]

Transcendental beliefs were widespread throughout America in the early nineteenth century. We see them in full fruition today. Thanks to transcendentalism, people were encouraged to trust their feelings and emotions because that's where God dwells.[5] If I could sum up transcendentalism in one word, it would be *self*. Within transcendentalism, your reason isn't the superior source of truth. Your inner self is, because *spirit* is superior. People were seen with infinite godlike potential, and the opinions of others stifled this inner, authentic, true self.[6] Who cares what people think? You do you, boo.

Let me take a minute to clarify the word *authentic*. I used to think it meant you weren't being fake or weren't a big liar, liar pants on fire. You weren't a hypocrite, a Fakey McFakerson. This is a biblical concept, and we should strive for this in our Christian walk.

But that's not what "authentic self" means in today's culture. Typically, it means trusting what your desires tell you is what's true for you. The truly authentic person is someone who outwardly expresses *their inner self*. Your outward "you" must match the inward "you." Society tries to pressure us to act against our true feelings and convictions, making us inauthentic. We must live our truth. YOLO!

It is ironic that today, in many cases, for someone to be their authentic self, *they have to deny reality to do that.* They have to be fake to be authentic. Ain't that a knee-slapper?

I agree there's a place for authenticity in the Christian life. But the Christian seeks authenticity differently: by recognizing their sinfulness, repenting, looking upward, and ultimately directing their focus toward God. This is where true authenticity lies.[7]

The transcendental movement to follow your authentic self seemed motivated by more than just a rebellion from society, but also *sexual* freedom.[8] When someone identifies as how they feel on the inside, whether it's a trans man, trans woman, nonbinary, two-spirit, queer—or even a mythological creature—this is their inner reality. Because following your authentic self is not just a societal trend.

It is *spiritual.*

Historically and spiritually speaking, Emerson's transcendental ideas paved the way for much of what we see today. But these ideas are more sinister than some realize.

Spiritual Giants?

New Thought spirituality can deceive people who are questioning their gender identity by making them think they are following God when they pursue gender fluidity. This can involve irreversible surgeries or lifelong hormone treatments.

How does this follow? If you are divine, *God's will is decided by what you feel or desire.* And the most enlightened are those who take the boldest steps to live in alignment with their inner divinity—their authentic self. Where Christians might think of spiritual boldness as proclaiming the gospel, denying cultural lies, or living in the mission field, New Thoughters might see it as having radical sex change surgery.

A way to describe this is what's called "expressive individualism." In his book *Strange New World,* Carl Trueman says it this way:

In a world where the inner voice is the key to the real person, the former is authentic while the latter presents a public image likely at odds with his private behavior. More pointedly, the trans person who was born male but claims to be a woman is to be lionized because that is an act of courage and honesty, whereby the outward performance is finally brought into line with the inner reality despite what society might say about such. All of this derives from authorizing—indeed valorizing—that inner voice of nature and then expecting, or even demanding that the outside world, from the public Square to the individuals' body, conform to this.[9]

Remember, in New Thought, being made in the image of God is equivalent to being God. Therefore, humans are intrinsically good. Jesus plays a role, but only to model for us what it looks like to live authentically. At a recent visit to a Unity center, I saw this expressed once again on the pamphlet they handed me: "We are each individual, eternal expressions of God. Our essential nature is divine and therefore inherently good. Our purpose is to express our divine potential as realized and demonstrated by Jesus and other master teachers."[10]

According to this, obeying God equals obedience to my feelings and desires. Following Jesus means learning from his example of perfect alignment with his Christ Consciousness or authentic self.

Can you see how this makes New Thought a perfect supporter of the LGBTQ+ movement? It not only approves of everyone having their own truth but lends a spiritual impetus—a way to include Jesus without surrendering to any outside set of moral or religious standards.

A prominent example of someone with these types of beliefs is Oprah Winfrey. Despite assumptions, she isn't a New Ager. She identifies as a Christian, and her spiritual beliefs are *much* more aligned with New Thought.[11] In a discussion panel on her show in 2009 exploring spirituality, the topic of homosexuality came up.

Michael Bernard Beckwith, founder and spiritual director of the Agape International Spiritual Center in Los Angeles (which is New Thought), had this to say about a gay man: "We're not talking religion. We're talking spirituality. People don't just happen to be gay. When people are born, they have that type of orientation, so he is gay by Divine right."[12]

If you believe you are good because the inner you is divine, then that means your intuition is your truth GPS. Whatever internal message you receive regarding your identity is more than a feeling. *It's from God.* If anyone disagrees or challenges this, they're not just coming against a person. They're coming against something divine.

They are against *God.*

In one shocking conversation I had with a New Thought reverend, she said mainstream fundamentalist Christians (uh, like me) are actually *anti-Christ* because of this. She said they are against the Christ within. They are against the message of Jesus. This is why Christians—no matter how loving or sincere in their attempts to help a gender-confused person find healing or peace—are seen as hateful, closed-minded, spiritually regressive bigots. *Christians are seen as being against what is good and godly.*

Twisted, isn't it?

My advice? Love them anyway. If you can, talk in person. It's very difficult to forget that people are made in the image of God when you're looking them in the eye. You can understand their perspective without necessarily agreeing with or endorsing their version of "truth."

New Thought teaches that truth is progressive because people progress. They liken this to a spiritual evolution. And accepting everyone's truth isn't merely tolerance. *It's a higher spiritual level of humanity.* One LGBTQ+ woman I spoke with told me she believes we are seeing a spiritual awakening of the human soul—unity manifesting itself. She also believes in Christ Consciousness, the law of attraction—and said she reads the Bible regularly. Of course, she believes she knows "higher truths" about its meaning and understands "true" Christianity. I can remember a time when I would have heartily agreed with her.

What about the Body?

New Thought's teaching that reality is mainly in the mind is similar to gnosticism. If you're not familiar with gnosticism, it comes from the Greek word *gnōsis*, which means "to know" or "knowledge." *Gnōsis* refers to a deep, mystical understanding of spiritual truths or the divine, gained through personal experience rather than intellectual reasoning. The mind can hold you back from a spiritual experience. It emphasizes an inner, intuitive connection with the divine, helping to uncover hidden truths about existence and the nature of reality. Gnostics divide the world into two realms: a divine realm, which is good, and a material realm, which is bad or evil. They believe in a "higher truth" not acquired through the Bible but through mysticism and that is known only to a certain special few. This is wildly unbiblical.

God created matter, and this matters (pun intended). God is spirit, but he created a material world he called *good*, including your body (Gen. 1:31). Jesus saw the body as so important that he decided to take on a body in the incarnation, something gnosticism shuns because the body is seen as evil since it's part of the material realm. Remember, in gnosticism and New Thought, the truest part of who you are is *spirit*. Your body, therefore your mind, holds you back from the supposed truth your spirit has, which is in your heart. This is why so many gnostic and New Thought teachings focus on controlling and overcoming the *mind*. But Scripture teaches that there is a *bodily* resurrection (1 Cor. 15:42–44). Can you see why this is significant? According to God, it's not only "spirit" that is important, true, and wonderful, but your body as well.

Gnosticism is repeatedly warned about in the New Testament.

(1 Tim. 6:20–21, 2 John 1:7–8; 1 John 4:1–3.) After Jesus's resurrection, gnostic beliefs were going around, saying Jesus only *appeared* to be a man but wasn't fully human. Rather, he was actually a spirit, like a phantom figure. There's no way he'd appear in an evil physical body. Gross. The apostle John, throughout his first letter, warns about the dangers of gnosticism.

The body shouldn't be ignored, mutilated, or hated. God loves it. Nancy Pearcey, in her book *Love Thy Body*, writes about this: "Christianity is often accused of being anti-sex and antibody. But in reality it is the secular ethic that is antibody. Gay activists downplay the body—our biological identity as male and female—and define our true selves by our feelings and desires. They assume that the body gives no reference points for our gender identity or our moral choices. In essence, the secular worldview has revived the ancient gnostic disdain for the body."[13]

Like a spiritual Trojan horse, gnostics aim to subtly introduce altered Christian teachings to believers, gradually shifting them toward gnosticism and seeking to reform the church from within. This is done by coming in looking like the "good guys," using the same language, practices, and virtuous demeanor. Don't be a sitting Greek caught off guard.

Tolerance or Tall Tales?

In the earlier stages of the New Thought movement, the topic of LGBTQ+ rights and acceptance might not have been as prominent or discussed as openly as it is today. New Thought organizations have evolved over time, with many becoming more progressive and inclusive. New Thought's spiritual emphasis on individual empowerment with spiritual growth is a clear foundation for inclusivity. Think of a mix of "you do you" and "you *be* you." New Thought doesn't *cause* gender confusion, but its philosophy *allows* any identity that resonates within you.

This makes sense. It's the logical conclusion for any belief championing following your heart, living your most authentic self, and progressing with the times. Progress in culture, having self-awareness, and knowing what you want can be wonderful. But in this case, truth and judgment—even if it's a proper judgment—are seen as a spiritual deformity, especially if it offends others. "You shall not judge!" and "Live your truth!" are the New Thought battle cry. This is how we can encounter people of a colorful variety of identities on social media, claiming that the Jesus they know would love and accept them.

In my research, I went to Unity Churches, Centers for Spiritual Living, and progressive churches with New Thought leanings. All of them proudly had LGBTQ+ flags displayed. In every service I attended, without exception, there was a focus on LGBTQ+ activism and guidance on being a supportive ally.

One church I visited even had preprinted name tags for your preferred pronouns. There was anywhere from a regular they/them, she/her to a ze/zir or xe/xem.[14] I've even heard about "neopronouns" (new pronouns) on TikTok and other online platforms where you can use a created word to serve as a pronoun without expressing gender. So this means words such as beep/boop,[15] Gods/Godself,[16] or pizza/pizzas[17] are perfectly acceptable pronouns. It's limitless.

Here are a few examples of the proliferation of the topic of LGBTQ+ rights and acceptance from some websites and brochures:

> We welcome all regardless of race, religion, nationality, gender identity, or sexual orientation. You are a beloved child of God and we love you just the way you are.[18]

> It is a profound act of self-love to celebrate the unique ways Spirit manifests in us and others. . . . We stand with the LGBTQIA2+ community as its members profess the truth of

their humanity, that their health and wellbeing are essential, that justice and equity are rights, not privileges, and that representation and visibility matter.[19]

Here's a New Thought website talking about why pronouns are so important:

> With so much negativity from the world, members of the LGBTQIA+ community have to cultivate a strong inner awareness of our innate wholeness, value, and worth. Just like our names, our preferred pronouns are personal. The focus that is currently placed on pronouns invites us all to look more deeply than outer appearances. . . . We know that we are each a unique, creative expression of the Divine. Our spiritual practices, including meditation and affirmative prayer, offer a foundation for each of us to touch our most authentic self and live, choose, and create from that awareness. Gender identity is one avenue of expression for our divinity. Respecting, supporting, and honoring the way someone understands themselves is to respect, support, and honor their divinity.[20]

On NewThought.org, which is the Affiliated New Thought Network, they have a pronoun workshop designed to help you clear up the difference between sex and gender:

> If you have ever wondered . . .
>
> > Are sex and gender the same thing?
> > Are males and females totally separate?
> > Why all the fuss about transgender?
> > What does "nonbinary" mean?
> > Should any of this matter to me?

. . . you are not alone. Join Rev. D as she sheds some light on these important questions.[21]

In one New Thought center I visited, they had a "Declaration of Principles" in one of their pamphlets.[22] I looked it up, and here are principles 5 and 10 from the International New Thought Alliance (INTA) website:

5. We affirm the freedom of all persons as to beliefs, and we honor the diversity of humanity by being open and affirming of all persons, affirming the dignity of human beings as founded on the presence of God within them, and, therefore, the principle of democracy.

10. We affirm our evolving awareness of the nature of reality and our willingness to refine our beliefs accordingly.[23]

You get the idea.

Want to bring Jesus and inner divinity into your identity as a trans woman? Want to worship a God who's all love and never judges? Or how about a metamystigorical interpretation of the Bible that subjectively fits with your identity as a therian or otherkin?[24] New Thought won't turn you down. It will advocate for you. Whatever your truth is, it will fortify it. There's nothing broken in you. You're whole. Just recognize the goodness of your true self! And remember, there's *always* a deeper spiritual, metaphysical meaning to someone's identity.

I do agree with some of the previous statements. It's abhorrent to discriminate on any level or think we are better than anyone else based on religion, race, or sexual orientation. The Christian view of being made in the image of God means love and respect are shown to *everyone*. My heart truly goes out to anyone who struggles with their identity in any way, and my disagreement does not mean I hate those I disagree with. I believe many are attracted to these beliefs because they've been hurt, and we would be wise to keep those hurts in mind as we make sense of this difficult cultural phenomenon. They need both love and truth, and we need to prepare our hearts to help them, especially if they *want* to come to church. To quote Nancy Pearcey again, she says, "Many people who experience gender dysphoria or same-sex attraction have had negative encounters in the church. They have been made to feel that they pose a danger to other people in the congregation, and that they must solve their sexual issues before showing up at church. . . . For Christians to be credible in asking others to repent, they must model repentance for their own failings that have pushed people away from the church."[25]

Perhaps the hurt many Christians have caused is why I struggled to share my personal issues with gender identity for so long. To love someone doesn't mean you always affirm them, especially if what they're believing about their identity is not true or is even harmful to them. But if we look at LGBTQ+ people with hatred, bitterness, or anger, we're missing the point entirely. They are not our enemy. We need to see them as Jesus sees them. Be the kind of Christian who is an example of 2 Timothy 2:23–26: "Have nothing to do with foolish, ignorant controversies; you know that they breed quarrels. And the Lord's servant must not be quarrelsome but kind to everyone, able to teach, patiently enduring evil, correcting his opponents with gentleness. God may perhaps grant them repentance leading to a knowledge of the truth, and they may come to their senses and escape from the snare of the devil, after being captured by him to do his will" (ESV.)

Buzzed on Love

Some might be wondering, "What's the problem? If the result is that society is more accepting and tolerant of the LGBTQ+ community, then isn't it right to do so and even helpful?"

This is a good question, and even fair to ask. It's one I wondered myself.

There's a forceful movement to reject even the most basic biological facts and redefine reality sheerly according to feelings. We see this all over, but it is particularly clear—and personal—on issues of sexuality and gender. Any resistance to comply with this move is met with harsh and swift social punishment. If you don't conform to the narrative (people make reality with their feelings), then you are considered hateful, fearful, and homophobic. Ironically, such people believe they are demonstrating *true* tolerance in this way. *They* are the ones who are open-minded and helpful. But does denying facts promote greater tolerance? Or does it result in more unfairness? Is our communal participation in these lies *actually* helping people? Is it right to lie to young boys and girls, telling them transitioning to the opposite sex won't harm them, when it entails being put on puberty blockers and hormones? Is undergoing major surgeries, losing healthy body parts, experiencing catastrophic mental health issues, severe disfigurement, and sexual dysfunction for the rest of their shortened lives helpful and right?

I don't think so.

None of this is ethical. Pandering to this crowd isn't helping. The only way to fight lies is to tell the truth.

I was reminded of this while recently watching the movie *Toy Story*. (Some people find wisdom in academic journals. I find wisdom in movies for eight-year-olds. Pass the popcorn.) Buzz thought he was a real spaceman, but Buzz was delusional. The other toys knew this, yet they were still all wowed by him. But Buzz believed in himself so much that he couldn't—and wouldn't—listen to any other voice that didn't affirm his "truth." Mr. Potato Head, specifically, made a good ally to Buzz, chiding Woody for his nonconformity.

Eventually, reality smacked Buzz in the face, and his reaction deserves some attention. Though he was heartbroken, he didn't double down. He didn't make excuses for himself. He believed the truth, and it set him free. Woody, despite having been a bit jealous of Buzz, was the only true friend he had. Woody was the one who refused to support the delusions. He told Buzz the truth the whole time and was treated with contempt for it. When Buzz finally knew the truth, it was Woody who helped him through it. *This* is love.

Christopher Yuan said it best: "Unconditional love is not the same thing as unconditional approval of my behavior."[26]

Tobacco Isn't a Vegetable

Whenever I get the chance to speak with someone who holds to New Thought beliefs, I specifically ask about identity and truth. I almost always ask the same question: Where do you draw the line?

For example, I asked a New Thought reverend, "If someone truly feels they were born in the wrong body, would you be supportive of their chosen identity?"

"Absolutely!" His answer wasn't surprising at all. He was a huge proponent of social justice and was an LGBTQ+ ally.

"This is what love is all about," he replied.

"Okay, so help me understand. What if their truth, or how they identify, is bad for them? What if I walk up to you and say, 'I'm a smoker with lung cancer. But *my* truth is that tobacco is a vegetable, so it's actually good for me.' I'll die if you don't warn me. What would you do?"

"Oh, I think that would be wrong," he said. "I would try my best to tell them that tobacco is bad for you and isn't even scientifically a vegetable."

"So you would correct my wrong thinking?"

"Absolutely. That's not cool . . . and sort of stupid."

Okay. Noted.

I took another angle. "What if it's something else? What if someone says they are a transgender person and also a transracial?

They were born white but actually identify as Black. They're following their heart and their truth."

"Well . . . I can't say that's the same thing."

"Why? What do you mean by that?"

He hesitated. "I'm not sure how to answer you."

I pushed him on this. "In your view, you said this is what love is all about. What's the loving thing to do? Would you tell the transracial person that this isn't true? Is this where you would draw the line?"

He was forced to move the goalposts. "Well, I think I would encourage everyone to just be their authentic self. Who am I to argue with that?"

I doubled down.

"All right, just so I'm understanding you correctly. If someone were to come up to you and say they have struggled their entire life with people accepting their identity as a nonbinary bird therian, this is their true, authentic self. Even though they were born a human man, they have shared *their truth* with others and have received judgmental and bigoted remarks. And they also smoke because they believe tobacco is a vegetable and it helps them cope with their troubles. They come to you for support. What would you say?"

He was silent for a few seconds. "I'm going to be real with you. I remember a time when I talked to people with similar identities, identifying as animals or fantasy creatures. I couldn't help but wonder if they hadn't created these identities to deal with trauma."

"So is what they believe actually true, or just *their truth*?" I asked.

"I believe that it's true for *them*."

"Would you ever consider challenging their truth?"

His response stunned me. Without skipping a beat, he firmly said, "*Never*."

He continued. "They can create whatever identity they want, but I would never say to someone that I don't actually think they truly identify that way. If that's their true self, and this form of themselves is within, then you affirm. Who's to say they don't have some spiritual truth that I don't, and they've just progressed more than me? To affirm is to love. And it's also the humble thing to do."

"Even if it's not true?" I asked.

"Even if it's not what *I* think is true."

"So . . . if they somehow have spiritual truth that you don't, can tobacco be a vegetable?"

He paused. "Yes," he said. "Tobacco can be a vegetable."

Where do they draw the line? There is no line. It's all spiritual evolution. Truth progresses and can't be fully known. The goalposts need to move to be relevant, tolerant, and obedient to your inner truth. Even if it gives you lung cancer.

In Him, Not in Us

Here's the problem. Identity in anything other than Jesus alone will leave us empty and longing for more. Those in the LGBTQ+ movement are looking for their identity in *themselves*. They think this will fulfill them.

They have it backward.

Identity grounded in self is identity grounded in falsehood and in the bondage of sin. It's self-idolatry. It's making ourselves the Lord and Savior of our lives. Jesus said in John 8:34, "Most assuredly, I say to you, whoever commits sin is a slave of sin" (NKJV). New Thought teachings on identity promise freedom but put us in bondage. The answer to our identity crisis isn't from within. Our identity can never be made complete in ourselves, especially when we're part of the problem. Nobody can call Jesus "Lord" and then live as though they are the lord.

Truth is, it's not a bad thing to want a new identity. This is the whole point of the gospel message: to end our identification with Adam (sin) and find our identity in Jesus, which reconnects us to our Creator. We were *created* to search for meaning and to discover our identity.

We're not divine. We're not whole. But we can *be made whole* by a perfect God who provides healing, not an escape from reality. You cannot reinvent yourself because you did not create yourself.[27] This is why Jesus says you must be *born again*. Being Jesus's disciple requires not an acceptance of self but a *denial* of self, bringing true peace and freedom (Matt. 16:24). Jesus didn't call you to be your authentic self. He called you to deny yourself.

Jesus didn't eat with sinners and tax collectors because he wanted to appear inclusive, tolerant, and accepting. He ate with them to call them to repentance. And this is where we will find true freedom: putting down our burdens at the feet of Jesus, accepting him as Lord of our life, and finding who we are *in him*.

I figured this out shortly after my season of gender confusion described earlier in the chapter. I was confused at this young age. But at age sixteen, I found Jesus. Suddenly, everything about my identity made sense. I knew who I was *in him*. Second Corinthians 5:17 says, "Therefore if anyone is in Christ, he is a new creation. Old things have passed away. Behold, all things have become new" (NKJV).

That was *exactly* how I felt: new.

I realized my identity struggle wasn't at all about dealing with the pain of not being a boy but about *accepting who I truly was* as a *girl*. That's the twist. Saying God "made" you gay, trans, lesbian, or "fill in the blank" and believe this is simply who they are. But many people are born with desires that are not in God's will or are harmful to themselves and others. Someone born with heightened sexual desires which plagues them their entire life does not mean they should live that way. Every desire we have isn't inherently good. Just because we desire something doesn't mean it should be acted upon. Your desires do not equal your identity. Believing someone should change everything to match their identity and desires simply isn't true. *It's the other way around.*

Being a female is an unspeakably wonderful thing in the eyes of God. Being a female isn't the deformed version of a man.

I love what Abigail Shrier says at the end of her book *Irreversible Damage*. Reading this paragraph had a huge impact on me. She says, "Young women have more educational and career options today than they ever have. Remember to tell your daughter that. . . . Tell her because it's natural to doubt. Most of all, tell her because it's true. She's lucky. She's special. She was born a girl. And being a woman is a gift, containing far too many joys to pass up."[28]

You are fearfully and wonderfully made (Ps. 139:14). This is what the creator of heaven and earth says about you. Accepting what he says is accepting the real, objective truth about your identity. Anything else is a lie.

Next, we're going to dive into an area that's saturated with New Thought. And virtually everyone, Christian or not, has been affected by this: self-help.

Unlearning the Lies

Now that we've shed some light on New Thought's connection to the gender and sexuality confusion we see all around us and the false hope it brings, let's take some steps toward eliminating any of this spiritual poison we might have ingested along the way.

1. Focus on Truth

Here are some recommended Scripture passages to read and ponder. To understand the context, I highly recommend reading the whole chapter where these passages are found:

- 2 Corinthians 5:17 (NIV)—"Therefore, if anyone is in Christ, the new creation has come: The old has gone, the new is here!"
- Galatians 2:20 (NIV)—"I have been crucified with Christ and I no longer live, but Christ lives in me. The life I now live in the body, I live by faith in the Son of God, who loved me and gave himself for me."
- John 3:5-6—"Jesus answered, 'Very truly I tell you, no one can enter the kingdom of God unless they are born of water and the Spirit. Flesh gives birth to flesh, but the Spirit gives birth to spirit.'"
- Jeremiah 2:13 (NIV)—"My people have committed two sins: They have forsaken me, the spring of living water, and have dug their own cisterns, broken cisterns that cannot hold water."

2. Stand Firm

I get it. I understand the temptation to compromise under the *intense*, never-ending drone of the voices saying—yelling—that if you don't affirm anyone and everyone who claims to be lord of their own identity, you're committing the highest of social and spiritual crimes. But you're really just joining a false religion that will lead you away from the God who loves you. Don't give in. Look up.

Here are some recommended resources on this topic that have been immensely helpful for me in this area:

Irreversible Damage by Abigail Shrier
Strange New World by Carl R. Trueman
Change of Affection by Becket Cook

The Secret Thoughts of an Unlikely Convert by Rosaria Champagne Butterfield

3. Pray and Proclaim

In a world that often defines us by external standards and fleeting values, find your identity in God. Here's a prayer for you:

Lord, I know my true identity can only be found in you. Let your truth sink deep into my heart, and may it overshadow any influences that try to shape my identity outside of your will. Help me resist the pressures of the world that seek to conform me to its standards. Instead, empower me to live a life that reflects your truth. Help me to stand firm in this truth, no matter the challenges I may face.

4. What We All Really Crave

The identity crisis is real, raw, and confusing. What we're truly looking for is fulfillment. We're going to find our identity in *something*. What—or who—we find our identity in determines our holiness, which affects our happiness. God wants us to be holy. Only *in him* can this be sustained.

CHAPTER 6

Loving Ourselves to Death

Self-Help and New Thought

> I don't think the self-help industry would be there if it weren't for the New Thought philosophy. They go hand in hand. New Thought is the foundation of the whole self-help movement.
>
> **—Rev. Dr. Kristin Hawkins, minister for**
> **Centers for Spiritual Living**

Would you like to be happier? How about more assertive or more likable? Would you like a bigger budget? Wouldn't we all love that?

If you answered yes to any of these, I can relate. Even when I was in my early twenties and had everything going for me (or so I thought), I longed for these things too. These desires, and others like them, aren't anything to be ashamed of. When it comes down to it, aren't we just aching to flourish? To be the best version of ourselves and live the best life we can live?

These desires are great unifiers. Everyone has them. And an entire industry has been built on this fact. Books, conferences, workshops, retreat centers, medical equipment, and more have been developed to help the masses achieve these goals. And although they might approach our felt needs from slightly different angles, these well-meaning (money hungry?) sources all shout one common answer: "You've got this. *You* are the missing ingredient!"

You to the Rescue

Imagine for a moment that you're trapped in a tower of a dark, depressing castle. Day after day, you look out a tiny window, hoping someone will appear on the horizon to rescue you from your lonely prison. Now imagine you finally see a figure approaching. As the horse and rider draw closer, you're finally able to see the rescuer clearly. And it's . . . you.

Whether this scenario makes you put on a cape or disappoints you, this is the simplified message of the self-help industry. The self-help phenomenon is all around us. Just go to your local bookstore and take a look at the self-help section. You're sure to see a number of blockbusters like Glennon Doyle's *Untamed*, Brené Brown's *The Gifts of Imperfection*, Rachel Hollis's *Girl, Wash Your Face*, Don Miguel Ruiz's *The Four Agreements*, Wayne W. Dyer's *Wishes Fulfilled: Mastering the Art of Manifesting*, or one of my personal favorites when I was in New Thought, Eckhart Tolle's *The Power of Now* (we'll discuss some of these in more detail in a bit). Some self-help books even use vulgar language in their titles to shock readers, but I'll, uh, spare the blush-inducing details for obvious reasons.

All these books express the same alluring selling point: *I know the secrets of how to improve your life so you can be the happiest version of yourself.*

Now, before I start getting ugly emails, let me put the brakes on for a second. Please know I'm not broad-brushing *all* self-help authors or their books. Some of them contain practical and genuinely helpful information. Many of these teachers aren't one sandwich short of a picnic when they hand out life advice. I've truly liked and benefited from this genre. Some of it's just common-sense good advice I wished more people followed, like setting boundaries, having good judgment, and applying logic. Every attempt to better ourselves doesn't equate to an evil intent to somehow awaken our inner divinity.

I reject the voices in Christianity that say all kinds of self-care is selfish and even satanic. I can't help but think of Christians who've had terrible traumas or mental and emotional health struggles. They need healthy coping mechanisms. A lot of people are struggling, and the last thing they need is added shame for seeking to understand themselves and break self-defeating cycles. Nor can we self-sacrifice to the point of burnout in the name of "not being selfish." Scripture teaches wise ways to watch what we're thinking and not be an insufferable pessimist but also not be a detached, humble-bragging optimist.

There is such a thing as caring for yourself in a healthy, God-honoring way. Look, neglecting yourself and your mental health is not God-honoring. *That's* satanic. Even so, there's no denying that the idolatrous self-reliance pendulum can swing way too far. It gives us heavy burdens we then blame God for.

Self-Help Pseudonyms

The term *self-help* was coined by a man named Samuel Smiles—who I'm disappointed to know wasn't a dentist on the side. He was a British writer who wrote a book by that title with a focus on courtesy, independence, and individuality.[1] Although his title and resulting literary genre have stood the test of time, it's also undergone a modern makeover to attract more consumers.

While researching for this book, I took a trip to a popular bookstore. I couldn't find the self-help section—not because it was missing but because it had a different label. The self-help books were there by the hundreds under the categories of "self-transformation" or "personal growth." If I were to choose a label, I'd add "self-reliance" because that's what we find in the root system.

Samuel Smile's *Self-Help* sentiments echoed the sentiments of Ralph Waldo Emerson, who heralded many of the principles of the self-help movement. His teachings on self-reliance, inner divinity, individuality, and the power of thought have deeply influenced and continue to mold self-improvement and personal empowerment philosophies. From vintage thinkers to modern self-help gurus, his wisdom is the blueprint that self-help authors can't help but borrow from. It's all about constant self-improvement, enhancing your mental, emotional, or physical lives—by your own efforts.

This leads me to another self-help section pseudonym I'd love to see: the "false gospel" section. Yeah, it might not be the best way to sell books, but at least it'd be accurate. Though not all self-help ideas are bad or even untrue, it's undeniable that many self-help messages are part of a false gospel. We'll talk more about this later in the chapter, but for now, let's just say it like it is: Self-help can be a repackaged gospel of works. You continually strive to be the best version of yourself.

Forget all the "being conformed to the image of Jesus" stuff. Booorrrinnng.

It's not hard to create a false gospel when we don't know the Bible or how to read it soundly. The self-help industry often exploits this vulnerability. In many cases, the Bible is presented as merely a spiritual book holding the secrets to your human potential. It's a book about *you* written to help *you* become prosperous, happy, and an overall better person. Biblical concepts are commercials for common sense and advice. Just imagine a title like *5 Ways on How to Use the Golden Rule to Create a More Positive Thought Life and Make Friends!* and you've got the gist.[2]

Many self-help materials modify biblical concepts to focus

on individual needs. These reinterpretations often disregard the broader biblical narrative, prioritizing personal insights over the original intent of the biblical authors.[3] In other words, rather than contextually reading the Bible to learn about God, self-help gurus reinterpret Scripture out of context to bolster their teachings. They then promote living your truth, embracing authenticity, thinking positively, having intuition, and bolstering the power of the mind as solutions to life's challenges—all with a Bible verse thrown in. Self-help (and its buddy, New Thought) made the misguided question "What does this verse mean to *me*?" trendy.

The self-reliance false gospel is all about pursuing our individual happiness rather than our holiness. It's about how to have our best life now because this is what Jesus wants. The implication is that the more we know about ourselves, the more we know about God who is within. Because if God is within, then self-knowledge is God-knowledge.

Of course, not all self-help teachers use the Bible or spiritual language in their approach. Many are secular and simply offer common sense advice. But whether there is a spiritual aspect to their guidance or not, the concept is the same: *You* are the authority. The more you discover your authentic self, your true self, the more happiness, prosperity, and comfort you will have.

And all of them can thank New Thought for their methods and ideas.

Cue New Thought

Regardless of the labels it carries, the modern American self-help movement traces its roots to New Thought authors and leaders. The all-time bestselling self-help books are *How to Win Friends and Influence People* by Dale Carnegie and *Think and Grow Rich* by Napoleon Hill.[4] Both have sold over one hundred million copies globally and consistently rank among the top-selling self-help books each year. (And yes, they were both front and center in the "personal growth" section of the bookstore I visited.) Both Carnegie and Hill were prominent New Thought ministers among many who spearheaded the self-help movement, marketing the Bible, God, Jesus, and the gospel as products to improve life.

Basically, they took the Bible and made it a self-help book.

The self-help movement is another example of how New Thought has blended into the culture. Early New Thought authors sometimes wouldn't use religious language when teaching New Thought concepts. This made New Thought blend right into everyday life. You'd see New Thought and pop psychology casually swapping their lingo in popular magazines and books. This blending was a hybrid of part metaphysical, part psychological, and part success advice, forming the foundation of the self-help movement we know today.[5]

We can also thank New Thought and the self-help movement for perpetuating the myth that we use only 10 percent of our brains.[6] I grew up believing if we were to use 100 percent of our brains, then we could achieve what Jesus was capable of. Even actors as legendary as Morgan Freeman believed in the 10 percent myth and even made a movie based on it named *Lucy*.[7]

No matter what approach early New Thought leaders took, here's their basic message: *Your reality is what you think.* Think yourself rich. Think yourself thin. Think yourself successful. Think yourself smart-ish. You name it. Change the way you think, and you will have the happiness and fulfillment you always looked for. It's centered on you. It's all within you. It's all about you.

To be clear, thinking positively is good. Having a hopeful attitude and believing in good things to come is a great approach to any day. And sometimes we do need to reshape our thought life to mature or have freedom from debilitating mental and emotional issues. Getting real here, I struggle with anxiety. It's not chronic, but I'm pretty certain my anxiety has funded a couple of my therapist's tropical getaways. So there's that. Through therapy, I've learned ways to deal with my thought patterns. I've learned new strategies without contradicting biblical truth. I now understand what triggers my anxiety. Over time, I was able to "rewire" my brain to function more peacefully in certain situations. And that's not New Thought or unbiblical.

A concept becomes New Thought when it asserts that our thinking alone can be the catalyst for and cause of the change in your life. It becomes New Thought when we believe our thoughts have the power to change and manifest reality. It becomes New Thought when the universe, or a divine source, responds directly to human thought.

Let me share some unsuspecting places that New Thought hides. Did you know many multilevel marketing businesses (MLMs) use New Thought books in their training? It's recommended reading for positive thinking, visualization, and manifesting. It's startling how many MLMs will also have a prosperity gospel presentation at some point.

Another example is Alcoholics Anonymous (AA). This program has helped countless people (including many I love) find freedom from substance addiction. However, I was shocked to discover that one of AA's main influences was the writings of Emmet Fox, a prominent New Thought author. "The Big Book," *Alcoholics Anonymous*, was being written while the authors were studying Emmet Fox's *Sermon on the Mount* book. This was a huge influence on the development of AA.[8]

The fact is we're made in the image of God, and this means we experience truth, love, and good things all the time. But Scripture says we're *shortchanged* in these things until we find our ultimate purpose in Jesus alone. There are objectively good and true concepts, teachings, and lessons in many self-help systems, including AA. But mixing truth with untruth can confuse people. More on that later.

The Fundamental Flaw

"Believe in yourself! Have faith in your abilities! Without a humble but reasonable confidence in your own powers, you cannot be successful or happy."[9]

Reading this encouragement from a self-help book about the potential of my mind and positive thinking captivated me. It left me feeling nothing but power. It even included Scripture references to this "power" within. So I knew it was legit. There was no denying this was God's will for my life.

I couldn't put the book down. I never knew that simply changing the way I thought would literally change the circumstances around me. Happiness, greatness, confidence, likability, assertiveness, wealth, romance, a fresh start, a positive perspective—there was a book or conference for that. But it wasn't just my perspective that would change. No, my thoughts could change my reality. I was magical. There was definitely *nothing* suspicious about this. What a serotonin rush!

A rush that eventually crashed into this really inconvenient thing called *reality*.

It didn't take long to realize that this "powerful thoughts" thing would require doing the work to be better. Eat better, think better, act better.

Just *be* better.

And this is how it gets you.

The inspiring quote at the beginning of this section is the first words you'll read in Norman Vincent Peale's tremendously popular self-help book, *The Power of Positive Thinking*. It's one of the most successful self-help books ever sold in American history. It also happens to be one of the most popular New Thought books ever sold in American history.

Peale was a popular New Thought author and minister. His influence is just one of many New Thought sources that have influenced our culture's views on positive thinking, self-reliance, following your truth, and, well, everything to do with yourself as the answer to your problems.

The theme is still the same: *self.* You're the chosen hero. You're not the problem. You're the solution. The downsides to this message are many, including the huge barrier it builds to accepting the gospel. And tragically, those who follow the religion of self-improvement ultimately become a slave to its never-ending, works-based demands.

That's the result of a fundamental flaw in how New Thought depicts humanity. Nearly every false idea today can be traced back to the belief that humanity is fundamentally good.[10] This creates the illusion of rediscovering something deep within and awakening our divine potential. Some people can't understand why they'd need a savior. *I'm my own savior. I am enough!*

New Thought began with healing, but it grew to promote personal prosperity and correct the "lie" that humans were inherently sinful. Humanity didn't need to be told they were sinners. They needed to know about their goodness and inner divinity, the Christ within, and that they are already whole. They just need to realize it. Supposedly, the lies of the religious fundamentalists had been holding people back. This was nothing but fear-filled religious propaganda, keeping humans from reaching their true potential.

Let's look at some popular examples of this ideology lurking in the pages of some of today's bestsellers.

Popular Examples

The authors I want to focus on say they're Christians. They talk about God, Jesus, and faith and quote Scripture on one side of their mouth. But out the other side, they talk about inner divinity, living your truth, manifestation, "I am" affirmations, and thinking and speaking positively. They offer a concoction of Christianity, culture, pop psychology, and what seems to be New Age, but it doesn't quite fit neatly into these categories. So what gives?

New Thought is what gives.

Keeping in mind the terminology we went through in chapter 3, let's look at some quotes to see if you can pick up on the red flags.

This first example is from Glennon Doyle's book *Untamed*, where she talks about what she calls her "Knowing":

> BE STILL AND KNOW. I'd read that verse many times before, but it struck me freshly this time.... There in the deep, I could sense something circulating inside me. It was a *Knowing*. I can *know* things down at this level that I can't on the chaotic surface.... What I learned (even though I'm afraid to say it) is that God lives in this deepness inside me.... I now take orders from my own Knowing.... Some call the Knowing God or wisdom or intuition or source or deepest self.... It doesn't matter *what* we call our Knowing. What matters ... is *that* we call it.[11]

I can't resist pointing out an irony here. The Scripture she's talking about is Psalm 46:10, which states, "Be still, and know that I am God. I will be exalted among the nations, I will be exalted in the earth!" Sounds good, right? I have heard many New Thought authors use this verse as a self-divinity verse.[12] It's notoriously used as a meditation verse to focus on knowing that our true self is inside, living as God. Just "be still and know" this is who you are, the Great I Am.

But there's more here. A plain reading of this verse shows it's about God's *judgment*. Check it out. Starting in verse 6, we clearly see this:

> The nations rage, the kingdoms totter;
> he utters his voice, the earth melts.

The LORD of hosts is with us;
    the God of Jacob is our fortress.

Come, behold the works of the LORD,
    how he has brought desolations on the earth.
He makes wars cease to the end of the earth;
    he breaks the bow and shatters the spear;
    he burns the chariots with fire.
"Be still, and know that I am God.
    I will be exalted among the nations,
    I will be exalted in the earth!"
    (Ps. 46:6–10, emphasis added)

I feel like if Beethoven's Symphony no. 5 and the hymn "It Is Well With My Soul" were a Bible verse, it would be this. Here, the author is acknowledging God's presence, authority, and control over all circumstances, reassuring believers that he is in charge, even in times of trouble or chaos. God has enemies and he's going to judge them. No matter what, God is sovereignly in control. He wins.

This verse is not about humans' inner divinity or the power of our thoughts, but God's sovereignty and power over humans. My brain cells are fist fighting trying to understand how I ever used this verse for a proof text on being divine.

Ironically, Doyle said she's read this verse multiple times and even had it tattooed on her wrist!

How does this happen? It's because of what I mentioned before about reading and interpreting Scripture. When we have a metamystigorical view of Scripture instead of a plain literal reading—like we would with any other book—we get what I call "cookbook theology."

Here's what I mean. Imagine someone—vegan or not—saying they got a recipe for Cheesy Fish Pie from a vegan cookbook. It uses real cheese and fresh fish. Besides this sounding disgusting, how in the world is this vegan? It doesn't make sense. The only way they could get this recipe from a vegan cookbook is if they read it with a personal bias, adding what they wanted, and picking and choosing the parts they like best and ignoring everything else. But they ended up with an outcome (a disgusting meal) that is incompatible with and *contradictory* to the very book they got the idea from. It's a vegan cookbook with vegan rules and guidelines, including *the* simplest boundary of veganism: no animal products!

People do the same thing with the Bible. By cherry-picking what suits them or aligns with their bias, they end up with something incompatible with the Bible's message—sorta like Psalm 46:10 being a motivational tattoo. This reminds me of someone getting a Chinese tattoo thinking it means "love" when it really translates to "potato," "fish pie," or "pickle juice."

Doyle's tattoo is fishy, unscriptural pickle juice.

Later in the same chapter of *Untamed*, Doyle explains that when she has a problem, she trusts this inner "Knowing" to guide her. At the end of her book, she even claims divinity, repeating "I am" affirmations multiple times in response to a list of questions about her identity.

No matter how disheartening the prior examples are, the quote I found most disturbing was the following quote regarding Eve from the garden of Eden:

Maybe Eve was never meant to be our warning.
    Maybe she was meant to be our model.
    Own your wanting.
    Eat the apple.
    Let it burn.[13]

This is a startling admission.

This perspective isn't unique. In one of the interviews I did for this book, I spoke to a woman in a New Thought church. I asked her about the serpent's lie in Genesis 3, about how the serpent deceived Eve by telling her she could be like God. Her response stunned me. Without skipping a beat, she said, "Oh no, honey, *that* sounds like truth to me!"

The implication is that *Satan* is the bringer of truth, and *Eve* was divine, just as God was. Satan's the good guy. And it's a lie that we *aren't* divine. Isn't that quite the narrative somersault?

Eve was *embracing* her divinity by eating the fruit. My New Thought friend told me that the truth of humanity's divinity has been hidden ever since. The serpent being the bad guy is merely a tactic fundamentalists use to prevent us from realizing the truth about who we really are. It's like she and Doyle are cheating off the same paper.

Brené Brown, another wildly popular author, says in her book *Braving the Wilderness*, "True belonging is the spiritual practice of believing in and belonging to yourself so deeply that you can share your most authentic self with the world and find sacredness in both being a part of something and standing alone in the wilderness. True belonging doesn't require you to *change* who you are; it requires you to *be* who you are."[14]

This is the religion of self. There is only autonomy, no submission. What Brown is suggesting is by turning inward and exploring the depths of our inner selves—what she refers to as our "wilderness"—we can connect with our true selves. This self-discovery enables us to genuinely belong to others with whom we share a divine connection.[15]

Unsurprisingly, Brown ends her book with an "I am" statement, similar to Doyle. She says, "Someone, somewhere, will say, 'Don't do it. You don't have what it takes to survive the wilderness.' This is when you reach deep into your wild heart and remind yourself, 'I *am* the wilderness.'"[16]

One New Thought teacher who emphasized the power of "I am" statements was Wayne Dyer. I used to enjoy listening to him speak and loved his books. Though this teaching wasn't limited to just him, he says this about "I am" statements: "The words *I am* are your sacred identification as God—your highest self. Take care how you use this term because saying anything after *I am* that's incongruent with God is really taking the Lord's name in vain!"[17]

I can feel my brain cells putting on their boxing gloves again.

These beliefs are not isolated to Glennon Doyle, Brené Brown, or other authors. All over social media, we see self-help slogans, affirmations, "I am" statements, and other teachings that are just fancy versions of New Thought concepts. Especially from celebrities.

One example is Demi Lovato, a famous singer who is more recently known for her continual change of genders. She recently said on her Instagram, "Like a serpent in the garden, I am truth, and I am darkness, I'm an angel, I'm a demon, just depends on what you're feeling."[18]

Jennifer Lopez, the wildly popular dancer, singer, and actress, shared a video on her Instagram in 2022 about how she starts her morning routine by reading affirmation cards. She then pulled out a card with a quote from Helen Keller saying, "Your success and happiness lies in you. Resolve to keep happy, and your joy, and you, should form an invincible host against difficulties."[19]

Seems super spiritual. So inspirational and practical. And, hey, sometimes it is. But here's a fun fact: What most people may not realize is this makes a lot of sense coming from Helen Keller. Though a great inspiration for many, she was a devoted Swedenborgian.[20]

Not only this, Lopez sounds like a professional New Thought practitioner with her beliefs on positive thinking. She said in an interview in 2021, "Your thoughts create your life. And so you have to think positive thoughts all the time. You have to force yourself to think positive thoughts at times. So I do a lot of different affirmations. I am whole. I am good on my own. I love myself. I love the universe. The universe loves me. God loves me. I am youthful and timeless at every age. I am enough."[21]

I hope you see a pattern here. Many assume this is New Age. It's not. This is New Thought philosophy repackaged as the self-improvement false gospel. It's shoved in our faces as a marketable new type of Christianity more palatable for the masses.

Spotting the Lies

Many self-help books with Christian undertones have New Thought in common when it comes to their spiritual views on human nature, the Bible, the gospel, the divinity of humanity, and many other New Thought teachings. This is no coincidence. These authors have adopted and embraced New Thought teachings, and may not even be aware of it. This is why we see authors like Glennon Doyle, Brené Brown, Rachel Hollis, Jen Hatmaker, and many others speak "Christanese." There's no shortage of self-help speakers, authors, and celebrities I could name. I want you to see the pattern and be able to spot it. Ultimately, the self-help message twists everything around and makes *us* the heroes, not the villains.

But as I mentioned, many self-help messages mix truth with untruths, making it difficult to discern. If you find yourself muddling through confusing content, here are a few guiding questions that might help:

1. Is this therapy, advice, or book unbiblical? Many ideas and modalities for mental health aren't in the Bible, just like there's nothing there for doing your taxes or curing sickness. But the point should be simple: Does this teaching go *against* the Bible and what God teaches?
2. After engaging in this content, am I getting a temporary high or euphoric feeling, leaving me unsatisfied and needing more of this material? Does this make me depend on these content providers rather than God? This is one reason why many Christians remain biblically illiterate. They

tend to rely on the intense feelings and experiences they get from spiritual leaders' messages instead of digging into Scripture to grow spiritually. If we remain biblically illiterate, we tend to view Scripture as self-help rather than as a way to know who God is.

3. Does this use any unsustainable New Thought or New Age philosophies to point *within* for the answers, or does this point me to God or Scripture?

Even this book, to some extent, is "self-help." (Gasp!) So while I encourage you to be discerning, there's no need to gasp every time you hear someone say they are reading a self-help book. What we need is clarity. We need to isolate claims and define our terms. And we need wisdom.

This message of making everyone their own hero and a victim at the same time goes beyond the practical and cultural to the spiritual. This message is subtle. But that's the danger of New Thought—it hides in plain sight. The original purpose of the entire self-help movement is more than just being able to manage depression, anxiety, or your life with wisdom and discernment. It's about following the true self. Follow you = follow God.

Smells fishy if you ask me.

A Heavy Burden

Let's get real here. You're not enough. And you're not intrinsically good. Neither am I. But this is actually *great* news. Reader, I feel your face as you read that. But before you think I'm using only 10 percent of my brain, hear me out.

Consider the source of the self-help message: It all starts and ends with our thinking, and the real you inside is perfect and divine.

Think about this. What must you *do* to find your true self? See beyond the movement and bookshelves to the spiritual implications. This deception offers peace but leads to spiritual bondage. *It's designed that way.*

Just imagine it. Control your thinking every second of the day. Constantly guard against negative thinking. You might miss a blessing or bring sickness and poverty upon yourself or your loved ones. Imagine the mental exhaustion after a day of repeating affirmations ten, no twenty, times a day. Or if you feel like you're not getting results, fifty times a day.

Oh, and are you meditating enough? Set aside time daily to meditate, seeking the stillness within and connecting you with your higher self. And make sure you're doing enough good for those around you. Don't be selfish. Hire a spiritual coach. Volunteer. Give your money. Work for social justice.

Not feeling peace? Do more! Order more self-help books and follow all the steps. Practice more gratitude. Maybe throw in some vision boards or ask people for more positive vibes.

Wait, you already did all that? You're still empty and depressed and struggling inside? Hmm, your true self must be really important if it's *this* challenging. Okay, time to try *more.*

Let's do everything all over again, except we'll add some Bible verses and do a gratitude *journal* this time. With sparkly pens! And for good measure, try to avoid friends and family who aren't affirming you and lifting you up.

Next, let's do the 3–6–9 method. (Yes, this is a real thing.) Just write down your desired manifestation three times in the morning, six times during the day, and nine times in the evening. Simple! And be sure to *affirm* your desires. Speak like it's true *now.* You must believe this for it to manifest, for any doubt at all will prohibit your results.

Still empty and restless inside? Hmm. Maybe stop thinking and judging altogether. Yeah, yeah, that's gotta work!

After doing all of this to the best of your ability and you still don't obtain fulfillment or find your true self, I have good news for you. Just constantly repeat all of this in any order at any given time to get your desired results.

Do more! Be better! Then wash, rinse, repeat!

Wow. Sign me up.

You might be wondering, "This is a bit much, isn't it? Aren't you overreacting? These practices *help* me."

Yes, they can. Temporarily.

This well will run dry, my friend. Many of the gurus know it. There's monetary and spiritual profit to be made off you if you are discontented and dissatisfied with your life. That's why you need another program. Or conference. Or book. Or strategy. Or affirmation. (More on this in chapter 7.)

I don't know about you, but self-reliance sounds like a lot of work.

And it is. Because the foundation is all wrong. Whatever we build on it will always leave us aching for more. When we start with the perspective of, "I'm doing this because I'm perfect inside the way I am, and I only need to discover this perfection, my true self, within," we fail right at the start. It's like trying to fill a bucket with a hole in it. It's a *broken* bucket. It's broken and needs to be *made* whole. It needs to be *made* new. Not merely *recognized* as whole or declared perfect. You're a broken bucket. Self-help is duct tape. But Jesus is a brand-new bucket.

We must acknowledge we are not perfect within and must be made whole instead of simply recognizing our wholeness. We need to start anew.

There's profit to be made off you if you're discontented and dissatisfied. The people in the self-help movement know this. Only Jesus offers the *true* satisfaction and contentedness you've been searching for your entire life. There's a reason why he's described as the Bread of Life, the Living Water. He alone satisfies.

Jesus said in Matthew 11:28–30, "Come to me, all you who are weary and burdened, and I will give you rest. Take my yoke upon you and learn from me, for I am gentle and humble in heart, and you will find rest for your souls. For my yoke is easy, and my burden is light" (NIV).

Jesus is basically asking, "Are you tired of being your own god? If so, give me that burden." Doesn't that sound much better? He cares about your problems. A lot. He feels them with you. You're not alone. He's enough for you. He makes all things new. Even buckets.

The True Rescuer

Recognizing our inner imperfection is the best thing we can do. It starts by acknowledging a fundamental truth about the gospel message, one that stands in stark contrast to the self-improvement philosophy. It should bring us to our knees as the beginning of true healing: *A denial of self to find yourself.* Jesus says plainly in Matthew 16:24–25, "Whoever wants to be my disciple must deny themselves and take up their cross and follow me. For whoever wants to save their life will lose it, but whoever loses their life for me will find it" (NIV).

Jesus doesn't save those who find themselves. He saves those who *die* to themselves (Luke 9:23–24).

Jesus isn't saying we need to live in poverty or never experience the pleasures of life. He's talking spiritually. When we discover our *true* condition as being separate from God, not *as* God, only then can we come to him.

You're not the hero. Once you come to terms with that, then true spiritual change can happen.

This is a huge hurdle for some people to overcome. Most people think they're good. The Bible teaches the exact opposite. It says we have all fallen short of the glory of God, and *nobody* is good, especially compared to a holy God (Rom. 3:10). Once we see our sin how God sees it, only then will we understand the cross. Thomas Watson once said, "Until sin be bitter, Christ will not be sweet."[22]

New Thought says to find yourself, but Jesus says to die to yourself. New Thought says you are born perfect. Jesus says you must be born again (John 3:3).

Second Timothy 3:1–5 says, "Understand this, that in the last days there will come times of difficulty. For people will be *lovers of self*, lovers of money, proud, arrogant, abusive, disobedient to their parents, ungrateful, unholy, heartless, unappeasable, slanderous, without self-control, brutal, not loving good, treacherous, reckless, swollen with conceit, lovers of pleasure rather than lovers of God, having the appearance of godliness, but denying its power. Avoid such people" (emphasis added).

This isn't a command to embrace yourself but a warning. What looks like a virtue is actually a vice. It will be made to look pleasing *and even godly*. But it's meant to leave you in bondage.

I couldn't agree more.

Loving ourselves like this leads to spiritual death.

Checking In: Reality

We're halfway through. Still with me? Are you starting to see the gravity and implications of New Thought beliefs and teachings? When I began to understand all of this, I had the urge to correct everyone constantly. But I found comfort (and a much-needed dose of humility) in an important truth: I am not the Holy Spirit.

Over the years, I've heard many amazing people share their stories of trauma and how the resultant pain shaped their beliefs. New Thought beliefs and teachings, often unbeknownst to them, offered incredible relief. Some might see much of what we've covered so far as having to rethink certain techniques or beliefs that have been instrumental in their healing journey.

I sympathize with this. I see why New Thought beliefs are so attractive. (Been there, done that. Wrote a book about it.) If New Thought were true, then that would mean truth—and subsequently, our identities—comes from within. A major problem with New Thought beliefs is that they distort reality. Are people seeking the truth, or are they seeking happiness? What if true happiness is found only in discovering what is true and real? What if finding the truth helps us understand our relationship with God, bringing genuine meaning and peace to our lives? I praise God that New Thought is false, because that means *truth can be known.*

For those of you who might be struggling with what to do with some of this information, let me encourage you. Take this one step at a time to the Lord. He'll guide you as he did me, gently and perfectly. Lean into it—tough stuff and all—because what Jesus offers is good and true.

No matter who you are, you are made in the image of God, worthy of respect and love. New Thought lies distort reality. They always promise more than they give. But truth matters. The *reality* of the Christian message brings perspective on what we were created for. Knowing truth and our identity in Jesus determines how we see the world. In Jesus, we find the most sacrificial love combined with the greatest power to draw us into a relationship with him. The gospel helps us understand why things are the way they are and why we were created.

This brings us to another popular—and sinister—New Thought teaching that casts a long dark shadow reaching into almost every living room, bookstore, and church in America: the law of attraction.

Unlearning the Lies

Now that we've shed some light on New Thought's connection to the self-help movement and the false hope it brings, let's take some steps toward eliminating any of this spiritual poison we might have ingested along the way.

1. Focus on Truth

Here are some recommended Scripture passages to read and ponder. To understand the context, I highly recommend reading the whole chapter where these passages are found:

- 2 Corinthians 12:9 (NIV)—"He said to me, 'My grace is sufficient for you, for my power is made perfect in weakness.' Therefore I will boast all the more gladly about my weaknesses, so that Christ's power may rest on me."
- Proverbs 28:26 (NIV)—"Those who trust in themselves are fools, but those who walk in wisdom are kept safe."
- Matthew 10:38–39 (NIV)—"Whoever does not take up their cross and follow me is not worthy of me. Whoever finds their life will lose it, and whoever loses their life for my sake will find it."
- Philippians 2:3—"Do nothing from selfish ambition or conceit, but in humility count others more significant than yourselves."

2. Stand Firm

Many self-help remedies address only our temporal or present needs. But the greatest need we have is a solution for our fallen spiritual condition. If we don't see this need, we'll never look for the solution. The answer to this need cannot be found within us. It must come from outside of us. The answer is found in the birth, life, death, resurrection, and ascension of Jesus Christ.

Here are some recommended resources on this topic that have been helpful for me in this area:

You're Not Enough (and That's Okay) by Allie Beth
    Stuckey
*The Truth in True Crime: What Investigating Death
    Teaches Us about the Meaning of Life* by
    J. Warner Wallace
Live Your Truth and Other Lies by Alisa Childers
Five Lies of Our Anti-Christian Age by Rosaria
    Butterfield

3. Pray and Proclaim

Our strength and understanding are limited. In a world that often encourages self-reliance, remember our ultimate trust should be in God, our loving and all-knowing Creator. Here's a prayer for you:

Father, I know true wisdom comes from you, and true strength is found in surrendering to your will. I confess my weaknesses, doubts, and fears, knowing you are the anchor of my faith. In times of uncertainty and trials, grant me the grace to place our trust in you, knowing your plans are greater than my own. May I boast in my weaknesses, knowing your power is made perfect in them. Help me to surrender my pride and self-sufficiency, replacing them with a deep trust in your providence. Amen.

4. What We All Really Crave

People want to better themselves. There's nothing wrong with that. What people are really looking for is to find happiness in themselves. But I have news for you:

You'll always let yourself down. Matthew 6:24 says, "No one can serve two masters. Either you will hate the one and love the other, or you will be devoted to the one and despise the other" (NIV). If you are the master, you are serving yourself. If Jesus is the master, you're serving him. But you can't make yourself the master and then call Jesus your Lord.

CHAPTER 7

Dreams Come True

*Toxic Affirmation and the
Law of Attraction*

> When you ask, you do not receive,
> because you ask with wrong motives,
> that you may spend what you get on
> your pleasures.
>
> **—James 4:3 NIV**

When I was eleven years old, I got my family a dream home.

I can still see it in my mind: a white two-story home with blue shutters, two acres of land, a private duck pond, and a long tree-lined driveway. Oh, also with bougie window boxes.

You're probably wondering how a child could afford such an incredible property. But I didn't buy it. I manifested it.

Or so I believed at the time.

I was taught to visualize my dream home multiple times a day, including all sensory details like its smell and paint color. I could make it a reality. My sisters and I were to imagine living in the home and were instructed to speak in the affirmative every time we thought of it. I was told this was a form of powerful prayer. We were to speak as if we actually had it—with no drop of doubt.

So that's what I did.

I stopped what I was doing several times a day and acted as if I lived in this house and spoke positively about what I loved about living there. So when my mother came to us crying one day after looking for homes, I assumed something was wrong. But that's not what happened.

She was crying tears of *joy*. She was overwhelmed by what she had found. What she described was the home I imagined—down to the fancy flower-filled window boxes.

Magnetic Thoughts

Although I didn't fully understand it at the time, this true story about my childhood beliefs manifesting our dream home were rooted in the New Thought practice called the law of attraction (LOA). This involves positive thinking, affirmations, visualizing, and manifesting.

LOA is deceptive and destructive—and probably at work in a church near you. So let's take some time to define it. Here's how TheLawofAttraction.com defines it:

> The Law of Attraction defines your ability to attract, into your life, what you focus on. Whatever you can imagine is achievable, if you take action on a plan to get to where you want to be. The true definition of the Law of Attraction is *like attracts like*. Whatever you give your emotional energy and attention to, is what will come back to you. . . . The Law of Attraction governs everything within our abundant Universe. It does not discriminate. It only exists with perfection whether you like it or not.[1]

If you can imagine it, you can create it. If it exists in the spiritual realm, you can manifest it in the physical realm. With the

LOA, the idea is simple: Your thoughts shape your reality. Your thoughts become things.[2] Your emotions are your spiritual GPS. You are a powerful magnet, and this power is emitted through your thoughts and feelings.

Every thought you have, every feeling you feel, and every word you say has a frequency or vibration. You always want to be on a positive frequency—or give out "positive vibes," as the cool kids say these days—to attract positivity. Remember, in New Thought, the things of God are positive. Any negativity is an absence of God.[3]

In one interview, I asked a New Thoughter about affirmations and the LOA.[4] "Do you practice the law of attraction?" I asked.

"Oh, absolutely. Yes. There's nobody I know that doesn't," she enthusiastically insisted. "You can't exactly escape it! But I think it's misunderstood as a positive-thinking fad when, really, it's much more than that. It's not that simple."

"How do you practice it?"

"Through positive thinking and affirmations. I repeat affirmations every day."

"What do you do if they're not true? Do you still repeat it?"

"Well, that's the goal. To *recognize* it's already true. It just needs to be realized."

"How would you do that through affirmations?"

"By *believing it*," she said. "It must reflect my inner truth. 'I am powerful, wise, well-liked, and whole' is what's true. I speak it and accept it as truth. Then it *must* manifest."

I suspected there was a logical conclusion to this type of prayer. So I asked, "Okay, so *who* are you praying to then?"

She cut to the chase. "To put it simply, *myself*!"

This isn't just her personal interpretation. This is the logical conclusion of affirmations. One New Thought blog site puts it this way: "Our role as human beings is to actualize our potential into our own experience. The impersonal God, the Creative Intelligence of the Universe, has provided everything we need to survive and thrive—as potential for us to actualize. That God becomes personal within and as each of us. . . . This is why we use affirmative rather than intercessory prayer. We are praying to ourselves to change our own mind, to come into alignment with our potential for good so that we actualize that good."[5]

But there's another surprising teaching that goes hand in hand with the law of attraction that most people don't realize.

Powerful Words

This next part might surprise some readers or even make you clutch your pearls. But stay with me here. You need to know this.

In chapter 3, we defined terms. I mentioned you would need to hold your horses until this chapter to know how New Thought defined prayer. Well, here it is: Not only do you want positive thoughts, but you also want to *speak* positive and affirmative statements as if they are absolutely true. New Thought prayers are called "affirmative prayers"—better known as affirmations.[6] We can thank New Thought for this popular practice.

Affirmations are positive declarations spoken out loud to bring forth results in the physical realm. Because words have power, people must take great care not to speak negatively. Negative words attract negative manifestations.

A crucial component of affirmative prayer is the power of faith—to pray with the *full* expectation of receiving results. Prayer is creative. Words matter. In New Thought, because everything is metaphysical, words have a vibrational frequency affecting the world around them. Therefore, they have creative power.

Rather than begging God for what you seem to lack—which is shockingly seen as a *lack of faith*—you make powerful declarations that you already have or are those things that are desired.[7] You must have no doubt and no questioning. Affirmations require absolute and unquestioned faith that you will receive your desired outcome. I once heard someone describe affirmations as "wish-craft." You craft your desires through thinking.

The belief that spoken words can manifest change has been around for centuries but was reintroduced into the American psyche through a French psychologist named Émile Coué. He would have his patients repeat positive phrases—affirmations—to themselves each day.[8] Affirmations went beyond psychology and took on a spiritual meaning when the baton was handed to New Thought. With its focus on positive thinking and humanity's divine potential, affirmations became preferred for personal transformation and shaping your own reality.

New Thought leaders such as Charles and Myrtle Fillmore inspired their followers to use affirmations to attract health, prosperity, and happiness.[9] But affirmations became truly fashionable once Louise Hay, a renowned New Thought self-help author and the visionary founder of Hay House Publishing, wrote about them. She claimed that affirmations and the power of her thoughts were responsible for healing her.[10]

Emma Curtis Hopkins, a New Thought leader, was practically a patron saint of affirmations. She believed that thought, not germs, made you sick.[11] She would instruct her students to repeat many affirmations for healing and wealth. Here's one she'd instruct for blindness: "'Let there be light.' You are bathed in a sea of light for God is light and He is all around you. You are in the glorious presence of God always. God is sight itself. You see with His sight. He sees through you and for you. You have perfect sight now. 'All is light.'"[12]

Affirmations are widely used in our society. Whether the goal is self-help, attracting prosperity or a life partner, growing self-esteem, or maintaining a positive attitude, affirmations are a part of our mainstream culture.[13] We see this practice in books, therapies, speeches, and, yes, even churches. More on that in the next chapter.

I Am Because I Said I Am

By far, one of the most important aspects of affirmations is "I am" statements. According to New Thought, what comes after you say "I am" holds creative power. Our words and beliefs shape our experiences and reality—but it's important to have the correct approach.

New Thought practitioners are often cautioned against negative affirmations. For example, saying "I am not sick" is a no-no. You say, "I am well!" because the focus in the former is on sickness, whereas in the latter, it is on wellness. You don't say, "I am not poor!" You say, "I am rich!" Therefore, speak positive "I am" affirmations to manifest your desired outcomes.[14] This can result in people affirming something that *isn't* true, but they must act, speak, and think as if it were.

Remember, *you're* the sovereign. "I am" statements are a declaration of someone's divine identity—just as Jesus declared his divine identity. Jesus is the example, the Wayshower of this inner divinity, the Christ within. Therefore, you're just as much the I Am as Jesus was.

A theme in affirmative prayer is that you are already whole, inherently good, perfect, and complete. Your only sin is your ignorance of this. In many of my great-grandmother's books, written in her handwriting, was: "I am whole. I am holy. I am good." So when you pray, you're just affirming what's within. In one New Thought center I visited, the prayer request card said this: "I now release the following prayer to the Christ within who does the work." This is why affirmations are simply prayers to *yourself*, whether you realize it or not.

At this point, you might be thinking, "Wow, Mel! This sounds so familiar! Sorta like a certain positive, smiling pastor from Houston!" Reader, you're a sharp one! If you've put these pieces together, consider this your official air high five. (If not, then stay curious. The plot thickens in the next chapter.)

Prayer in Christianity is different. Prayer is talking to God but understanding we're not confiding *within* us but *beyond* us. It's not contemplative meditation, sending positive vibes, or positive thinking. It's communication with the holy God of the universe, making our requests known, and him responding in his sovereignty, providence, and power for his purposes and glory (Rom. 11:33–36; 1 John 5:14–15). New Thought strips sovereignty from God and hands it to humanity.

God wants to humble us. Satan wants to put us on a pedestal.

God says to die to yourself. Satan wants you to live for yourself.

God alone says he is the Great I Am. Satan says *you* are the Great I Am.

As one New Thought teacher says, "Keep believing in you, the God in you, the Great I Am that I Am that I Am. That's enough."[15]

Okay, Satan.

What's the Big Deal?

I have a dear friend who is a devout Christian and works as a victim advocate at the local police station in my city. She has seen some of the most horrendous things happen to women and children. When these people walk into her office, the first thing they see is a board with statements they have probably never heard before: "You are beautiful. You are not alone. Don't give up."

These are not statements they will confess over and over again as a self-sovereign to create a new reality for themselves. These are encouraging statements about human value and the truth of their situations as they already are. Affirming someone in and of itself isn't bad or wrong. Often it can be helpful and healing. But affirming something *true* is what makes it genuinely beneficial. If we've learned anything about New Thought, it's that it can distort what's good to fit its narrative, which can lead to confusion or misapplication of positive ideas.

Here are some helpful ways to distinguish New Thought affirmations from other forms of encouragement:

- New Thought affirmations focus on the self, not a holy and sovereign God. We demand control instead of submitting to the control of God.
- Affirmations are used as a sort of incantation, sometimes leading to a *denial of reality*. For example, say someone is obviously sick or going through a tragedy. Instead of facing the truth—they have a terrible flu and probably need a doctor—they affirm that they are healthy and well. They are, in essence, claiming their *own* truth, whether it's true or not. A lie needs at least a little legitimacy to gain credibility. As Georg Christoph Lichtenberg powerfully put it, "The most dangerous untruths are truths moderately distorted."[16]
- Affirmations are notorious for taking Scripture out of context to force biblical support. Many New Thought authors cite various Bible passages to support the ideas of affirmative prayer, the divinity of humanity, and the belief that our words have creative power, claiming these concepts align with what Jesus taught.
- Affirmations always make you the good guy. The spiritual default posture of affirmations is that you are inherently good and you deserve nothing but positive things to come your way. In this light, it's difficult to see our flaws.[17] In Romans 7:18, Paul says, "For I know that nothing good dwells in me, that is, in my flesh. For I have the desire to do what is right, but not the ability to carry it out." (In verse 24, he says he's wretched! Paul, the greatest Christian missionary who ever lived, sees himself as unrighteous, wretched, sinful, and unworthy in the presence of a holy God.)

I used to read Scriptures like this and think, "Oh no! I

can't talk about myself like that! It's too *negative*." But this makes perfect sense in light of Scripture.

One of the main issues with affirmations is the disregard of sin. If we think we don't have a sin problem, then why in the world would we need a savior? If we're blessed, victorious, wealthy, worthy, healthy, and full of light, love, unicorns, rainbows, potatoes, and happiness, why do we need salvation?

- Just because you hear someone being positive, saying nice things about themselves, and speaking Scripture does not always mean they're using affirmations. The question to ask: Is this *true*? Or are they cherry-picking Scripture?

To say, "I trust God at all times because he is my refuge" (Ps. 62:8) or "As I lose my life for Jesus, I will find it" (Matt. 10:39) is different from saying affirmations to manifest into your life.

You might be thinking, "Mels, does this mean I go around all the time just wallowing in the fact that I'm a horrible person? Can I not see anything positive in myself because doing so would mean I'm somehow taking away glory from God?"

No.

Having a healthy self-worth or self-concept does not mean you're taking glory away from God. It means you're recognizing who you are in Christ, knowing you were worth the price paid to redeem you from death.

Knowing what you're good at isn't prideful. Boasting in it is. Liking who you see in the mirror isn't vanity. Having an excessively high opinion of yourself is. Getting compliments and enjoying your own company isn't arrogant. Only constantly wanting affirmation is.

Common sense and biblical wisdom imply that our actions

and words impact our lives and relationships. This does not equate to our thoughts and words having superpowers.

I also want to point out the difference between "thinking positive" and what I'm talking about in New Thought. There's nothing wrong with being an optimist and having a generally happy demeanor. Thinking positive, in and of itself, is not New Thought. We should strive to have an optimistic mindset in general. This *does* affect our mood, attitude, and how we treat people. An optimist *discovers* reality. They have a generally healthy attitude about whatever they encounter. This is biblical.

A New Thoughter believes their thoughts and words are able to *create* reality. They believe anything that comes upon them that's negative (sickness, poverty, hardship, etc.) they attracted to themselves through their thinking. This is unbiblical.

An optimist can look *to* God. A New Thoughter thinks they *are* God.

Wanna Know a Secret?

One of the most well-known examples of the law of attraction in pop culture is Rhonda Byrne's book *The Secret*. This book (which expands on the documentary by the same name) took the country by storm and has currently sold over thirty million copies. At the beginning of *The Secret*, Byrne shares how she discovered the LOA, which is a part of the book that is often overlooked but which I find crucial.

(Time to put on my mysterious narrator-voice hat.) She was given a *mystifying* one-hundred-year-old book. What she read changed her life forever by revealing an *ancient*, long-suppressed *secret*! Only a special few knew of this powerful secret, and she was here to tell everyone about it. (Takes off hat.)

That mysterious one-hundred-year-old book? It's called *The Science of Getting Rich* by New Thought author Wallace Wattles. The book would have been considered self-help at the time.

(Chapter 6. Same play, different scene.) Wattles wrote this book with the same concept New Thought author Napoleon Hill did: If you think rich, you'll grow rich. The LOA is how we achieve this.

Riding the success wave, Byrne continued to write books rehashing the same concept, expounding on the LOA. Take a look at her explanation of magnetic frequencies and the role they play in the LOA and attracting your desires: "Everything in the universe is magnetic, and everything has a magnetic frequency. Your feelings and thoughts have magnetic frequencies too. Good feelings mean you're on a positive frequency of love. Bad feelings mean you're on a negative frequency. Whatever you feel, whether good or bad, determines your frequency, and like a magnet you attract the people, events, and circumstances that are on the same frequency!"[18]

Think of the consequences of this mindset. The car accident you had? The cancer you were diagnosed with? The job you got? The twenty dollars you just found on the ground? The punch you just got in the throat? It's *all* because you attracted it somehow. This is (supposedly) a *law* as constant as gravity.[19]

This teaching isn't restricted to just Byrne. Eric Butterworth, a New Thought author, shares a similar sentiment in his book *Celebrate Yourself*:

> Every person is a living magnet, drawing to himself things, people, and circumstances in accord with his thoughts. The man may say, "But I was not thinking about accidents!" However, in the subconscious mind there must have been patterns of belief in accidents of a possibility, resistance of careless drivers, being on the road, and others....At this time, you may not understand it, but something in you has attracted it....Accept the obvious fact that it has happened, and know that there is that in you that is equal to it. And most importantly, determine that you will grow through it and thus rise to a state of mind where such a thing cannot happen again.[20]

Now just imagine for a second how much effort that would take to "rise to a state of mind where such a thing cannot happen again." What does that mean? When is it good enough? A somewhat unknown fact is that Eric Butterworth had a profound impact on Oprah Winfrey. She is on record—as a Christian—saying that the book *Discover the Power Within You*, written by Butterworth, changed her view of life and religion. She said *this* was the book that showed her why Jesus really had to come, to show us the Christ Consciousness within us all. Butterworth was also the first Unity minister to appear on *The Oprah Winfrey Show*.[21] Another interesting fact about *Discover the Power Within You* is that Maya Angelou wrote the foreword to it.

With well-known names like these, it's no wonder how these ideas became so influential in our world.

Abraham and Esther Hicks

Speaking of recognizable names, one of the New Thought teachers who fascinated me most was Esther Hicks. I listened to her teachings on the LOA quite often. However, Esther wouldn't say the teachings were hers. She would attribute them to Abraham—the spirit she channels (occult soup, anyone?).

But Abraham doesn't claim to be just one spirit. Channeled through Esther, he—or they—explains itself to be a group of collected consciousness from a nonphysical dimension.[22] This reminds me of the encounter Jesus has in Mark 5:9 with a group of spirits named Legion. Yikes.

I once heard someone say Abraham is an example of the spiritual awakening we're seeing in the LGBTQ+ community. Because "Abraham" technically has no gender and is a "they," it shows the spiritual potential of humanity, and *this* is why we need to embrace the spiritual potential of humanity, however that looks. Tragically, Abraham is only one of the channeled sources of information about the LOA. Pick up any LOA book, and you will see channeled material.[23]

These "secrets of the universe" are coming from spirits that are being channeled through humans who write them down, with the books becoming bestsellers.

The Appeal: It "Works"!

The LOA, affirmations, manifestations, and "I am" statements are attractive for various reasons. Not only do they offer people an illusion of control in a world gone mad, but many people are led to believe these practices align with quantum physics and science. They hold emotional, spiritual, and pseudoscientific allure, drawing those seeking to connect with "quantum physics" and the unseen frequencies of the universe.

Another reason these practices look so attractive is because *they often appear to work*! Just like the home I got for my family when I was a child. (Uh, you're welcome, Mom.) It seemed like I thought it, I spoke it, and—bibbidi-bobbidi-boo—it happened. The fact that it seemed to yield results was one of my biggest spiritual obstacles when I was leaving New Thought.

A lot of people, especially on social media, claim to use the LOA with success, such as manifesting health and wealth. This is a staple of New Thought beliefs. As I'm writing, I just went to TikTok and searched "how to manifest." Many videos popped up, some with *hundreds of thousands* of views. Here's a sample of the claims:

"I manifested an 'A' on my test!"
"This manifesting method is foolproof."
"Never manifest the wrong way again!"
"Try this manifestation technique for instant results!"

Unfortunately, ideas like this sell millions. The more fantastic the success, the more people will be attracted to the sensational nature of the LOA. But here's the deal. Many of these results have common sense explanations or are spiritual hocus-pocus. But if it helps people, what's the problem? Here are a few points to ponder:

- **It's temporary.** Yes, the LOA might help you. For now. But sooner or later, those results and subsequent satisfaction from them will wear off. Whatever method you used to achieve those results? You'll now have to rely on. It's like spiritual Botox. It definitely "works." But it's not sustainable. You'll need another fix. Then another.

   Imagine a buff guy at the gym. He takes steroids to pump himself up and inflate his self-worth. Sure, he can bench more and feel good about himself when he flexes in the mirror. But it's a false strength. It's temporary. He's dependent on the steroids for results. He doesn't realize that the effects of these drugs on his body are going to cause lasting damage. Perhaps he doesn't care. Because, hey—*this works!* It brings the results he desires and makes him happy.

- **Critical thinking is negative thinking.**[24] Many times, for the LOA to yield results, you must turn your brain off. No negative thinking. No doubting. But what if someone is doing their absolute best to bring in positive energy, visualizing with no doubts, and they still have no results? Then it must be somebody else's fault. Someone else is bringing in the negative energy. This can cause people to avoid those they think are causing the "bad vibes."

   Additionally, it can lead to self-deception by not allowing opposing thoughts or opinions to question what you're trying to manifest. You live in your own echo chamber. You mind control yourself. So, of course, people think it's foolproof. They won't allow themselves to think otherwise because they are desperate for results.

- **Thinking better makes us act better.** This one is biblically accurate and a no-brainer. Making better choices typically leads to a better outcome in life. I hate to break it to you, but if you think you manifested an A in class, it most likely wasn't because the universe was in your favor. You probably paid attention in class, studied, or didn't have a difficult time figuring out the right answers.

- **There's a social incentive for this to work.** Look, it doesn't take a genius to see how many views these sorts of videos get. Ideas like this sell by the millions. Promising health, wealth, and prosperity is a clever way to become popular. So the more outrageous your stories about success in this area, the more people will be attracted to the sensational nature of these teachings.

- **Sometimes we _make_ it fit.** There's a scene at the end of _Cinderella_ where one of the stepsisters is trying on the glass slipper. Instead of accepting that her toes are the size of sausages, she gets frustrated and says, "I'm going to _make_ it fit!" (She's just living her most authentic self.) And indeed, it does (sorta) fit for a few seconds as everyone gets excited. But then it flies off, almost shattering. This is what I see when I think of people manifesting and visualizing. We _force_ it to work by our own actions. For example, I remember a time I wanted to manifest red tulips. I can still see these tulips in my mind: long red-stemmed in a tall clear vase with a red bow tied around it. *Chefs kiss.* I visualized them for weeks, but nothing was happening. Knowing our wedding anniversary was coming up, I hinted to my husband about wanting red tulips. When the day arrived, I was very pleased to see that my husband managed to track down red tulips. Sure, the vase wasn't the right size, and the tulips were smaller, not _exactly_ what I was visualizing. But he pulled it off! My hero. Considering tulips were out of season, I saw this as proof that it was the

LOA. But see what I did there? I *made* it work. And others do the same thing. We then credit the LOA. (Then many turn around and market their experience to others.) It's similar to a case of selective hearing. We selectively listen and reinterpret information to confirm our preferred beliefs.

- **Of course, occultic practices "work."** People find occult teachings and practices attractive because they "work." That's precisely the problem. Our interest tends to be justified because of the supposed science, or pseudoscience, behind the method.[25] I agree with my friend and apologist Hillary Morgan Ferrer when she says, "'Occult' doesn't mean 'not true.' It's not synonymous with 'doesn't work.' Occult means *secret* or *hidden*. There are almost always short-term 'benefits' to dabbling in the occult. It wouldn't entice anyone otherwise."[26]

- **It works for the wrong reasons.** Sometimes you get results because of demonic influence. This is what the devil does. He can't get rid of Jesus. But he can distort him. He can show you another Jesus who likes what you like, dislikes what you dislike, and believes what you believe.

  I remember talking with someone a few years ago who started out as a Christian but felt like she needed "more" of God in her walk. She wasn't satisfied with just the Bible and started reading occultic material, including *Conversations with God* by Neale Donald Walsch and *A Course in Miracles*, among others. She claimed they were inspired by God. She ended up invoking her own spirit guide, claiming it was in line with her Christian values. She wanted to be able to experience what these authors did. But it didn't go well for her. She had her spirit for a while and claimed it gave her *wonderful* advice that truly helped her. But over time, the spirit became manipulative. It wasn't the kind, helpful being she thought it was. This was demonic. She immersed herself in Scripture and called out to Jesus to forgive her. The being left, never to come back again.

Like eating hot sauce to get rid of indigestion, people try to use New Thought methods to get rid of the very issues it causes.

Demons aren't afraid of your mind power. They aren't afraid of your positivity. They aren't afraid of your high frequency. They aren't afraid of your good works. They aren't afraid of your positive vibes. They aren't afraid of your affirmations. There's only one thing they're afraid of and will flee from: the name of Jesus.

These points aren't just limited to the LOA. This is true for *all* New Thought and occultic practices. A mixture of all of the above was how we "manifested" our home.

Didn't Jesus Teach This?

Since LOA is New Thought, it markets itself as being aligned with Christianity. As mentioned before, these concepts are deemed spiritual truths that Jesus and the Bible teach. Scriptures such as Matthew 7:7, which says, "Ask, and it will be given to you; seek, and you will find; knock, and it will be opened to you," are broken down into a practical New Thought formula: ask, believe, receive.

Several New Thought authors write books that appear Christian by incorporating Scripture and Christian terminology to teach the LOA. Books like *Why Did This Happen to Me?* by Joseph Murphy and *How to Use the Power of Prayer* by Harold Sherman are marketed to Christians as books on how to practice the LOA.

I personally practiced the LOA, *thinking it was what Jesus taught.* I even hired an LOA coach to teach me more super spiritual things and how to yield results. (The strange things you can find on Craigslist, amIright?) She said she was a Christian and believed

Jesus practiced these laws of the universe too. For it to work, we just needed to harness the power of our minds.

The LOA is marketed as being ancient and interwoven throughout all religions and spiritualities. For some reason, people seem to eat stuff up when you tell them it's ancient. Perhaps they feel it indicates that something is more sacred and spiritually genuine. Some of the teachings of the LOA may not explicitly reveal the *real* motive behind it. It's not so much about vibrations, frequencies, an embarrassing misuse of physics, and creepy collective spirits talking to us. Instead, it's about *you*.

Reader, this is the part about the LOA that should shake us to our core: Its message isn't about love or unity. It's not about treating others how you want to be treated. It's not about coexisting in harmony. It's advertised that way. But don't be fooled. It is totally, utterly, unequivocally *demonic*.

Let me show you what I mean.

This is an example from *The Secret*, which we discussed earlier in this chapter. It is perhaps the most fitting example I can come up with because it explicitly reveals the core message of New Thought.

> You are God in a physical body. You are spirit in the flesh. You are Eternal Life expressing itself as You. You are a cosmic being. You are all power. You are all wisdom. You are all intelligence. You are perfection. You are magnificence. You are the creator, and you are creating the creation of You on this planet.[27]

I'm sorry. But if I may put this plainly, this is garbage. (Keep in mind this book has sold *millions*.)

Let's fix this. (Clicking my red pen.) Here's how it *should* read:

> *Jesus* is God and a physical body. *Jesus* is spirit in the flesh. *Jesus* is eternal life. *Jesus* is a cosmic being. *Jesus* is all power.

Jesus is all wisdom. *Jesus* is all intelligence. *Jesus* is perfection. *Jesus* is magnificent. *Jesus* is the Creator, and he created the creation of you on this planet.

Since I'm in an editing mood, let's look at another one. This is also from *The Secret*:

The earth turns on its orbit for You. The oceans ebb and flow for You. The birds sing for You. The sun rises and sets for You. The stars come out for You. Every beautiful thing you see, every wondrous thing you experience, is all there, for You. Take a look around. None of it can exist, without You. No matter who you thought you were, now you know the Truth of Who You Really Are. You are the master of the Universe. You are the heir to the kingdom. You are the perfection of life.[28]

Click.

The earth turns on its orbit for *Jesus*. The oceans ebb and flow for *him*. The birds sing for *him*. The sun rises and sets for *him*. The stars come out for *him*. Every beautiful thing you see, every wondrous thing you experience, it's all there, for *him* and because of *him*. Take a look around. None of it can exist without *him*. No matter who you thought you were, now you know the truth of who *he* really is. *He* is the master of the universe. Because of *him*, you are an heir to the kingdom. *He* is the perfection of life.

There. That's better. Get this: the entire underlying premise behind the LOA is *you are God.* This is anti-gospel. This is anti-Christ.

Think of the long-term effects material like this has had on people, which we're now seeing demonstrated in our country. Tell people they're God? That has devastating consequences.

Destined to Fail

The LOA is not without controversy. Critics argue it is overly simplistic and unrealistic and can potentially lead to victim-blaming, where people who face challenges and hardships are blamed for not thinking positively enough. It has also contributed to a destructive amount of entitlement.

Author Barbara Ehrenreich, in her book *Bright-Sided: How Positive Thinking Is Undermining America,* would agree to a point. She also has an entire chapter dedicated to how the positive thinking movement destroyed the economy.[29]

You'd think a popular belief like the LOA, which teaches about love, acceptance, and inner trust, would yield good results in the long run, but *it encourages people to look in the wrong place for fulfillment.*

If you're told the answers are found inside you, you are doomed to fail from the beginning. You're the standard. You're the answer. But it's really the unholy trinity of me, myself, and I. Not only that, but telling others they can just manifest what they should actually be working hard toward is irresponsible. It could possibly lead to some deeper issues. People are robbed of learning important life skills like studying, wrestling with tough decisions, or thinking critically through major life decisions.

Furthermore, because "love" is seen as the highest emotional frequency one can be on, anything bringing fear is seen as unloving. Many people in New Thought look at many Christians as being fear-oriented with their "negative" talk about hell and sin. Can you see why they're resistant to the true gospel? You can't have the good news without the bad news, but they can't let in the bad news!

The LOA is tempting. It seems to bring happiness. Many New Thought teachers say the LOA is really the law of *love.* In this way, it's marketed as being a core doctrine to the positivity New Thought is so well known for. The law of attraction—the law of *love*—is the most powerful force in the universe, they'll say. But that's a lie. The type of love New Thought provides is not a virtue but a vice. It uses virtuous words like *love, joy, peace,* and *desire*. But it delivers entitlement, denial, apathy, and greed.

The LOA isn't biblical. It's *anti*-biblical. It's occultic, not Christian. It makes Jesus your life coach and God your loyal servant. But "believing in Jesus" is not a magic formula. And God isn't your golden retriever.

Unfortunately, speaking things into existence, declarations, and inner power aren't confined to the secular masses. In the next chapter, we're going to dig into another side of New Thought that is more personal for Christians: the Word of Faith movement.

Unlearning the Lies

Now that we've shed some light on New Thought's connection to the law of attraction and the false hope it brings, let's take some steps toward eliminating any of this spiritual poison we might have ingested along the way.

1. Focus on Truth

Here are some recommended Scripture passages to read and ponder. To understand the context, I highly recommend reading the whole chapter where these passages are found:

- Matthew 6:25, 33 (NIV)—"Therefore I tell you, do not worry about your life, what you will eat or drink; or about your body, what you will wear. . . . But seek first his kingdom and his righteousness, and all these things will be given to you as well."

- James 4:3 (NIV)—"When you ask, you do not receive, because you ask with wrong motives, that you may spend what you get on your pleasures."
- 1 Timothy 6:10 (NIV)—"For the love of money is a root of all kinds of evil. Some people, eager for money, have wandered from the faith and pierced themselves with many griefs."
- Romans 1:25—"They exchanged the truth about God for a lie, and worshiped and served created things rather than the Creator."

2. Stand Firm

If you're a Christian, it's important to reject teachings like the law of attraction and instead trust that God will provide for your needs. This reminds you to rely on God's plan and provision rather than self-centered ideologies.

Here are some recommended resources on this topic that have been immensely helpful for me in this area:

> *Mere Christianity* by C. S. Lewis
> *Game of Gods* by Carl Teichrib
> *Law of Attraction: A Gateway Drug to Spiritual Heroin* by Jon Clash

3. Pray and Proclaim

We are not God. We are not the Great I Am. There is only one Great I Am, and when we surrender to this truth, we will grow in wisdom and truth. Here's a prayer for you:

Lord, help me remember that my power and purpose come from you, and may I never exalt myself to a status reserved only for you. Protect me from false beliefs that seek to replace you with my own desires.

4. What We All Really Crave

At the core of this teaching is something we all yearn for and isn't necessarily all bad: power and control. We all need to have some sense of power and control to live happy and healthy lives. But teachings like the law of attraction elevate humanity to godlike status. It's in the *surrender* of this kind of power and control to God that brings us what we're really looking for: peace.

CHAPTER 8

Prosperity Now

New Thought and the Word of Faith Movement

> The Word of Faith movement sort of has an interesting secret that they don't want the world to know about. . . . The WoF movement is the cousin to the New Thought movement.[1]
>
> **—Rev. David Alexander, spiritual director**
>
> **at Spiritual Living Center**

In 2011 I left my New Thought beliefs and entered a season of intentional biblical discipleship. I read my Bible faithfully and developed a growing desire to study, understand, and trust it. I quickly realized that many of the deeply cherished beliefs I held all my life were entirely unbiblical. Though they'd been cloaked in Christianese and wrapped in a Bible verse or two, there was no hiding the ugly truth.

The law of attraction is total garbage.

Speaking things into existence, believing in the creative power of my words, and attributing negative circumstances to a lack of faith?

In the bin.

Believing God *always* wants me to be healthy and prosperous and that I should always speak as if I'm healthy and wealthy?

Rubbish.

Believing I have the same power as God because I am divine? Creating and manifesting my desires because I'm a child of God? Believing that whatever adjective follows the affirmative words "I am" creates my day?

All trash.

I spent a lot of time sorting through these teachings and more, repenting for my unbiblical beliefs and my distorted view of myself and God. I was being freed from the lies.

Then, imagine my shock when I saw those same deceptive New Thought teachings I had repented of—being taught using the same Scriptures—in an unexpected place: *the church.*

The Movement

I discovered a distinct movement within Christianity that says a hearty "amen" to the previous list I'd tossed in the garbage can. This movement is called Word of Faith (WoF). Though this term is synonymous with the prosperity gospel, the "Word of Faith" name wasn't *given* to them.[2] The people in this movement fused "Word" and "Faith" together to reflect the movement's core doctrine that your words, when infused with faith, can shape your reality and manifest positive changes. I guess you could say they named *and* claimed it. (Ba dum tss!)

What people may not realize is that this belief is a mix of New Thought with a side of Pentecostal tradition.

I had never known what Word of Faith was until I saw these similarities *after* I left New Thought.

Now, not all Pentecostal or charismatic Christians believe what we'll discuss in this chapter. But there are demonstrable connections between New Thought and WoF. Any historian worth their fancy quill pen knows this. We will look at several of those connections. Many unsuspecting church attendees have no idea how convoluted some Sunday sermons are, especially in some charismatic and Pentecostal cultures. Some Christians can be more vulnerable to spiritual experiences driven by a desire to "give the Spirit room" and to have "mountain-moving faith." With the best of intentions, trusting pew sitters might believe a New Thought–influenced message because someone tossed in a Bible verse or two (never mind the context). On top of that, it was delivered by a spiritual authority they might have been trained not to question. My goal is to help readers learn to unmix the mess so we can discern truth from lies.

Before we dig into some of the most significant problems with the WoF, let's take a brief look at how it started.

The Grandfather: E. W. Kenyon (1867–1948)

Essek William Kenyon is considered the grandfather of the WoF movement.[3] He was a Baptist pastor whose teachings were popular among Pentecostals. Most of the core theological doctrines of WoF can be traced back directly to Kenyon. His teachings included:

- Human nature is spirit, soul, and body, but is primarily spirit.
- God created the world by speaking words of faith and does everything else by faith. We are intended to exercise the same kind of faith.
- In the fall, human beings adopted Satan's nature and gave up their divine dominion to Satan, making him the legal god of this world.
- By our positive confession or affirmative declarations

with the "God kind" of faith, we can overcome sickness and poverty. All sickness is a spiritual condition.[4]

A plain reading of Scripture doesn't lead to these beliefs. So where did he get these teachings from? From two sources. The first was a divine healing movement in the late nineteenth century called the "faith cure" movement. This taught that God guaranteed healing to all believers as part of the atonement. Illness disappeared when someone truly believed and lived as if God had already healed them.[5] Kenyon adopted much of these teachings, believing sickness is a *spiritual* rather than *physical* problem.[6] He supported the New Thought belief that the proper response to illness is to ignore symptoms of sickness and refuse to acknowledge or affirm it verbally.[7]

Kenyon was also significantly influenced during his years attending Emerson College, which was founded by Charles Wesley Emerson, who was a Unitarian minister. Transcendentalism and New Thought dominated the curriculum.[8] According to one expert, it's nearly certain it was here that Kenyon regularly sat under an instructor named Ralph Waldo Trine, a master expositor of New Thought and author of one of the most widely read New Thought books of all time.[9] It is undeniable that Kenyon had an extensive collection of metaphysical books and had a keen interest in reading them.[10]

The question isn't whether he was exposed to New Thought. Even *I* have an entire library of New Thought books I read with great interest (and brain hurt) for research for this book. The question is, *How did Kenyon respond to them?* Even though he denounced New Thought, he recognized people were getting results from its methods. The metaphysical influence seen in Kenyon's work supports the fact that he adopted—not rejected—these ideas. Furthermore, he remained in contact with many New Thought students from Emerson and spoke highly of the college.[11] It's clear from Kenyon's own works that the literature he was exposed to and the lasting relationships he had with his teachers and classmates played a significant role in what he would go on to write and teach.

Interestingly, while Kenyon found New Thought teachings intriguing, he regarded the movement as a counterfeit version of Christianity. In an attempt to retain what he found relevant and discard the rest, Kenyon ended up developing a "new type of Christianity" that he called "practical Christianity."[12] What's further shocking about the "practical Christianity" name is it's the *exact same name* that Unity used and was known for in the early 1900s. Kenyon claimed that *his* version was the authentic one.[13] It's as if he wanted to offer a superior Christian alternative to New Thought.

The question is, In trying to create a fresh approach to adapt and respond to New Thought, did he unwittingly concede these metaphysical ideas at the expense of biblical ones? I believe he did.

For Kenyon, there was more to God's redemption story, and he viewed himself as the messenger of this information.[14] His teachings supposedly revealed "a wealth of an almost unknown truth of the Word of God."[15]

One detail of my research stunned me: Kenyon taught that Jesus's physical death on the cross isn't the basis for redemption. Why? Because it was *physical*. Remember, to Kenyon and many WoF teachers, our true self is *spirit*. He believes that because sin is spiritual, Jesus's physical sacrifice on the cross was not enough and wouldn't reach the actual problem.[16] This is why many WoF preachers teach that Jesus had to die a *spiritual* death in hell and be spiritually reborn to restore his divinity. This key teaching explains why Kenyon and other WoF teachers believe humans can also be "godlike" when they're reborn. (More on that later.)

This also helps explain why the intellect is criticized in WoF circles. If "spirit" represents ultimate reality, then our physical senses perceive something secondary. Our intellect takes a back seat. The mind is seen as holding the Christian back from experiencing the fullness of God. This should be seen as a red flag. If anyone ever tells you to turn off your brain to accept questionable theology, run!

Many strange behaviors and teachings result from this type of thinking in WoF circles, such as claims of visiting heaven, rolling around on the ground screaming, visitations from Jesus himself, and blowing the wind of God on viruses.

However, it's simply not true that Kenyon was an incognito ninja New Thought minister who was trying to dupe Christians. But he is the source of most of the distinctive and controversial teachings of the WoF movement.[17] The *most* that could be said is Kenyon was significantly influenced by metaphysical teachings, and this is undeniably clear in the legacy he created.[18]

The Father: Kenneth Hagin (1917-2003)

If Kenyon is the grandfather of the WoF movement, Kenneth Hagin is the father of the WoF movement we know today. Hagin was the founder of Rhema Bible Training College, was a big fan of Kenyon's work, and is heralded as a highly respected prophet and teacher in the WoF movement.

It's crucial to look at Hagin. It's extensively documented that he plagiarized many of his teachings from none other than E. W. Kenyon.[19] Hagin also claimed to have performed and experienced numerous healings. So when God supposedly told him to take the same faith he had exercised for healing and to apply it to finances, he began teaching prosperity and the power of words.[20]

Why is this important? Because Hagin caused the spiritual ripple effects we see today. He took many of Kenyon's metaphysically influenced teachings and combined them with the Latter Rain Pentecostal teachings, giving birth to the WoF movement we know today.[21] What's the Latter Rain movement, you ask? Think of a modern day of Pentecost 2.0 in the mid-1900s with an emphasis on eschatology. Latter Rainers believed God was sending a new wave of his power, just like he did on the day of Pentecost. This would help prepare the world for Jesus's return. They focused on things like speaking in tongues, creating the fivefold ministry, healing, and having leaders with special spiritual powers. But the movement quickly became controversial. Excessive emotionalism, spiritual elitism, and fringe behaviors were justified, among other controversial teachings. Many Pentecostal denominations distanced themselves from this movement. Even so, it had a big impact on the WoF movement.[22]

Though Hagin had many—and I mean many—unusual and questionable teachings, the most relevant here are his unique teachings about health, wealth, and positive confessions.[23]

The WoF movement has had several prominent leaders and televangelists over the years, including Kenneth Hagin, William Branham, John G. Lake, Kenneth Copeland, T. D. Jakes, Oral Roberts, Benny Hinn, Joel Osteen, Todd White, Bill Johnson, and Creflo Dollar, among others. Oral Roberts University has significantly influenced many of these teachers. They either received their education at this university or have strong associations with it, which is known as a prominent Word of Faith college.

Connecting the Dots

New Thought teachings were everywhere in the 1900s. Many Christians, greatly influenced by Kenyon, were trying to find a way to assimilate them into their existing beliefs. New Thought was teaching health and prosperity. It claimed there was power in our words. Kenyon sought to give this right to Christians rather than denounce it altogether. It was hard to deny the rapidly spreading ideas. New Thought was like the unnamed "positive thinking" religion for everyone. From magazines to pop psychology and books, it was as accessible as the air they breathed.[24]

The WoF movement was a response to this trendy positive thinking movement. But it wasn't a biblical response. It was a *syncretistic* one, a pick-and-choose-whatever-feels-good belief system that ironically ended up adopting some of the very ideas it claimed to deny.[25]

Throughout the rest of this chapter, I'll draw some connecting lines between New Thought ideas and WoF teachings. But before I do, I'd like to provide clarification:

- I'm *not* broad-brushing the people in the WoF movement as being unsaved. There is diversity within this movement. I'd even say some of it is orthodox. But there's tremendous error being taught by WoF teachers, and it needs to be made clear *why* they're in error without being overly critical and downright awful about it. There are dear brothers and sisters in Christ in many of these churches who need a lifeline. My own story attests that people can be in error and still be saved. My torch and pitchfork are for New Thought ideas, not people.

- I want to make a distinction between charismatics, Pentecostals, and the WoF. While many Pentecostals and charismatics *are* associated with WoF, others within these groups *adamantly* oppose WoF teachings. The WoF is a radical extension of the Pentecostal charismatic movement.[26] I don't think it's accurate (or biblical) to lump all who are "charismatic" or "Pentecostal" into the WoF group.

- My goal is to uncover the presence of New Thought teachings in mainstream Christian settings while recognizing that many people I care about are part of this movement. We must confront the true origin of these teachings and discard what is not of God, throwing it in the theological bin where it belongs.

We *ought* to call out bad theology. It's not divisive to do so. It's divisive to *teach* bad theology.

In Romans 16:17, Paul says, "I urge you, brothers and sisters, to watch out for those who cause divisions and put obstacles in your way that are contrary to the teaching you have learned. Keep away from them" (NIV).

To explain, imagine you're a medical student. Your intelligent professor has taught your class how to make a certain medicine with *very* specific ingredients. Any variation to this recipe will result in permanent damage—even death—if someone takes it. You're minding your own beeswax, staying true to what you were taught, then—bam!—another teacher crashes in, teaching your class a different recipe for the same medicine, contradicting your professor. You are *not* being divisive when you object. *They* are being divisive because they're butting in with the contrary teaching. You're simply staying true to what you were taught *because there are consequences if you don't.*

We're required to examine what WoF teaches, as it contains harmful beliefs that are unbiblical.[27]

Though there are many nuanced problematic teachings in WoF, my main goal is to show that WoF does *not* align with the Bible but with New Thought in these areas. So let's take a closer look at some of these connections.

Connection #1: Healing

One of the original teachings of New Thought was that healing happens in the mind. If you're sick, it's because you're being a big negative-thinking ninny. If you're sick, it's not your body needing correction. It's your thoughts.[28] Your mind is *way* more important than your body. Closely related was the teaching that it's *always* God's will to heal, with healing being one of Jesus's main teachings and reasons for being on earth. John 10:10 is used as a proof text for this, which says, "I came that they may have life and have it abundantly."[29]

WoF has a similar formula for healing: If you have enough faith, believing with *no* doubt, you will *always* receive healing. WoF leaders regularly quote Scripture passages such as Mark 11:24 and Matthew 7:7 to demonstrate that this is God's will for humanity. Kenneth Hagin himself claimed that through his faith, he was miraculously healed after reading Mark 11:24.[30]

In my research adventures, I had a phone call with a woman at the International New Thought Alliance (INTA). I was asking about New Thought and health, and I was surprised by what she shared with me. "I feel like a fraud," she said.

"Why?" I asked.

"Because I haven't mastered this thing. I'm very frustrated I haven't manifested my healing."

I thanked her for sharing that with me and asked a follow-up question. "Why do you think it hasn't manifested?"

She seemed hesitant to answer but said, "Well, it will. I mean, I'm not *going* to be well, *I am* well!" she emphasized. I wasn't prepared for what she said next.

"I go to this little Pentecostal church down the road from my house every now and then, and I'm very well received. I don't agree with everything and don't believe they have the full Truth, but they're getting there! They teach things I've always believed, and I enjoy their New Thought declarations of health and wealth."

... 'Scuse me? Their *what*?

I asked for specifics. "What do you mean by that? I don't think many Pentecostal churches would agree with New Thought teachings."

"Oh, I don't think many do! But when it comes to their affirmative prayers and understanding we're all whole in Christ, I couldn't agree more."

To be clear, I don't think she fully understands the vast differences between New Thought and charismatic Pentecostal doctrines. But I understood how she could see similarities if she was in a Pentecostal church that was actually WoF. What she was alluding to is what we went over in chapter 2 about the intrinsic wholeness of humanity, which says it's an illusion that we're broken.

Many WoF teachers would agree with her. In my research, I attended a WoF church in my area. Afterward, I talked with one of the pastors. I read this aloud without telling him the source: "Words are the first level of the creative process. So, when you say, 'I am,' the words that follow 'I am' are summoning creation with a mighty force because you are declaring it to be a fact. And that is why it is extremely important you choose your words wisely." I quoted Matthew 7:7 as one Scripture to support it.

He said he absolutely believed that. He unapologetically advised me to speak and act as if I received healing and abundance. I then asked if he could elaborate on how people bring sickness to themselves or why God wouldn't heal. "Well, it's not God's will that we get sick. It's his will to *always* heal! To make us healthy! We're always able to bring that healing. That means the responsibility to get well isn't on God! 'Cuz he wants that! It's on the person praying or the person being prayed for," he said.[31] What he didn't know was that what I read him was a paraphrase from *The Secret* about the law of attraction.[32]

In New Thought and WoF, there's no room for excuses. If you don't receive healing, it's never because of God's sovereign will at work. He's certainly not allowing your pain and suffering for any greater purpose. The fault lies with you and your lack of faith.

New Thought and WoF do differ in how they describe Jesus's role in healing. For example, Phineas Quimby believed that when Jesus healed, he wasn't really performing a miracle but correcting someone's wrong thinking. In WoF, healing would absolutely be seen as a miracle performed by Jesus. However, both would agree that all of us have the same power as Jesus and the apostles and should always be healed.[33]

The good news? *None of this is biblical.*

Scripture is clear: Jesus's main priority was to preach the gospel, not physically heal everyone. Neither did the apostles always heal. A simple reading of the New Testament shows this. In 1 Timothy 5:23, Paul is instructing Timothy on how to care for himself for a stomach ailment. He doesn't tell him to have faith and "believe to receive" his healing or speak like he's well. No, he simply gives him instructions on how to relieve the sickness.[34] At the Pool of Bethesda, Jesus healed only one man among many. In Mark 1:29–38, he was healing in Galilee, but the next day, he woke up and left, *knowing that everyone was looking for him.*[35] His reasoning made sense: "Let us go somewhere else—to the nearby villages—so I can preach there also. *That is why I have come*" (NIV, emphasis added). Paul himself pleaded with Jesus to heal him three times in 2 Corinthians 12:8–9, but Jesus's answer was, "My grace is sufficient for you."

The question I would pose to someone who believes it's *always* God's will to heal is this: Is Jesus *alone* enough for you? If you never had a single miracle, healing, or spiritual experience, would his grace be sufficient for you? How we answer this question reveals much about our heart posture toward Jesus.

Connection #2: Prosperity and "The Good"

"When Christians are poor, do they talk as if they had chosen poverty? . . . They are poor because they can't help it, and their whining is pretty good evidence! . . . Do not allow yourselves to believe in misery. . . . Decree against it! . . . There shall nevermore be any poverty known among us!"[36]

Reading this, you'd think you were front and center at Lakewood Church listening to Joel Osteen, but this is a quote from Emma Curtis Hopkins, one of the prominent women in the New Thought movement. Surprise!

Though Joel Osteen would agree with her. He believes, "When you face adversity, don't be a crybaby. . . . Instead, have the attitude of a victor. . . . You must get out of that defeated mentality and start thinking and believing positively. God wants you to be a winner, not a whiner."[37]

Both quotes are great examples of teachings in the prosperity gospel. Prosperity was a later focus in New Thought, but it developed with women like Hopkins. She claimed that right thinking can not only heal you but bring prosperity and success in all areas of life. She had a teaching called "The Good," which was an early version of the prosperity gospel. She would speak an affirmation saying, "My Good is my God," and "There is Good, and I ought to have it."[38] The general idea with "The Good" is that God has provided everything good and wouldn't allow us to desire what wasn't possible. You're *entitled* to wealth.

She taught many ideas someone might hear from a WoF pulpit on any given Sunday—none of which are found in the Bible. Things like:

- Jesus was the first prosperity teacher.[39]
- Prosperity is a law.
- Speak positively to experience abundance.[40]

These were spiritual teachings taught in New Thought well before they were mainstream in WoF. Hagin was the first to bring these New Thought teachings into the WoF landscape after a supposed visit from God himself. As mentioned before, Hagin claimed God told him to take the faith he used with healing and apply it to *money*. (Yeah. No need to test against Scripture. Because *God* told him *directly*.) But what's interesting is these "visits from Jesus" came in the same year he started reading Kenyon's work.[41]

The central belief of the prosperity gospel should startle Christians: *through right thinking, humans possess powers that were once attributed solely to God, including the abilities to create health and abundance.* This is the premise for Napoleon Hill's wildly popular book, *Think and Grow Rich.* Charles Fillmore, the cofounder of Unity, wrote an entire book called *Prosperity* in 1945 about lessons and laws of abundance. He even changes Psalm 23 to say, "The Lord is my banker. My credit is good. . . . Though I walk in the very shadow of debt, I shall fear no evil. . . . Thou fillest my wallet with plenty."[42] Can you believe it?

Another New Thought book, called *You Can Be Prosperous* by W. I. Hoschouer, published in 1947, teaches this as well. He claims prosperity can be obtained through faith, which is "a divine force connecting man inwardly with God and making God's power available to and active in man."[43] There's even a tiny pamphlet my grandmother had by Emmet Fox called *The Magic of Tithing.* He sprinkles in Bible verses like Malachi 3:10 and Luke 6:38, which supposedly promise blessings when you tithe. God will open the floodgates of heaven when you tithe and also give you divine protection. He says this is a law of God.[44] When we harness these laws, then we can access divine laws for prosperity and health. These concepts are widespread in WoF teachings and churches, as seen in this quote: "Just as there are spiritual laws that set prosperity in motion, there are also laws that set poverty in motion. . . . We need to know what the laws that govern prosperity are so we can abide by them. We need to know what the laws that govern poverty are so we can stay away from them. . . . As long as you are thinking, talking, and acting [in] poverty, you are going to get more of it than you can stand."[45]

No, this isn't from a New Thought author—this is cowritten by Gloria Copeland, wife of WoF preacher Kenneth Copeland. Surprise!

Kenneth Copeland is no stranger to prosperity preaching. (And if ever there was a preacher who truly excelled in causing second-hand embarrassment when watching him, it would be Kenneth

Copeland.) He has videos about the supposed laws of prosperity and even a three-step plan for manifestation. (Yes, he actually teaches this.)[46] He's not the only one. WoF preachers like Paula White, T. D Jakes, Benny Hinn, Jesse Duplantis, and more are not shy in telling believers it's their divine right to be healthy and prosperous.

It wasn't until the 1940s and 1950s that Pentecostal preachers—like Hagin—started speaking of spiritual laws, financial blessings, and the power of the mind for health and wealth. It was a part of the American mood. They didn't fight against it but instead found it *irresistible*. It was here the gospel was made into a tool for health and wealth.[47]

Again, the prosperity gospel isn't biblical. A simple reading of Scripture tells us Jesus and the apostles were *not* rich. We instead see:

- Wealth is not necessarily a sign of God's blessing. *Contentment* is. Paul said in Philippians 4:12–13, "I know what it is to be in need, and I know what it is to have plenty. I have learned the secret of being content in any and every situation, whether well fed or hungry, whether living in plenty or in want. I can do all this through him who gives me strength."
- We never once see Jesus warn about being poor. But we see repeated warnings about the snare of riches.
- And no, being poor doesn't make you more pious. Look, it's not a sin to be rich or virtuous to be poor. No matter what we have in life, we are to steward it correctly and for the glory of God.[48]

Connection #3: Positive and Negative Confessions

We discussed affirmations in chapter 7, which means your thoughts and words have power to manifest your reality. WoF has a different name for this teaching: positive confessions or declarations. In WoF, prayer is speaking to God, but it's also speaking to things and circumstances and commanding them to do what we say.

WoF and New Thought both have teachings about negative thoughts and words. In WoF it's called negative confessions—speaking negatively and receiving negative results. In New Thought, it's called "denial." A denial is a verbal rebuke of the power of any negative condition to limit, bind, or defeat us.[49] You can't just blindly say them. You have to *feel* them. Your emotions are a powerful tool for what results you get. You use the power of your words and feelings to dismantle negative thoughts.[50] Binding and rebuking is a common WoF version of this. Instead of negative thoughts being rebuked, usually, it's a negative *spirit* that is rebuked.

Both come to the same conclusion: Because humans are divine spirits (more on that later), when we are redeemed, we have power to rule over our circumstances by speaking words of faith. This is seen as a spiritual power. The same concept works with wanting health and wealth and avoiding sickness or poverty.[51] In WoF, you never *ask* God whether it's his sovereign will for you to have anything or to be healed. You speak it as if you have it.

Consider my previous conversation with my INTA friend who was frustrated she couldn't manifest her healing. What I didn't mention is I tried three more times to ask her about her sickness. She *refused* to talk more about it, changing the subject every time. I understood why. As a New Thoughter, she believes there's power in her words. If she said, "I'm sick," or spoke as if she had an illness, then she'd be sick. Her healing wouldn't happen. I could sense she regretted even mentioning it to begin with.

Ironically, Kenyon denounced New Thought affirmations, but it's clear he agreed with its methods. He believed New Thought used the right process with the wrong theology and was exploiting truths belonging to Christians.[52] Again, he was trying to *redeem* New Thought teachings and recycle them in the church.

When it comes to positive confession, Kenyon here is key. These teachings are from him but are *distinctly* New Thought in origin:

- Faith is a force, a power to be yielded and used to control outcomes.
- Understanding your inner spiritual self is the key to manifesting what you want.
- "Right thinking" and speaking in the present tense bring things into existence—healing, wealth, a relationship, a Cadillac, good weather, your missing sock, etc.—to manifest in the material world.[53]

Kenyon also taught that people who used Jesus's name had a unique power, and even unbelievers could benefit from the power of spoken positive words. He used John 14:14, which says, "If you ask me anything in my name, I will do it," and said we should change "ask" to "demand."[54] You don't merely *ask* God for healing or wealth. Psshhh. That's for the pathetic peons who don't have enough faith. No, you *demand* it.

Another deceptive version of positive confessions comes in the form of *declarations*. One of today's biggest champions of declarations is Joel Osteen. His "I am" declarations, positive thinking message, and prosperity teachings are *uncannily* similar to New Thought. This is not a coincidence. Joel's father, John Osteen, was a good friend of the Unity movement and of a successful Unity minister in Texas named Howard Caesar.[55] Joel is familiar with New Thought ideas, and you see this influence in his teachings.[56] While many Christians sharply disagree with Joel and his teachings, New Thought leaders praise him. One New Thought leader says, "Joel Osteen is a lot like a Unity [New Thought] minister, but he's just waving a Bible around while he says [New Thought] things. Then, every once in a while, he diverges off into a little fundamentalism to keep people happy. But essentially, he's giving a very positive [New Thought] like message."[57] This should give us pause.

Again, WoF teachings on positive and negative confessions are unbiblical. They are built on biblical half-truths such as:

1. God can do marvelous things when we trust him.
   True, but God is not obligated to do these things.
2. Thinking and speaking positively is generally a healthy thing to do.
   True, but it is not true what we speak is bound to laws manifesting our reality. Revelation 3:17–18 says, "You say, 'I am rich; I have acquired wealth and do not need a thing.' But you do not realize you are wretched, pitiful, poor, blind and naked. I counsel you to buy from me gold refined in the fire, so you can become rich; and white clothes to wear, so you can cover your shameful nakedness; and salve to put on your eyes, so you can see" (NIV). Here, we see Jesus tells the Laodiceans they are the opposite of everything they were confessing. If WoF teachings were true, it would be impossible for Jesus to give them this report.[58]
3. We should pray with expectant faith.
   True, but it does not mean we demand *everything from God.* I don't understand how this is acceptable for Christians to do to God our Father when we wouldn't even put up with this type of behavior from our own children. Can you imagine little snot-nosed ten-year-old Jimmy coming to you and *demanding* you bless him?
4. Jesus's name has power!
   True, we ask in Jesus's name, but that doesn't mean God will give you everything you ask for. That's hard for some to grasp, but this is why his control is so beautiful. Pray often with all your heart and mind. But this isn't some sort of magical incantation forcing God to bend to our will.

Praying "in Jesus's name" doesn't equal "abracadabra." We pray according to the will of God, letting our *requests* be made known to God (Phil. 4:6).

These teachings have consequences. Interestingly, the reasons WoF has for speaking things into existence are the same given by New Thought: because you are divine. Which brings me to my last line to draw.

Connection #4: Little Divine Gods

Both WoF and New Thought share a remarkably similar teaching of inner divinity. Thanks to Kenyon, WoF (disturbingly) has what's called the "little gods" doctrine.[59]

Perhaps because of the backlash they've received, I don't know many WoF preachers today who would be forthright and say, "We're gods."[60] But this teaching is still implied and admitted behind closed doors. *Why* can you heal, speak things into existence, control the weather, and have godlike powers? Because in WoF, you *are* godlike.

Besides Kenneth Copeland, one of the most outspoken WoF teachers about the "little gods" doctrine is a well-known WoF figure I mentioned briefly before: John G. Lake. He said that "God intends us to be gods...There is a God-power and a soul force in the nature of man that God is endeavoring to bring forth. ... The inner man is the real governor, the true man that Jesus said was a god."[61] Can you guess who one of his theological inspirations was?

None other than E. W. Kenyon.[62]

If this weren't surprising enough, Lake is one of the only WoF preachers with a direct and undeniable link to New Thought. Lake was connected to a lesser-known New Thought minister named Albert C. Grier. But this was more than just a "connection." Before Lake was well known, he co-served in a New Thought congregation with Grier, becoming lifelong friends.[63] They did divine healing ministry together, and when Lake started his own ministry, his new congregation was mostly members of the New Thought congregation.[64] He owed much of his success to Grier and his New Thought teachings. Furthermore, Lake was one of the first WoF teachers to talk about spiritual forces and laws of the universe that we could control with "faith."[65]

John G. Lake is one of the most influential leaders in the early WoF movement who has influenced countless Christians with these kinds of teachings. But there's more to this "little gods" doctrine.

Here are some main points in WoF about this teaching:

- Part of the purpose of Jesus's coming was to show us this potential and restore humanity to godhood.[66]
- This is why we should be able to perform miracles as he did—and then some. Jesus wasn't unique in his incarnation, but *all* Christians are incarnations of God just as much as Jesus was. Kenyon taught that when we realize our divine potential, we become like "supermen," graduating from a lower class of Christian.[67] Kenneth Hagin also shared this view.[68]
- One correlated teaching between WoF and New Thought is how they view "being made in the image of God." New Thought's view, as discussed in chapter 3, is different from that of WoF, but both believe we're godlike.[69] In WoF, to be made in God's image means we are *exact duplicates* of God. This was Kenyon's teaching that humans are made in the same *class* of gods as "little gods."[70] This is called "deification," which is the elevation of humanity to gods, or potential gods, and demoting God to look more human.[71]
- Chapter 3 discussed how New Thought authors explain humanity as being potential "gods in embryo." Kenyon has a startlingly similar teaching, except he says, "Every new

creation is a superman in the embryo."[72] We just need to tap into our powers the way Jesus did. This has created a legacy of some Christian leaders making wild claims of having fringe (sometimes cringe) spiritual powers.

Again, these teachings are unbiblical. Scripture says we are made in God's image and likeness, not after God's *kind*. WoF teaches we *become* godlike through the atonement, and New Thought teaches we are *already* godlike.

Imagine putting someone in a room with just a Bible to read. They have no prior knowledge of WoF or the Bible. They would *not* come out with WoF or New Thought teachings. WoF represents a unique blend of specific Pentecostal traditions and New Thought teachings. It's a fundamental feature that characterizes the WoF movement.

Both New Thought and WoF tend to demote the Bible's authority and elevate personal experience. They then interpret the Bible *through* those experiences, not the other way around. Why? Because the authority is shifted. Both the WoF and New Thought teach that Christians share the same authority as Jesus. Feelings are confused with the voice of the Holy Spirit. With all the connections we've made, it's not surprising that WoF also shares New Thought's methodology for "hearing from God." Who needs a Bible when you can just look and listen within?

The Lust for Power

A final observation that can't be ignored is that WoF amplifies the desire for spiritual encounters. In my research, I couldn't help but notice a repeated effort to justify exaggerated displays of power as something biblical. This is where *many* strange (and sometimes downright silly) behaviors are enabled in the name of the supposed power of God. The implication is that the more spiritual experiences someone has, the more favor they have from God. And the more *power* they have. Those not experiencing miracles or successful declarations lack power. Sadly, some people lose their faith because they think they aren't as favored by God because they don't have outrageous spiritual encounters. Someone having extrabiblical mystical experiences means they are *super spiritual*. They have higher spiritual knowledge. They're *special*.

If somebody tries to challenge what they feel God is directly telling them? *What? How dare you! How can you say God didn't tell me that? Look at all the super-spiritual stuff that happens to me! How can you possibly question if God spoke?* Online, we see hundreds of thousands—sometimes millions—of views of captivating personalities claiming spiritual power in the name of God.

Can you see how spiritual arrogance creeps in? The heavy reliance on subjective encounters and self-centered spirituality, along with an anti-intellectual bias, can become a big problem in WoF. This includes a disdain for people who choose to study Scripture systematically with faithful interpretive methods. *What? You only read and study your Bible? Boorrriinnng.*

This attitude can make people feel like second-rate Christians. I hope no one has made you feel that way. But if they have, know that God values your trust in him and your commitment to spreading the gospel infinitely more than counting your weekly spiritual encounters with him so you can impress Judy McSuperChristian at the church's casserole swap party.

WoF makes the same mistake New Thought does: It shifts the sovereignty of God to the sovereignty of self *as a divine power.* The prosperity gospel places a burden on people. This is what false gospels are *supposed* to do. They make sensational claims and then make it impossible for you to achieve them.

The positive WoF message is attractive. People want to hear it. Thousands of people flock to positive-thinking Happy Jesus, who promises prosperity and health. *That's* a Jesus people like. He's easy to follow, and he gives you the desires of your heart. Following Happy Jesus, seeking constant victories through manifestations and miracles, leaves people empty and always yearning for the next spiritual high.

Don't worship experience and power over truth. When we lust for power, we are tempted to experiment with spiritual experiences, venturing where God forbids us to go.

Take Jesus after his baptism, for example. He is hungry after fasting for forty days. The devil comes to him, saying, "If you are the Son of God, command these stones to become bread" (Matt. 4:3 NET). The devil's logic is: If you have power, why don't you use it to meet your own needs?[73] It's also the underlying logic within spiritual experiments—you can direct power at your own command to suit your own needs. But it's not the logic of Jesus or Scripture.

It's the logic of the devil.

Jesus was tempted to use spiritual power to fulfill his personal goals and needs.[74] It's a bit of a paradox: Some of these Christian communities talk about spiritual warfare and being fully equipped with God's armor—which they're called to do. But at the same time, they're embracing the things they say they're against. In their quest to stay relevant, they're magnifying personal experiences, and ancient mysticism is becoming a big part of these "faith experiences."[75]

The fruit of the WoF movement isn't good. It mocks the gospel and Jesus's message. While many WoF teachers have sound theology on certain matters, they allow some teachings in their churches that should be rejected.

This is only one area where New Thought has affected the church. In the next chapter, we'll cover one of the most influential movements taking the church by storm. It contains surprising New Thought elements many may not be aware of: progressive Christianity.

Unlearning the Lies

Now that we've shed some light on New Thought's connection to the Word of Faith movement and the false hope it brings, let's take some steps toward eliminating any of this spiritual poison we might have ingested along the way.

1. Focus on Truth

Here are some recommended Scripture passages to read and ponder. To understand the context, I highly recommend reading the whole chapter where these passages are found:

- 2 Corinthians 12:7–10 (NIV)—"Therefore, in order to keep me from becoming conceited, I was given a thorn in my flesh, a messenger of Satan, to torment me. Three times I pleaded with the Lord to take it away from me. But he said to me, 'My grace is sufficient for you, for my power is made perfect in weakness.' Therefore I will boast all the more gladly about my weaknesses, so that Christ's power may rest on me."
- John 4:24—"God is spirit, and those who worship him must worship in spirit and truth."
- Luke 22:42 (NIV)—"Father, if you are willing, take this cup from me; yet not my will, but yours be done."

2. Stand Firm

Pray for those who are in WoF, and also be prepared and equipped to know what you're up against. Here are some recommended resources on this topic that have been immensely helpful for me in this area:

Counterfeit Kingdom by Holly Pivec and R. Douglass Geivett

The Word-Faith Controversy by Robert M. Bowman Jr.

Blessed by Kate Bowler

God, Greed, and the (Prosperity) Gospel by Costi W. Hinn

The New Book of Christian Martyrs by Johnnie Moore and Jerry Pattengale

3. Pray and Proclaim

Here's a prayer for you:

Lord, help me to stand firm against teachings that don't align with your Word. Keep my heart focused on your will, which may sometimes involve challenges and suffering. Help me endure this with faith and patience. Give me the humility to seek your truth above all else. Help me to always remember the example of Jesus, who submitted to your will, even in the face of suffering.

4. What We All Really Crave

Christians want to feel loved by God and yearn for spiritual potential. This isn't wrong. But it's a lie to think that God does not have sovereignty and providence over our own.

CHAPTER 9

A Different Gospel

New Thought and Progressive Christianity

> I am astonished that you are so quickly
> deserting the one who called you to live
> in the grace of Christ and are turning
> to a different gospel—which is really no
> gospel at all.
>
> **—Paul in Galatians 1:6–7 (NIV)**

I said a quick prayer, walked into the church, and sat down. I grabbed my pamphlet from the front and sat in the back, as was my custom when visiting new churches. The introvert code requires I sit where hopefully nobody sees me and close enough to the front that my thirty—*ahem*—year-old eyes can see the screen. This particular visit was to a progressive church in my area.

I visited several progressive churches as part of my research, and I discovered this one through an announcement at a New Thought church I attended. They said this progressive church was organizing a prayer labyrinth walk.[1] That wasn't something I was going to participate in, so instead, I attended the regular weekend service.[2]

Sitting in the back, I was shooketh at the choice of opening song: "Revelation Song." *Holy, holy, holy is the Lord God Almighty, who was, and is, and is to come.* This beautiful biblical song is based on Revelation 4 and the wonder, holiness, and never-ending worship of Jesus alone. Hearing it in this setting was ironic and unexpected.

I listened to the sermon, taking notes. Afterward, I approached the reverend to ask him some questions. But what he said took me by surprise. He mentioned I might want to come back next week because he was only a visiting reverend. And he wasn't visiting from another progressive church *but from a New Thought church.*

Apparently, this was a common thing in my area. Clergy from New Thought and progressive churches in my area work together. From time to time, they do what they call a "reverend swap" for a Sunday service. I did end up coming back the next week to talk to the progressive pastor. I caught up with him after service.

"Thanks so much for talking with me," I said.

He warmly welcomed a conversation with me. He wasn't intimidated in the slightest. "Sure, I'm happy to talk about this stuff. I love it."

"I'm curious to know more about this reverend swap. How did you become acquainted with New Thought churches in the area?" I was surprised because the term *New Thought* is unfamiliar to most people, even though the teachings are throughout society.

"Well, we all share a unique bond, spiritually as well as with serving the community through social justice. They get that the gospel is *really* about love."

He explained that even though he wouldn't consider himself New Thought, he embraced Christ Consciousness and believed this informs us how the Bible should be interpreted. He was a devoted ally to the LGBTQ+ cause. As a progressive, he denied most major core doctrines of Christianity, such as the Trinity, Jesus's sinlessness, and the Bible being the Word of God. He was a universalist and open to a wide range of theological perspectives. He prioritized personal spiritual growth, inclusivity of all religions, and social justice as *the* highest spiritual virtues. For him, Jesus was open and inclusive to people of all faiths and lifestyles, especially those in the LGBTQ+ community. He explained Jesus was a social justice activist, fought for the oppressed, was a feminist, and would denounce most of what evangelical Christians believe today. (In many progressive spaces, *evangelical* is a derogatory term.)

Interestingly, after he gave his beliefs, he ended with a caveat that, without exception, *every single* progressive pastor I spoke to gave: "But this is just what *I* believe."

"Yeah, I've been hearing that a lot. How do you determine what's true then?" I asked.

"Everyone needs to decide what's true for them by what resonates from within."

Sounds familiar. Chapter 3. Same song, second verse.

He continued. "We need to be intentional about accepting people that are different than us because we don't have it all right. It's about diversity. Everyone has a piece of the truth, and when we all come together, we are closer to seeing what that is."

I challenged this. "What about Christians who believe the Bible alone and believe Jesus is God alone and the only way to be saved?"

He *physically recoiled* at this remark. Without hesitation, he said, "Oh no, those are the *bad guys*. They're the literalists who are closed-minded and cause a lot of hate and division. I doubt they'd even come to one of my services and hear what we'd have to say." The irony of his statement was so superb I thought my head would explode.

I continued. "Can you really blame them for believing a plain reading of Scripture and simply being obedient to what it says? Even if they're uncomfortable with what they're reading, they consent to it. What would you do if you came across a Scripture that made you uncomfortable?"

He enthusiastically said, "I would interpret it through the lens of *love*. This is what it means to be holy. As long as we're doing the loving thing, then we're holy. It's about acceptance."

I brought it back to New Thought. "So you would agree that New Thought is in line with these ideas?"

"Absolutely. I like the Jesus I hear from them, and they like the Jesus they hear from us. This is a Jesus that works for everyone."

Doctrine Deniers

If there's a road most taken away from the biblical Jesus, it's progressive Christianity.

If you're not familiar with progressive Christianity, it's a movement aimed at giving Christianity a spiritual "facelift" diverging from historic biblical Christian beliefs and practices. It originated with the emergent church movement, which arose in the late twentieth and early twenty-first centuries.[3] John Pavlovitz, who is well known in the progressive Christian movement, describes progressive Christianity this way:

> The truth is that Progressive Christianity is so diverse that it simply cannot be neatly defined or summarized, but here are some things that most who claim the label probably agree on:
> We believe that a God who is eternal, isn't land locked to a 6,000 year-old collection of writings, unable to speak in real-time to those who seek. Revelation can come within and independent of the Bible. . . . We believe that social justice is the heart of the Gospel, that it was the central work of Jesus as evidenced in his life and teachings; the checking of power, the healing of wounds, the care for the poor, the lifting of the marginalized, the feeding of the hungry, the making of peace.[4]

Progressive Christianity, in its most aggressive form, seeks to modernize historic biblical Christian beliefs and practices, often drawing from postmodern thinking, sometimes questioning historical biblical teachings, and often reinterpreting the Bible to be more inclusive of heterodox ideas, practices, and lifestyles. This movement has evolved into what is often referred to as "woke" Christianity today, which tends to promote religious and spiritual open-mindedness, social justice, diversity, and a departure from historic biblical Christian doctrines.

In practice, some progressive Christians focus on personal spirituality, social justice, and LGBTQ+ inclusion. They can also overemphasize and redefine the teachings of Jesus related to love and compassion. Many of them deny the beliefs, creeds, doctrinal statements, and scriptural views of historic biblical Christianity we went over in chapter 3.[5]

As we've seen from previous chapters, this is similar to New Thought. The website ProgressiveChristianity.org is a spiritual networking site sharing almost identical spiritual values to New Thought.

On this website, they list the core values of progressive Christianity:

> Progressive Christianity is inherently always evolving and progressing. Please take these lightly but seriously. They are not dogma, they are simply a starting point to establish conversations and a foundation of values and beliefs that we have observed Progressive Christians generally share. It's okay if you don't agree with all the words or all the parts. We support your authentic path. You can use these in your faith communities and with family and friends to talk about what it means to you to be a Progressive Christian in today's world. Here is to always progressing!

1. Believe that following the way and teachings of Jesus can lead to experiencing sacredness, wholeness, and unity of all

life, even as we recognize that the Spirit moves in beneficial ways in many faith traditions.

2. Seek community that is inclusive of all people, honoring differences in theological perspective, age, race, sexual orientation, gender identity/expression, class, or ability.

3. Strive for peace and justice among all people, knowing that behaving with compassion and selfless love towards one another is the fullest expression of what we believe.

4. Embrace the insights of contemporary science and strive to protect the Earth and ensure its integrity and sustainability.

5. Commit to a path of life-long learning, believing there is more value in questioning than in absolutes.[6]

Notice the confusing caveats in the first paragraph:

"Take these lightly . . ." but also take them seriously.

"This isn't dogma . . ." But then the values and beliefs given look a lot like dogma—But then deny the values and beliefs any authority *even as you affirm them.*

"We support your authentic path . . ." But the implication is that if you disagree, you won't be supported.

Ironically, even some progressives might dismiss this website as not aligning with what progressives actually believe, which shows the diversity of this movement. But the previous statements do overwhelmingly align with many progressive leaders' teachings and beliefs. The commitment to remaining in constant doubt and refusing to submit to any sort of "set doctrines" is like trying to catch smoke.

Compare this with the International New Thought Alliance, which has a similar role of being an umbrella organization for New Thought. If you remember from chapter 5, they have a "Declaration of Principles" that is comparable to the previous list. But they also have a social justice statement:

The members of INTA hold a basic unifying Principle which we believe is the foundation for the new paradigm of a just society: namely, there is a Divine Presence which is the Source of all there is and which lives in, through, and all people. Therefore, all persons are worthy and deserving of dignity, justice and respect, regardless of national origin, class, creed, race, ethnicity, physical ability, sexual orientation or gender identity. Reflecting this idea, INTA celebrates the diversity of all people, and rejects and strongly disavows all forms of racism, sexism, or any other "ism" that negates the Truth of any person. The International New Thought Alliance offers information and takes appropriate action wherever possible to create and support a just and equitable society.[7]

In regard to New Thought's commitment to progress, one site states, "'New Thought' is not a name or expression used to designate any fixed system of thought, philosophy, or religion, but the term itself conveys the idea of a growing or developing thought. When New Thought is molded and formed into a system, it ceases to be 'New' Thought."[8]

Many New Thought philosophies can be found on ProgressiveChristainity.org, and vice versa. This isn't surprising, seeing as how many of their core values are the same. No wonder some of them do reverend swaps.

When I first started learning about progressive Christianity, I was stunned at the similarities between what progressives believed and what I believed in New Thought. I didn't realize how *progressive* I was. I followed New Thought teachings, but politically and socially, I was progressive without realizing it. My view of Jesus was more mystical, but I was progressive in my view on the Bible, universalism, embracing all spiritualities, and welcoming the ever-evolving LGBTQ+ community—and probably would have listed my preferred pronouns in my Instagram bio. I also was a big supporter of social justice, though some New Thoughters have a different name for it: spiritually guided activism.[9] To clarify, "social justice" simply means the pursuit of a fair society by addressing inequality and discrimination. It aims to ensure equal opportunities and rights for everyone. This is good and biblical. As Christians, we should fight for equal rights and opportunities for others, which Christians have done for hundreds of years. But social justice has evolved, especially in progressive spaces. Instead of Jesus's death and resurrection being the heart of the gospel, social justice has become the focus.

In my conversation with the kind progressive reverend, it became abundantly clear that New Thought and Progressive Christianity share quite a bit of DNA. Not only do they glorify uncertainty, but they're resolved in their desire to please the masses under the banner of "love."

Many people assume the DNA link is New Age spirituality. There is some spiritual overlap due to the acceptance of diverse beliefs in New Age and progressive Christianity. However, there are *significantly* more similarities and partnerships between progressive Christianity and New Thought. The reason why we are seeing such a blend of the two has to do with the spiritually inclusive nature of New Thought and how it's stealthily become a dominant, yet hidden, spirituality of America.

Progressive Christianity isn't just a new sect of biblical Christianity trying to get closer to what the Bible teaches or seeking truth no matter what. They believe they are *improving* Christianity, not just merely redefining it.

The Secret Glue Sauce

But why were there so many connections? What was mixed in with all of this to make it seem so similar? In many ways, progressive Christians have more in common with New Thought than they do with biblical Christianity.

Some progressive teachers, like Richard Rohr, for example (who too many Christians quote online because they think he's a Christian), seem to hold a hodgepodge of spiritual beliefs. He teaches a strange pseudo-spirituality about the Universal Christ and other Christianese beliefs, yet spiritually diverges in other ways. Many New Thought churches, teachers, and websites look up to him. I've even heard him quoted at their services. But putting Rohr in any category is like trying to catch the laser from a laser pointer. And he's not the only one.

Many teachers in progressive circles have created a version of Jesus and Christianity that seems more relevant in the culture today yet seem to claim a different spirituality entirely. Why?

I discovered there is a sort of "glue" binding them together that explains these similarities: mysticism. This is the belief that one can attain direct knowledge of God, spiritual truth, or ultimate reality through personal experiences such as intuition or insight. Some people claim there isn't a perfect definition of mysticism. Admittedly, it can be vague. But in the context of New Thought, mysticism is a way of believing and practicing spirituality where people focus on having personal, direct experiences with something greater than themselves, like God or a divine power. People usually achieve this by going beyond the rules of organized religion to seek *their own* understanding of the divine.[10]

To be clear, there are mystical elements in biblical Christianity. We have a supernatural worldview. But for the Christian, experiences should always be interpreted *in light of Scripture*. Spiritual experience untethered from Scripture may give results but may bring encounters with something or someone other than the one true God.[11]

We touched on transcendentalism in chapter 5, connecting it to the spiritual aspect of defining our inner identities or authentic selves. Transcendentalism shifted the focus away from ideas about theology and God to personal experiences. People became more interested in promoting interfaith dialogue and creating a more ecumenical atmosphere where people from different religions could come together and learn from each other. This resulted in using *mysticism* to describe similar experiences in religions that aren't just Christian.[12]

Mysticism helps us to understand why there seem to be so many connections between New Thought and progressive Christianity. The following Venn diagram helps us understand these connections more clearly.

This diagram helps explain the overlap and why I could see so many New Thought teachings within Progressive Christianity yet see they were different too. New Thought and progressive Christianity drink deep from the well of mysticism, yet both consider themselves Christian.

THE CONNECTIONS

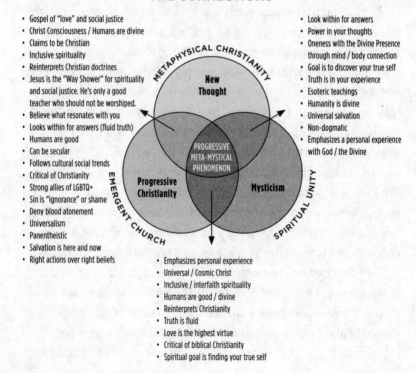

- Gospel of "love" and social justice
- Christ Consciousness / Humans are divine
- Claims to be Christian
- Inclusive spirituality
- Reinterprets Christian doctrines
- Jesus is the "Way Shower" for spirituality and social justice. He's only a good teacher who should not be worshiped.
- Believe what resonates with you
- Looks within for answers (fluid truth)
- Humans are good
- Can be secular
- Follows cultural social trends
- Critical of Christianity
- Strong allies of LGBTQ+
- Sin is "ignorance" or shame
- Deny blood atonement
- Universalism
- Panentheistic
- Salvation is here and now
- Right actions over right beliefs

- Look within for answers
- Power in your thoughts
- Oneness with the Divine Presence through mind / body connection
- Goal is to discover your true self
- Truth is in your experience
- Esoteric teachings
- Humanity is divine
- Universal salvation
- Non-dogmatic
- Emphasizes a personal experience with God / the Divine

METAPHYSICAL CHRISTIANITY

New Thought

PROGRESSIVE META-MYSTICAL PHENOMENON

Progressive Christianity

Mysticism

EMERGENT CHURCH

SPIRITUAL UNITY

- Emphasizes personal experience
- Universal / Cosmic Christ
- Inclusive / interfaith spirituality
- Humans are good / divine
- Reinterprets Christianity
- Truth is fluid
- Love is the highest virtue
- Critical of biblical Christianity
- Spiritual goal is finding your true self

In this light, the secret sauce of this type of mysticism teaches only partial truths. Christians are lured into these teachings when they hear biblical terms. This explains why it's hard to pin down the teachings of someone like Richard Rohr. If progressive Christianity, mysticism, perennial traditions, Catholicism, and New Thought had a baby, it would look like Rohr.

But this isn't necessarily true of *all* progressives. Because of their fluid view of truth, this means what one progressive considers to be the spiritual path working for them may not be the one for someone else.[13] It brings to mind a book by Thaddeus Golas called *The Lazy Man's Guide to Enlightenment*. His entire thesis was simple: Enlightenment doesn't care how you get there. It's about *the experience*, not truth. This could be the perspective of many progressives.

I'm Certain That Nothing Is for Certain

Another similarity is found in this blend of New Thought and progressive churches: the relativistic dance of how they uncover their "true self."

No matter whom I talked to, whether in a progressive or New Thought church, there was fundamental agreement on certain beliefs while also being inclusive, allowing room for other beliefs. Their goal was to remain open-minded, even if they contradicted themselves. Inclusion is the goal, not truth. This, to them, is "loving your neighbor as yourself."

The New Thought progressive reverend I spoke with was a perfect example of this. In our conversation, it was difficult to get him to definitively say what he believed. He would speak out of both sides of his mouth, saying one thing, then backpedaling to the opposite. He even said, "Certainty is the enemy of love."

I immediately responded, "Are you *certain* of that?"

He didn't miss a beat. "No, I'm not, actually."

He was *uncertain*. My brain cells were kung fu fighting.

Not everyone I talked with was so inconsistent, but they were all candid. Truthfully, I found his positions confusing. He even conceded multiple times that he sounded like a hypocrite because he was saying what he believes is true, but at the same time believed truth to be evolving. But he didn't think this mattered at all because we should always be ready to learn and change our minds. To him, this was a sign of spiritual maturity. As we discussed in chapter 4, defaulting to a relativistic position is the higher moral ground. The reverend said, "To say we *know* is seen as arrogant and even morally wrong."

I wonder if he *knows* that *knowing* is wrong. (...those kids were fast as lighting...hiya!)

The sermon the reverend gave that morning was ironically about idolatry. The crazy thing was that if you didn't know this was a progressive church, his sermon would've sounded biblical! He spoke about Moses, the golden calf, and making idols. He even gave a prayer at the end asking God to destroy our idols so we could get closer to him. So I asked the reverend afterward, "What if God were to answer that prayer? Would you be willing to melt your own golden calves to pursue what's true in order to get closer to him?"

"Yes, I would. I love Jesus and want to do what God wants me to do." Of course, *love*, *Jesus*, and *God* are subjectively defined.

Part of his message was how the Israelites worshiped many gods, and this was wrong to do because there was only one God. "You mentioned in your sermon today that it's wrong to worship many gods. In light of this, if you met someone who believed in many gods, would you tell them that's not true, and Jesus was sent by God to tell us to believe and follow only him?"

He barely paused before answering. "Absolutely not. I would *never* tell someone that."

He was dancing quite a dance. I picked up my theoretical tap shoes and danced along as best I could. "Reverend, if I may point out, you just gave a message about tearing down idols to know who God actually is and to put aside our false idols to allow him to reveal himself. If we ask this of him, then he gives it to us, and we don't like it and reject it, then *how is this not a golden calf?*"

He surprisingly sat back, crossed his arms, and laughed. A few seconds later, he said, "Yes. That sounds very hypocritical."

His candor was refreshing, but I was floored at the fact *he simply didn't care if he didn't make sense.* Nothing fazed him. He wouldn't adjust his views even if he *knew* they were wrong.

He remained in constant uncertainty. This is a staple of this type of progressive Christianity—but this is also shared in the shifting relativistic nature of New Thought. And I have a theory of why.

First, let's review a crucial New Thought belief: Somewhere inside us all, there's an inner goodness within that's divine and perfect. This is your true authentic self. Everything else is the false self. To get to the true self, we must deconstruct everything false, which are the things society has built upon us.

This journey of self-discovery—via deconstruction—is a key component in the progressive Christian life.

Deconstruction has become a trend in Christianity, sparking controversy about everything from definitions to motives. But it's important to know that this type of deconstruction is different from simply putting your beliefs to the test to make sure they're biblical, with the goal of rebuilding a solid faith in Jesus. No. This postmodern trend is often meant to help you find your true self—your own truth about who Jesus is and what works for you—and to dismantle everything else.

What are you dismantling? Social constructs. A social construct, in this lens, is a false sense of yourself that has, in essence, been built by the powers and culture around you. In other words, your false self *is a social construct.* In this view, this version of "you" isn't real. It exists only because it's been built by society and accepted by those around you. Your true self is underneath this false self.

If your false self is a social construct and finding your true self is your ultimate goal, *life becomes an unending search for and removal of what is false*. Every thought you have, every feeling you feel, must be analyzed. You're left wondering, "Is this a construct or my true self?" Can you see how this would lead to a life of nearly constant uncertainty? This sounds exhausting.

I believe this is the reason for the constant drone of uncertainty I heard from every reverend I spoke with, whether in a New Thought center or a progressive church. Uncertainty is venerated because if any truth or belief is built within you at all, then it's from what's been conceived in society—*rebuilding your false self*.

Tricky, isn't it?

There's an allure to ambiguity. If you claim you aren't sure about anything, then you don't seem so closed-minded. You're one of the cool kids, changing with the times. But there's an irony here. Everyone is included, *except* if you believe what the fundamentalists do—also known as the "bad guys."

The Uncertain Progressive Metamystagorical Jesus

New Thoughters and many progressives both think they are improving what Scripture teaches. My friend Alisa Childers says, "Progressive Christianity is not simply a shift in the Christian view of social issues. It's not simply permission to embrace messiness and authenticity and Christian life. It's not simply a response to doubt, legalism, abuse, or hypocrisy. It's an entirely different religion—with another Jesus—and another gospel."[14]

This was abundantly clear in my conversation with the progressive reverend. Toward the end of our time together, I asked him if he would become a "bad guy" if it meant what biblical historic

Christians believed was objectively true. His response was telling: "No. I don't want to be associated with them or what they believe. I don't want to be seen as a bad guy because I know how people see them. I wouldn't be able to handle that. And they make sin out to be something that sends us to hell. I think sin is an adventure. Maybe it's semantics, but I get my answers from within, and that's not sinful at all. It's the only part of me I know is whole and trustworthy."

It broke my heart that he thought he was already whole. His Jesus—progressive, metamystagorical Jesus—is a false Jesus that can't save him or anyone else. These types of progressive Christians say they follow Jesus, but really they follow a caricature of Jesus. I saw this online recently from a progressive site:

> From the gospel stories, it's quite evident to me that what made Jesus unique was that he was his most authentic self. Profound!
>> And that goes for you too!
>> [You say to Jesus:] "I want to be like you."
>> [Jesus:] "You be like you! That's how you be like me."[15]

Biblically, this is a *foreign* concept. If the world loves this type of Jesus, then let me never love the world. This is salad bar Christianity, picking and choosing what we like and don't like, tweaking beliefs to fit in more with the world (never mind that Jesus never did this). Those who pick and choose what they like from Jesus's teachings are only a Jesus follower by name, not practice. The only way to get to this point is to simply change what Jesus said (as recorded by the eyewitnesses) in order to fit your idea of what Jesus should or shouldn't be.

Ironically, some progressive Christians accuse Bible-believing Christians of trying to confine God within the "box" of the Bible by searching for truth about him, viewing this as a selfish need to control. Meanwhile, they often adapt their understanding of God to fit modern cultural values, selectively embracing aspects of Jesus, God, and the Bible that align with inclusivity, but denying the parts they don't like. Yet they claim it's biblical Christians— who take the Bible literally—who are creating our own version of God. This seems misleading. True freedom lies in submitting to what God says, not in shaping God to fit our preferences.

Those who see Jesus as all-tolerant, fully-inclusive, only-affirming, and nonjudgmental don't want to acknowledge he said things like, "Whoever is not with me is against me" (Matt. 12:30 NIV), "I am the way and the truth and the life" (John 14:6 NIV), "Repent" (Matt. 4:17 NIV), "If you love me, obey my commands" (John 14:15), and, "leave your life of sin" (John 8:11 NIV). Jesus didn't eat with tax collectors because he wanted to appear inclusive, tolerant, and accepting. He ate with them because he loved them and wanted to call them to repentance.

This is the Jesus of Scripture. And *this* Jesus can save you. But some do not want him. In Christianity, the Bible is supposed to change *you*. But in some forms of progressive Christianity, *you* are supposed to change the *Bible* because it's outdated and can't be understood without a modern lens.

This mindset reminds me of a scene in the animated version of *The Pilgrim's Progress*, the beloved allegory of the Christian journey. Christian (the main character) sets out on his journey, and Obstinate (the stubborn) and Pliable (the double-minded) both try to stop him. They think they're being good friends, telling him to stop his nonsense and come back to the city of Misery, where people ignorantly live evil, sinful lives—and love it. Christian refuses, telling them about the good king, who alone can rid him of the heavy burden growing on his back (sin). He tells his friends, "You can read about it here in this book! See?!" He holds up the book (Bible), but Obstinate's reply might as well be today's modern war hymn: "No, I don't see! And quite frankly, I don't *want* to!"

Both New Thoughters and progressive Christians claim the

name "Christian" but then live as their own god. Ideas once considered unique to New Thought are embraced within the walls of progressive churches. They both regress back to the lie that is central to their belief: *You* are your own sovereign. My friend and fellow apologist Dr. Frank Turek put it this way:

> Progressive Christians will tell me, "Frank, you get to define who a Christian is and who isn't?" Let me give you a straightforward analogy here, a simple thought experiment. If we were all at the base of Mount Sinai when Moses came down with the Ten Commandments and said, "Here they are. Yahweh gave us these ten commandments, and we look at those ten commandments and go, "We don't like those ten, we got our ten." Should we call ourselves followers of Yahweh? Of course not! We're not followers of Yahweh; we're followers of ourselves.[16]

Checking In: Mercy and Grace

Here's me just checking in with you again. Hey. How are you doing? Brain hurt yet? Let's do a heart check.

As you've gone through these last few chapters, notice how there's a hierarchy problem between humanity and God. This reminds me of a time when I was mixed up in New Thought, I was frustrated with a certain lack of spiritual and theological depth in the church. But there were a precious few who put stones in my shoes along the way. One of them was a woman who challenged me on my "mindset" mentality by quoting Romans 8 in a way that left a lasting impression on me. Yes, our mindset can influence our mental and spiritual state. But spiritually speaking, we are often in conflict with God's "mindset" because ours is different from his. Scripture says humans have a sinful nature, referred to as "the flesh" in the Bible, and our minds are set on what this nature desires (Rom. 8:5–6). This is part of our identity, and our sinful nature stands *in opposition* to God's nature (Rom. 8:6–7). When a propeller airplane takes off, it naturally veers left unless corrected to steer right. This concept also applies to Spirit-minded Christians. We shouldn't follow our inner inclinations but go against them. Because of our sinful nature, we are always "course correcting." One of my favorite hymns expresses this concept:

> Prone to wander, Lord I feel it
> Prone to leave the God I love.[17]

The truth is, if we align our thoughts and lives with the Holy Spirit instead of our own desires, we will know we belong to him (Rom. 8:9–10). (Really, just go read Romans right now.)

If New Thought were true, it would rob the mercy and grace of God, which is foundational to the gospel. Judgment is getting what you deserve. Mercy is not getting what you deserve. Grace is getting what you don't deserve. New Thought being a lie means no matter who you are or what you've done, God eagerly offers you his love, grace, and mercy. My heart yearns for people to see their need for God's mercy and grace.

Do the various interpretations of Christianity feel a little overwhelming? Take a moment to stop and pray. Know that God is carrying you through any struggles or questions you have. I am reaching through these pages, praying for you. I think of all the Christians in the past who stood up for truth in times of great lies and think of those today who carry that torch forward. Can you imagine them praying for the future church in moments like this, where there's a strong temptation to give in and give up, or for Christians to have the discernment to see through the devil's schemes? Perhaps they couldn't deny the depth of God's mercy and grace and how desperately the world needed to hear about it. Those who have been lured by lies need to know there's something better for them.

I wish I could stop the book here and say there aren't other areas of the church that have been affected by New Thought philosophies and teachings. But there's one more area I need to put a spotlight on. And it might ruffle a few feathers.

Unlearning the Lies

Now that we've shed some light on New Thought's connection to the progressive Christian movement and the false hope it brings, let's take some steps toward eliminating any of this spiritual poison we might have ingested along the way.

1. Focus on Truth

Here are some recommended Scripture passages to read and ponder. To understand the context, I highly recommend reading the whole chapter where these passages are found:

- Luke 9:18–20 (NIV)—"Once when Jesus was praying in private and his disciples were with him, he asked them, 'Who do the crowds say I am?' They replied, 'Some say John the Baptist; others say Elijah; and still others, that one of the prophets of long ago has come back to life.' 'But what about you?' he asked. 'Who do you say I am?' Peter answered, 'God's Messiah.'"
- Luke 9:23–26 (NIV)—"Then [Jesus] said to them all: 'Whoever wants to be my disciple must deny themselves and take up their cross daily and follow me. For whoever wants to save their life will lose it, but whoever loses their life for me will save it. What good is it

for someone to gain the whole world, and yet lose or forfeit their very self? Whoever is ashamed of me and my words, the Son of Man will be ashamed of them when he comes in his glory and in the glory of the Father and of the holy angels.'"

- 1 Corinthians 1:18, 23—"The message of the cross is foolishness to those who are perishing, but to us who are being saved it is the power of God. . . . But we preach Christ crucified: a stumbling block to Jews and foolishness to Gentiles."

- Galatians 1:8–9—"Even if we or an angel from heaven should preach a gospel other than the one we preached to you, let them be under God's curse! As we have already said, so now I say again: If anybody is preaching to you a gospel other than what you accepted, let them be under God's curse!"

2. Stand Firm

Here are some recommended resources on this topic that have been helpful for me in this area:

Another Gospel? by Alisa Childers

Hijacking Jesus by Jason Jimenez

Stealing from God by Frank Turek

Critical Dilemma by Neil Shenvi and Pat Sawyer

The Deconstruction of Christianity by Alisa Childers and Tim Barnett

Cynical Theories by Helen Pluckrose and James Lindsay

Richard Rohr and the Enneagram Secret by Marcia Montenegro and Don and Joy Veinot[18]

3. Pray and Proclaim

Various interpretations of Christianity abound. Remember that God is unchanging and that his teachings are the foundation of our faith. Here's a prayer for you:

> *Lord, help me to discern the difference between cultural trends and the eternal truths. Help me to stand firm against any teachings that may lead me away from your path. I pray for those who may be drawn to progressive Christianity. May your Holy Spirit work in their hearts, leading them to a deeper understanding of who you really are. Help me, as a Christian, to engage in loving and respectful dialogue with those who hold differing views, always seeking to share truth, the gospel, and your love.*

4. What We All Really Crave

I once had a Christian friend deconstruct and go progressive. Her reasoning wasn't based on facts. She simply said she didn't want to tell people what to believe anymore. She was done fighting. She wanted to feel accepted and free. How much of the pull toward a deconstructed Christianity is due to a misunderstanding or unwillingness to see the nuanced truth and compassion—even if difficult—in historic faith? Remember that what you're really looking for is found only in Jesus and him alone. He *is* the endgame.

CHAPTER 10

The Schuller Secret

*New Thought and the Church
Growth Movement*

> If you want to be popular, preach
> happiness. If you want to be unpopular,
> preach holiness.
>
> —Vance Havner

For seven years I attended a nondenominational Christian church, while—though I didn't know it at the time—believing some of the core ideas of New Thought. Our church wasn't heretical by any stretch of the imagination. I went weekly and was very involved. I helped with community outreaches, volunteered regularly in church ministries, and attended some women's Bible studies. (I even baked a casserole or two.)

But in hindsight, it is interesting that my incorrect theology went unchallenged. Never *once* did I have any sort of epiphany that the New Thought beliefs I had were unbiblical. I definitely had all the information I needed to navigate a better life though, including resolving marital problems, boosting self-esteem, managing stress, or finding a way to personally relate to virtually every biblical figure.

Don't misunderstand me. Those are good and important topics churches *should* talk about. But in 2011, when I discovered I had unknowingly adopted some New Thought beliefs under the guise of Christianity, I felt like I had been theologically throat-punched. I felt *embarrassed*. How could I have believed in these teachings for *so* long? I decided that much of the blame was on me. It was *my* responsibility to read and study my Bible. But something was bothering me about church culture that I couldn't quite put my finger on. It wasn't until some time went by and I was talking to a church friend that I realized what it was.

We were hanging out in the foyer (cuz . . . *doughnuts*) and talking about some new equipment the church had just bought. I admit, I was miffed. "I don't get it," I said. "Why do we need *four* brand-new flat-screens? Why not recycle the ones we already have that aren't being used in the other rooms?" I gestured toward another building. "Not to mention this . . ." I pointed to a large poster advertising the next sermon series—Finding Your Purpose: Serving Others and God. I knew part of the "serving others" meant inviting people to church. "I know my life has a purpose. I want to serve God and others, and yes, people should come to church, but I can't help but feel like this is eight weeks of a self-discovery session. I want something . . . deeper." It's not that it was a terrible message. The message was good and needed. But for some reason, I felt like I was being theologically shortchanged.

Then my friend said something I'd never heard before. "Oh, but this is a *seeker* church. *Loads* of churches are seeker churches. That's just what they do. They spend millions to draw people in, and you gotta have the right look and feel to do that."

A "seeker" church? What did that even mean? I didn't know.

It was this simple sentence that catapulted me into investigating how thousands of pastors adopted a marketing model to grow their churches—one that, while understandable and attractive, for some of these churches may be more entangled with New Thought than we'd like to believe.

But I'm getting ahead of myself. What I'm talking about is what many of us know as the "seeker-sensitive" model. Of course, being sensitive to prospective or new believers isn't a bad thing. These churches, big or small, are aware Sunday service is mainly for Christians, but people new to the faith may be in attendance. Some of these newcomers are exploring Christianity, testing it out, or just giving church another shot. And that's *great*. It's good when a church acknowledges these visitors and makes them feel welcome. But is there a limit to that? And what are the ultimate goals of that approach? Some of these churches avoid using complicated religious words that make sense only to long-time Christians. Instead, the pastors wisely use plain language that anyone can understand. But there's an understanding: For most churches, the Sunday service is *mainly* for Christians. They are the primary audience. While non-Christians are wanted and welcome, the focus remains on taking care of the Christian community's needs.

With that in mind, I believe there's a more appropriate name for this: the seeker-*centered* model.[1] This refers to when a church develops a marketing strategy with a focus solely on nonbelievers, a concept rooted in what is known as the "church growth movement." In other words, "seeker-centered" is what potentially happens when "seeker-sensitive" goes wrong.

To be clear, not all seeker-sensitive churches *do* go wrong. For example, some churches whose Sunday morning services focus on reaching seekers also have additional church services and programs dedicated to discipleship and spiritual growth of believers. More than one approach exists. My focus, however, is on a model that prioritizes increasing church attendance over nurturing the spiritual growth of believers.

But what if there's a complicated history behind this model? Part of the seedbed for the seeker-centered design has much to do with the overall pragmatic, entrepreneurial attitude of America making its way into the church. Although the full historical background and nuanced origins of the church growth movement[2] are beyond the scope of this book, and although there's no question that much good has come from well-meaning biblical churches and people connected to this model, it's … complicated. I need to stress that my perspective here is not coming from a place of spiritual pride or looking down at fellow believers; my goal is to highlight a subtle influence of New Thought on a particular category of growth-oriented churches.

And it started with a positive-thinking reverend in a fancy crystal cathedral.

The Origins

Robert H. Schuller has had a profound influence on the way we do church today. Schuller was a minister best known for his program *The Hour of Power,* which he ran from 1970 to 2006. I remember watching him as a child. His messages were always powerful and positive, and his church, the Crystal Cathedral in Southern California, was crazy impressive. It looked like crystal because it was made almost entirely of glass.

Schuller had his theological beginnings in a reformed school called Hope College in Holland, Michigan. He attended the respected Western Theological Seminary, but as time went on, he seems to have abandoned many of the Reformed doctrines he learned there. This was likely due to the influence of two well-known New Thought teachers who influenced his ministry, Norman Vincent Peale and Dale Carnegie.

When Schuller first started preaching, he thought people didn't come to his services because he wasn't inspiring enough and he was overly theological. Carnegie's book *How to Win Friends and Influence People* influenced Schuller's preaching style to become more positive. Peale's book *The Power of Positive Thinking* and his New Thought message of prosperity transformed the topics Schuller preached on and how he did ministry.[3] In essence, both

Peale and Schuller replaced the simple and pure message of the gospel with positive thinking.

Schuller's version of Christianity appeared deeply traditional in many ways. He wore a ministerial robe and quoted Scripture, and traditional music was played on the beautiful church organ. Many people who attended his church would think they were hearing an uplifting Christian message. But his messages were more focused on self-esteem, the power of the mind, and positive thinking than on the gospel.

Was the congregation even aware of some New Thought ideas shaping his messages? His preaching style can be narrowed down to five basic principles:

1. **Possibility Thinking:** This is a rebrand of Peale's New Thought positive thinking.[4] God always wants you to do bigger and better things. (Think of a spin-off of a Joel Osteen message except with a robe, more organs, and fewer Colgate smiles.) He believed that "possibility thinking"— not the gospel—is why God put him on earth.[5]

2. **Impress the Unchurched:** Schuller believed he was a missionary to reach those who didn't go to church. But he didn't believe that the way to do that is with the gospel. Rather, be nontraditional. Use marketing strategies. Have new shiny things, like an impressive building. Maybe one looking like crystal. Sermons were called "messages," and the focus was not on theology but on felt emotional needs and how God wants you to succeed. Schuller also called the church a community church for the sake of seekers who don't understand denominations.[6]

3. **Don't Be Controversial:** Schuller's focus was on the positive aspects of Christianity. He didn't talk of sin, hell, wrath, or anything considered negative. He was a universalist who believed it was "utterly ridiculous" to ask someone to

change their faith. He thought it was an "extremist view" to say only one religion was true.[7]

4. **Humans Aren't Rebellious, We're Mistrusting:** Schuller wrote in his book *Self Esteem: The New Reformation* that "positive Christianity does not hold human depravity but human inability."[8] He said, "Essentially if Christianity is to succeed in the next millennium, it must cease to be a negative religion and must become positive. . . . Too many prayers of confession of sin and repentance have been destructive to the emotional health of Christians by feeding their sense of nonworth. . . . I am; therefore, I can. I am a child of God. I am somebody. . . . These positive affirmations can become commonplace in the church of Christ that is reformed to glorify God by glorifying his children."[9] To Schuller, our biggest problem isn't sin but not realizing our own worth. We're not born sinners, but instead, we are afraid to trust God. Humans are good on the inside. To Schuller, Christianity has it backward, with too much centrality on God. He said, "Classical theology has erred in its insistence that theology be 'God-centered,' not 'man-centered.'"[10]

5. **Self-Esteem Messages:** Work the emotions. This is the focus. Either tell people they're *awesome* just the way they are, or tell a tearjerker story. Schuller resonated with Peale's storytelling abilities and captivation with psychology mixed with New Thought mind power and optimism. He decided this gave him more insight into the human condition than theologians did.[11] He encouraged people to believe in themselves, to have faith in God, and to love. It was self-help optimism in the name of Jesus.[12] Schuller's goal was similar to Joel Osteen's: They want people to feel good about themselves and not feel like sinners.[13]

By now I'm sure you see the influence of New Thought ideas in every one of those principles. But there's another legacy Schuller is known for: He had a knack for knowing how to grow a church. The New Thought beliefs he adopted from Peale helped inform his understanding of how church should be conducted. He developed church growth strategies that bear a resemblance to a kind of seeker-centered model. Of course, not *all* seeker churches were shaped by Schuller, but resemblances to his model for church growth can be found in many.

His goal wasn't to please Christians. He was unapologetically set on impressing the *unchurched*.[14] At one point, Schuller went door to door asking unbelievers what they would want in a church. On the surface, I think gathering information about your demographic is smart. We *should* be willing to go out and talk with unbelievers and hear what they have to say. But Schuller's motives were more than just curiosity. He took that information, used the data to shape his ministry, and from that created a model for church growth that prioritized growth above all else. Here's what one of Schuller's closest friends had to say about this:

> [Schuller] realized that giving Bible studies on Sunday morning during a worship service would turn off most of the unchurched people entirely. . . . Then he asked the people what sort of a church they would want to attend. They wanted light, beauty, tranquility, beautiful music, friendly people, programs that suited their needs, sermons that weren't boring, better yet, sermons that weren't even sermons! They wanted a place where they could feel comfortable. . . . He decided at that point that he would never again use his pulpit as a teaching platform.[15]

This method took off. Schuller's model became a marketing tool for a popular Christianity that *really* worked. Schuller accomplished for church what Disney did for amusement parks.[16] But it didn't stop with him.

The Legacy

Being a smart marketing master for church growth, naturally, Schuller turned around and marketed his methods. In 1969 he established the Robert H. Schuller Institute for Successful Church Leadership. In a 2005 Crystal Cathedral newsletter, Schuller said this about his institute: "Many of our alumni left our Institute sessions with renewed vision and encouragement to establish or grow some of the most remarkable and recognized congregations in America, and around the world, TODAY . . . in 1970, where could a pastor go to learn successful principles for personal, spiritual nourishment and church growth?"[17] At his leadership institution, Schuller shared the secrets to his success with decades of church leaders eager to achieve results. This included many of America's most recognizable church pastors and entrepreneurial leaders, including some you might have heard of.

Let me be clear. I am not personally attacking Christian leaders, who may be admired by many, but showing a difficult truth about some forms of the seeker model. Because of the many notable pastors influenced directly by Schuller and because of these pastors' outsized influence on a portion of the global church for decades, we must be willing to ask tough questions about *methods*. How much influence did New Thought have on shaping this model? What inspired Schuller's seeker methods? What were his motives? What were these motives grounded in? When other Christian pastors built on these seeker concepts to grow their churches, how did that foundation shift? While many pastors and Christian leaders were influenced by Schuller and implemented many of his strategies with success, *I'm not suggesting they agreed with all his beliefs*. For most pastors, it's clear Schuller's *methods* were adopted over many of his *doctrines*. And for some churches, approaches that resemble Schuller's may originate from other sources. However, his influence is significant and worth examining due to his prominence and popularity.

Popular pastors who adopted these methods remarketed these ideas in their own books, seminars, and trainings, which in turn have influenced thousands of pastors and been incorporated into mainstream churches, big and small, broadly influencing our church and ministry culture today.

Strengths and Challenges

What are you saying, Mel? That it's all bad and I need to leave my church?

Well, I don't think it's that simple. Let me tell you why.

But first, let me pause for a moment. I rewrote portions of this chapter several times, especially this section. I listened to thoughts from my brothers and sisters in Christ and pastors who shared a wide range of insights about the seeker movement—from those who love seeker churches to those who have been hurt by them, outgrew them, or left them, and many perspectives in between. I made every effort to listen objectively. And the reality is, it's complicated. It's an easy but inaccurate cheap shot to say that all churches influenced by a seeker model are entirely unbiblical and you should avoid them. Another cheap shot would be to argue that methods and theology are totally separate, so seeker churches are harmless. I don't believe that either is true. Lots of good happens in them. But some of them have also been deeply shaped by methods and beliefs that we should think critically about.

We must be willing to ask hard questions no matter where we fall on this. Are there potential risks from adopting a seeker approach in church? Are there things we can learn from the seeker model? What impact does this model have on the long-term spiritual growth and discipleship for seekers *and* believers? Does Schuller's old methodology affect today's theology? How about our practice?

Decades have passed since the seeker model's creation. This

gives us ample time to objectively observe its long-term effects, both its strengths and its challenges. Let's take some time to explore these. First, in the spirit of presenting the seeker model *in the best possible light*, let's start with the strengths.

Strengths

1. INTENTIONS ARE IN THE RIGHT PLACE

Many pastors who use this model genuinely love God and want to spread the gospel. They truly believe this model is an effective way to help people be more receptive to hearing about Jesus in a way maybe they never have before. Their goal *is* biblical: to be wise in the way you act toward outsiders and make the most of every opportunity (Col. 4:5) and to become all things to all people for the sake of the gospel (1 Cor. 9:22–23). Their goal is to contextualize the gospel without compromising with the culture.[18] In many ways, these churches might be a great start for someone who's new to the faith and may have an emotional hurt to overcome before they can grow in their faith. These churches also argue that their intention does not revolve around money and numbers but sharing the gospel.[19]

Many seeker churches, though not all, tend to be large, which allows for more hands to assist with community outreach. These churches are intentional about prioritizing outreach, organizing wonderful events and missions that help communities locally and across the nation.

2. CHURCH DOESN'T HAVE TO BE BORING

One thing seeker churches do very well is they can *read the room*. I personally loved this about the seeker church I went to for years. It's great walking into church knowing that an amazing variety of talents and gifts will be expressed, especially in the arts. (I have this perspective as a semi-professional-ish artist myself. Shout-out to all my canvas sniffers!) It's wonderful how the unique and creative talents of others can be incorporated into a song or message. The aim is to avoid sticking to tradition merely for tradition's sake. If something is biblical, it should be followed.[20] But if there's flexibility regarding things like the type of music, whether the pastor can wear casual clothes, or hosting fun events that don't compromise the biblical message, then why should it be an issue?[21] The effort that goes into making a fun and welcoming place for kids (especially tweens and teens) is valuable too. There are incredible benefits of kids loving to go to church.

Many of the seeker churches I researched for this book had a high priority on events and fellowship for all ages. To be able to hang out with fellow believers on a regular basis can be the highlight of the week for some Christians. In many ways, seeker churches get fellowship and community *very* right.

When it comes down to it, we don't need to be stuck in legalism or rigidity. There's nothing wrong with playing drums on stage with the pastor in jeans in quality lighting. It's perfectly fine to have snacks and coffee in the foyer with some awesome books for purchase that the congregants might enjoy. Let them have their lights and eat their doughnuts.

3. It's a Safe Place to Hear Truth, and It's Practical

Many people love seeker churches because they are the opposite of what they may have experienced in a legalistic church. I was one of those people. In seeker churches, people have been able to take steps toward healing from past abuses. The welcoming environment and atmosphere felt removed from a negative experience they had in another church. They felt cared for and able to relax. There's nothing wrong with being modern and contextualizing the gospel message. This is *smart*. We'd be wise to realize that we don't need to be stuck in 1952 to preach the gospel effectively. The bottom line is that seeker churches create a welcoming environment for those unfamiliar with or hesitant about church, making it easier for nonbelievers to engage with the message of the gospel.[22]

Another strength of this model is that the sermons and teachings of seeker churches often focus on how biblical principles can be applied to real-life situations, making faith feel more actionable and relevant. Nobody can argue about the pragmatic effects of the seeker model. There's quite a bit that works.

4. THEY SPEAK MODERN LANGUAGE

Many seeker pastors are gifted and engaging speakers. In strength #1, I mentioned that one of the main intentions of a seeker church is to *contextualize* the gospel. This means they focus on sharing the gospel and biblical ideas in a way that makes sense to unbelievers, breaking down tough concepts so the average person can easily understand them. This is particularly helpful for the younger crowd or brand-new believers who might have a difficult time understanding certain biblical teachings. Many of these pastors have great audience awareness, which is important for good communication.

5. PEOPLE *DO* GET SAVED

This one is the most important. It's biblical to seek out the lost. Many people have heard the gospel in seeker churches—*maybe for the first time. Many* people have been saved in seeker churches and are showing good fruit. Look, if God wants to get your attention, he'll get it. Just from my own personal experience, I've seen numerous lives changed from attending a seeker church service because they heard the gospel in a way they've never heard it before. Many of them are strong Bible-believing Christians to this day.

Also, can I say that there also needs to be more grace given to the expectation of pastors? Yes, pastors need to be *shepherding*, but shouldn't Christians be more intentional with their Bible reading and study, rather than expecting the church to handle all the theological heavy lifting? One way that some seeker churches address this is they offer small groups or Bible classes that are separate from the Sunday sermons to help people in their spiritual growth, as well as some of them offering additional church services aimed to shepherd people toward deeper discipleship.

These are some of the biggest strengths of a seeker church.

Then what's the problem, Mel? If people are truly saved in these churches, and people feel good and are getting hope, why are you picking on them?

Well . . . this is where it gets complicated.

Challenges

1. DISCIPLESHIP

A goal of the seeker model is to grow the church to share the gospel. But how much attention is given to making disciples after they receive the gospel? I heard from numerous people who attended seeker churches (including some pastors) that lack of a deeper biblical and theological growth was their number one concern.

As a reminder, one of Schuller's foundational happy lies was "possibility thinking." For Schuller, positive thinking was almost as important as the resurrection of Jesus Christ.[23] Schuller saw the gospel as the theology of self-esteem.[24] This makes discipleship a path to personal success and achievement, which is not the biblical gospel. How much of this informed Schuller's model? Do we really not see the *why* and the *what* related here? I think we need to ask that hard question.

But the method works—sort of, at least. One study for the Hartford Institute for Religion Research (in 2008, arguably around the height of the church growth movement) showed that for megachurches (most of which operated on a seeker model), spiritual growth peaked between three to five years, then declined over time.[25] The same study acknowledged that it is widely understood among pastors that while new attendees are consistently joining the church, many also leave just as frequently.[26] Another study from 2023 extracted the mission statements of five hundred megachurches (of two thousand or more). Only *two* out of the five hundred declared discipleship as their mission.[27] One three-year study done in 2007 by Willow Creek, a very influential seeker church, found that 25 percent of their congregants reported they were not growing spiritually at all, and 63 percent of those who felt stalled in their spiritual growth had been attending the church for over five years.[28] Now, it is *excellent* that the church was pro-actively working to gauge this, see it as a problem, and respond. But these numbers at the height of the church growth movement indicated that even long-term members were feeling a lack of deep spiritual growth—though to be fair, that sense of stagnation might have been just as common in nonseeker churches.[29]

Theologically, the danger could be that the seeker church creates a perpetual merge lane. Some people are always "approaching" but never actually growing.[30] Yes, seeker churches might be gospel-centered and meet felt needs. But are they making *disciples*? That is a crucial question—and one for all churches, seeker church or not.

2. THERAPEUTIC THEATRICS

Picture it: You're an unbeliever who has been invited to church on a holiday. You watch an elaborate performance where the pastor drives a shiny BMW onto a stage filled with fancy props, and you're pretty sure there are people hanging from the rafters to perform in the air later. The pastor is charming, funny, and entertaining. He uses theatrical displays to work your emotions, using life story after life story to get you in the feels to make his point. It's self-improvement application with a gospel message. A strength of a typical seeker church is that they're not boring. But with the intention to impress the unchurched, can theatrics and emotional self-improvement appeals go too far?

One of Schuller's happy lies had to do with how he viewed humanity and sin. In his view, every problem we face, whether personal, in society, or even the presence of sin and evil itself, comes from people having low self-esteem. So the goal to reform the church is to build up our self-esteem and focus on felt needs. This is the main thesis of his book *Self Esteem: The New Reformation.* Has he succeeded in this goal?

Furthermore, the seeker marketing model needs a leader with a captivating persona and a modern style to attract the seeker. And it really *works.* According to a study by the Hartford Institute for Religious Research, the reasons people were attracted to a large seeker church were the worship style, the senior pastor, and the church's reputation. What kept them there? The worship style, the senior pastor, and the church's reputation.[31]

A study of 727 larger churches, many of them seeker-oriented, revealed that almost half of the churches surveyed spend between 39 to 52 percent of their yearly budget on staff costs.[32] Many of these churches (to their credit) are transparent about their yearly budgets, not to mention many *do* try to invest wisely in how they spend their money, such as gospel outreach.

In one conversation I had with a pastor from a seeker church in the South, he shared their yearly budget and how much went to maintaining the church and outreach. In essence, he said the quiet part out loud: If we make them feel good emotionally, we see numerical and financial growth. But doesn't that prompt us to ask what's *not* being said? What kind of environment would this create? What temptations would it put before the pastors of a church shaped by this model?

3. AN OBSESSION WITH EXCELLENCE

The Schuller model can function like a business model. It's designed to deliver success and excellence *similar to a business.* From perfect branding to the latest technological advances, things must run well. This isn't entirely bad. In fact, the pursuit of excellence often comes as much from a desire to reflect God's glory and greatness as from any business goal. (Not to mention . . . it's pretty!) But could there be a temptation to rely too much on the need for excellence to make the church more inviting and intriguing to unbelievers? One pastor in an article about why he left his seeker church explains that "what you win people with is what you keep people with."[33] No pressure.

During my research, former staff members and even former pastors of seeker churches expressed that they would feel like they were often walking on eggshells due to such high standards. Furthermore, since excellence is such a high priority, I discovered that some staff members might not actually be Christians. The argument is that if an unbeliever is the best musician for the concert, hire him. What if someone with sketchy theology—but a high profile—has an eye for church aesthetics? Well, just slap a church bumper sticker on their car and put them on payroll.

Staff (and volunteers) can be told their service *is for God*, so they often feel guilty for wanting to say no. Is there a risk that they overextend themselves, believing it's for the kingdom, when in reality the focus may be more on increasing numbers? To be fair, the risk of overwork is high in any mission-oriented organization, whether seeker church or not, and all organizations should be mindful of that risk.

There's nothing wrong with having a healthy standard of cleanliness or aesthetics in *any* church. But when the focus is to look good in order to attract others, what happens to the standard? Has the pursuit of excellence led to lowering crucial standards, sometimes turning the focus to style over substance?

4. PERSONALITY-DRIVEN LEADERSHIP STRUCTURES

In some seeker churches—as in large churches of all sorts—there can be a divide between the congregants and the lead pastor, requiring some sort of privileged position to speak with your own pastor. I jest, but this is one of the biggest challenges that I came across in my research. If your church requires a user manual for how to interact with your pastor,[34] or pleasing him (with the guise of pleasing God) is the priority of the church, then what are the consequences to the staff and congregation? What are the consequences to the *pastor* when it comes to accountability? If they can't be corrected because they're "in charge," then it's time to reassess. How does the seeker model impact lead pastors who hold significant positions of power? How does this environment influence the way others perceive the pastor? The pitfalls described are not solely found in seeker churches, since any large organization faces these problems. My focus here is on the specific ways those problems manifest themselves in churches following the Schuller model.

When pastors become more like CEOs and celebrities instead of shepherds and preachers, we lose something important. Pastors *should* have authority that is respected, but it is authority rooted in God's Word.

A Biblical Church

I've highlighted just a few strengths and challenges of the seeker model. The bigger picture is to look at the purpose of the church: to serve others, study, and teach Scripture. We're also commanded to obey the Great Commission.

Scripturally speaking, the church is to:

1. Pray (Acts 2:42).
2. Teach biblical doctrine and equip the saints for ministry, helping them discover and utilize their spiritual gifts for the body of Christ (Eph. 4:11–12).
3. Provide a place of fellowship for believers to encourage and love one another (1 Thess. 5:11; 1 John 3:11).
4. Help those in need (James 1:27).
5. Spread the gospel. In Matthew 28:19–20 we are given the famous Great Commission. Jesus instructed his followers to go and make disciples of all nations, baptizing them and teaching them to obey his commands. In Philippians 1:18, Paul says he is grateful that the gospel is being spread, even when it's done with false motives.

God adds to the local congregation when the church as the body of believers is organically being what it was designed to be. The church is not a building. It's a community of believers united in worship, growing in faith, supporting one another, and carrying out the mission of spreading the gospel message of salvation through faith in Jesus Christ. We are to "contend for the faith that was once for all delivered to the saints" (Jude 3).

With a world that's becoming more and more hostile to the Christian message, it's important for us to ask, Does this model train Christians for spiritual war? How much of it has been influenced by Schuller's New Thought motives and how much has been influenced by the Bible? Is it both? Some? Neither?

Let's take two very biblical and virtuous intentions: discipleship and gospel-centeredness. Seeker churches may prioritize being gospel-centered, perhaps placing less emphasis on discipleship efforts that foster deeper spiritual and biblical growth. On the other hand, some non–seeker churches may prioritize discipleship. Their primary focus is on the spiritual growth of believers, with minimal outreach efforts, and they may overlook the need for contextualizing the gospel. Sometimes assessing these intentions creates an "us-vs-them" mindset. But shouldn't the church excel in *both* discipleship and sharing the gospel? It seems that upholding one over the other produces its own set of challenges.

Seeker churches vary widely in style, methods, and growth strategies. What one church emphasizes may differ from another, creating a spectrum of strengths and challenges. Though I believe the intention was pure even for the subset of churches that adopted Schuller's church growth model, time has revealed its effects more clearly, allowing us to ask thoughtful questions from all perspectives.

And where we find happy lies, we need to lovingly root them out. Even if they're in our own backyard.

CHAPTER 11

Beyond the Happy Lies

*Finding True Wholeness in
Authentic Christianity*

> You are inherently whole, good, perfect,
> and divine.
>
> —Satan, garden of Eden, BC (The New
> Melissa Paraphrased Translation)

I sat in the far back of the tiny New Thought church. As usual, I took notes during the positive and inclusive message and found the reverend afterward to ask her some questions. She gladly agreed. We talked for over an hour.

With almost everybody I interviewed, I always saved one question to ask at the end, which I posed to her: "Have you ever heard of the serpent's lie in Genesis 3?" To the average Christian, this might seem like an obvious question. Many have heard it before. But it was this concept that ultimately brought me to my knees when I left New Thought because I had discovered what it really was. It never occurred to me that deceit could look and act like love, light, and Jesus.

She looked confused. "Well . . . how about you remind me of it."

"It's in Genesis 3 where the serpent deceives Eve by questioning what God said and telling her she can be like God. Many Christians recognize the serpent's lie—that humans can be divine or god-like—as the core deception of all humanity. What do you think that means?"

Her demeanor completely changed. Out of everyone I interviewed for this book, her response is one I will never forget. It was unique from the other interviews and conversations I'd had. She looked taken aback. She said she'd never heard of this before. Then she punted the question back to me. "What do *you* think it means?"

I didn't skip a beat. "Oh, I think Christians have a point!"

Her face tensed. Then she asked, "How so?"

I was surprised. She seemed almost intrigued. I shot up a small prayer and went on. "Well, if I were the devil, I'd think I would want people to think they're already happy, whole, and divine so they wouldn't believe the *true* gospel. The truth is we can only truly have peace when we realize our brokenness. He says to come to *him*, not look within. That only brings emptiness, not completeness."

She was quiet. "I guess I never thought about it that way." She looked physically uncomfortable with my answer. But I also noticed something else: She looked *tired*. She had just given a positive, hour-long message about our divinity, wholeness, and abundance. She smiled the whole time, beaming about how loved we all were and sharing jokes with the congregation. But here, in front of me, without anyone else around, was a different woman. A *broken* woman. It's as if she *wanted* to believe what I was saying. So I asked her a candid question. "Do you believe this?"

Her answer astonished me. "I *won't* believe that." I immediately knew exactly what she was saying.

She was *choosing* not to believe it.

This is the exact sentiment shared with me by another person I spoke to in a New Thought church. He said he has days where he *wants* to believe in a separate, personal, fatherlike God who saves us from ourselves. But metaphysical Christianity challenges him to go *beyond* this. He saw this as more virtuous. My reverend friend in this current conversation shared the same point of view.

I knew we didn't have much time left. We had already been there for a while, and we both needed to go soon. I made eye contact with her and said, "I don't pretend to know everything you've gone through or how you got here. But one thing I do know is the wholeness and rest you are looking for aren't inside you. It's in Jesus *alone*."

To my astonishment, she didn't resist this but also didn't accept it. She only half smiled, nodded, and explained she had to go. I thanked her, gave her a hug, and left. I don't know if I'll ever see her again, but I think of and pray for her often.

Did God Really Say?

Think of the worst times in your life. New Thought would have you look within during these times. If you're God? Then *this is the best it gets*. But there's something freeing and wonderful about crying out to God and telling him *I can't do this*. That you can't handle it. You need him. He is the only one who can carry and help you. There's peace in knowing you are not alone, just left to rely on yourself. You can surrender and trust in Jesus.

It doesn't matter who you are or what you believe. There's one thing our heart and soul yearns for: Jesus. He doesn't say you come to the Father through your

goodness,
morals,
wisdom,
mystical experiences,
tolerance,
love,
or positive vibes.

No, you come to salvation, to wholeness, to truth only through *Jesus*. This is the endgame. This is what every person I talked to is truly looking for.

The lies Satan whispered in the garden were half-truths, which are basically pretty lies with more makeup on. The serpent asked, "Did God really say . . .?" Satan always begins by distorting what God says. In this way, it's clear to see how New Thought has taken the words of God and twisted them into something more mystical, positive, and culturally acceptable. To Adam and Eve, Satan said,

> *You will not die.* False. Sin brought death.
> *Your eyes will be opened!* True. But not like they thought.
> Their eyes were opened to their sin and what evil and death are.
> *You will be like God, knowing good and evil!* False and true.
> They would know good and evil, but not as gods.

It was Satan who said in Isaiah 14:13–14, "I will ascend into heaven, I will exalt my throne above the stars of God. . . . I will be like the Most High" (NKJV).

Ironically, in humanity's desire to be gods, we become more like Satan.

False Light

New Thought doesn't discard God altogether. It adds him to a sort of spiritual soup, like in 2 Kings 17:33: "They worshiped the LORD, but they also served their own gods in accordance with the customs of the nations from which they had been brought" (NIV).

They worshiped the Lord, *but* . . .

I hear people all the time say they worship God. They *love* him, they say. They read their Bible, they believe the gospel, they say. *But* . . .

- They believe in the law of attraction.
- They talk about Christ Consciousness rather than the risen Jesus.
- They believe humanity is divine.
- They believe Jesus was just a good teacher, a swell guy, showing us our human potential.
- They believe the Bible is limited and only one of many spiritual books with truth.
- They believe our spiritual identity can come in the form of multiple genders—and species.
- They believe truth progresses and can't be fully known.
- They believe our words and thinking can manifest healing and abundance.
- They believe all these occult practices can be used for *good*.

No. God said *don't do what they're doing*. I have a better way. Follow me. But they stubbornly stuck their fists in the air and did what they thought was good in their own eyes.

This is a repeated theme in the Bible that is eerily (but not surprisingly) similar to today: Everyone loves Jesus, but not Jesus *alone*. In the Old Testament, the prime sin of the Israelites was idolatry. God compared their worship of other gods along with him to adultery. They want him along with their other spiritual side chicks. But a plain reading of Scripture shows that Jesus demands our whole heart. This is inconvenient for people who want to say they love Jesus but don't do what he says.

Some think they are walking in light. But it's backward. They don't understand they are actually walking in darkness because *they are afraid of the light*. Jesus says in John 3:19–21, "This is the verdict: Light has come into the world, but people loved darkness instead of light because their deeds were evil. Everyone who does evil hates the light, and will not come into the light for fear that their deeds will be exposed. But whoever lives by the truth comes into the light, so that it may be seen plainly that what they have done has been done in the sight of God" (NIV).

Jesus warns us to be careful "that the light within you is not darkness" (Luke 11:35). New Thought is darkness, and it can be difficult to discern. It's like a twist villain in a movie—a character you think is kind, loving, and good until the end when the dramatic irony is revealed. Our hearts sink when we discover that the beloved good guy was actually the bad guy all along. We read about one of the greatest twist villains of all time in 2 Corinthians 11:14. His name is Satan, and Scripture says he disguises himself as an angel of light, and often uses his favorite strategy: self-exaltation cloaked in false humility.

Satan brings a message that *looks* like light. It looks good, pleasing, and like God, but it's not. Compared to the light of God, it is darkness, and this darkness deceives people. People claim to know Jesus, but they walk in darkness. This also means they're in a false truth. Jesus is the Light, and only he can purify us (1 John 1:6–7). Only Jesus offers you *true* satisfaction and contentedness you've been searching for your entire life. He alone satisfies.

He preached he is the Bread of Life (John 6:35), the only way to the Father (John 14:6), the Good Shepherd who came to lay down his life for the sheep (John 10:11). He was God in human flesh (John 1:1), equal with the Father, King, and Lord of all creation (John 8:58). He is the Light of the World (John 8:12). Follow *him*, and you won't walk in darkness.

Happy Shiny Things

New Thought offers an enticing bargain. It creates a false Christianity promising power and popularity, all while quoting Bible verses. But as we've seen, the offer comes at a steep cost. It is all too easy to lose the simple gospel message offering true salvation and encouraging Christian maturity.

It reminds me of the movie *Indiana Jones and the Last Crusade*. (That's right. I don't watch only *cartoons* to share sage-like wisdomish things.) Indiana is looking for the "Holy Grail." He discovers its location in a chamber guarded by a knight. He learns the true Grail grants eternal life while the counterfeits bring death. Indiana walks around the room, looking at all the pretty, shiny cups. But he skips them all and spots an old, plain, dirty clay cup. Without missing a beat, he says, "Now *that's* the cup of a carpenter." It was modest. But it was authentic.

New Thought is just one of many shiny goblets telling humanity they can be their own god. This brings *death*. We must stand firm and never bow the knee to this sinister lie and resist the temptations it offers.

In 2 Timothy 4:2–5 (NIV), Paul pleads with Timothy about what you, Christian, are facing today. I join him in this plea. Paul writes,

> Preach the word; be prepared in season and out of season; correct, rebuke and encourage—with great patience and careful instruction. For the time will come when people will not put up with sound doctrine. Instead, to suit their own desires, they will gather around them a great number of teachers to say what their itching ears want to hear. They will turn their ears away from the truth and turn aside to myths. But you, keep your head in all situations, endure hardship, do the work of an evangelist, discharge all the duties of your ministry.

We must pray for and reach those who are caught up in these teachings. Prayer is a powerful weapon and can help give us perspective when trying to reach the lost. We must also proclaim the gospel to them. Ultimately, New Thought offers people a different gospel and another Jesus. It offers the happiest of lies. Second Corinthians 11:3–4 says, "I am afraid that just as Eve was deceived by the serpent's cunning, your minds may somehow be led astray from your sincere and pure devotion to Christ, for if someone comes to you and preaches a Jesus other than the Jesus we preached, or if you receive a different spirit from the one you received, or a different gospel from the one you accepted, you put up with it easily enough" (NIV).

So then, where should you start when trying to reach someone with New Thought beliefs?

- Realize you're not the Holy Spirit. God does the saving. But it's helpful to know what New Thought is so you can spot it and ask thoughtful questions. Hopefully, this book has helped with that.
- There's an intense emotional incentive to make the Christian message more palatable. Don't do this.[1] People need to know truth, even if it's hard. This is a major reason why people compromise the gospel and one reason why New Thought spirituality has gone unnoticed for so long. Christians don't want to offend others, so they water down the message to make it more inclusive and tolerant. But in the process, they remove the Stumbling Block. We're entrusted with the gospel to proclaim it, not compromise it.[2]
- Watching people believe lies is frustrating. But keep in mind that people aren't your enemy. Remember, the real battle is not with flesh and blood but with unseen forces (Eph. 6:12). This is a spiritual battle. You need spiritual armor. New Thought makes your enemy look like your best friend. The devil is full of dark schemes designed to look like false light. Be strong in the Lord and wear his armor to stand against the devil's schemes (Eph. 6:10–13).
- Know your Bible and speak the truth. When a massive group of people believes in lies that comfort them, the only explanation is that the Father of Lies is behind it. Satan's ultimate

weapon isn't power. It's deception. If Satan's primary tactic in spiritual warfare is spreading lies, then our most effective defense in the battle against him is the opposite: spreading truth. The antidote to deceit is truth.[3]

- Be ready to answer hard questions. Christians are attracted to New Thought beliefs because they *seem* to give solutions to spiritual questions. You don't have to be a New Thoughter to believe in New Thought beliefs. Chances are, someone you know has been infected by this spirituality and they *truly* think it's biblical. But the truth is they're just hungry to know who God is. Their intention is to search for truth, but they have stumbled on a shiny goblet. My hope is this book has prepared you to help challenge their positions with love and logic.

Whole-iness

During the numerous interviews I did for this book, I heard constant affirmations of completion, wholeness, and happiness, but at unsuspecting moments when someone let their guard down, what I saw most plainly was *pain*.

Many people who are attracted to New Thought spirituality have been deeply hurt and wounded. In my numerous interviews with people from New Thought centers and beyond, some shared their stories of deep wounds, finding no comfort from Christians or the church. One woman shared a personal story with me from her childhood, which I won't be repeating, out of respect for her. But she shared that she would never again give up her power to anyone or anything outside of herself. I gave her a hug and thanked her for sharing something so personal. I had the opportunity to talk with her about the gospel.

It's important to remember the reasons why people are attracted to a spirituality like this. People embrace New Thought beliefs through inspiration or desperation. They are thirsty for these ideas because they're desperate to change their situation. They're searching for wholeness. But New Thought offers a counterfeit. They're seeking meaning. But New Thought offers more confusion.

What Jesus has to offer is truly what they are looking for. He doesn't always take away our pain, but he bears it with us. He's the only one who can truly make us whole in our brokenness. As the old hymn says,

> What can wash away my sin?
> Nothing but the blood of Jesus.
> What can make me whole again?
> Nothing but the blood of Jesus.[4]

Only he can make us whole. He doesn't call us to just be happy. Anyone can do that. He calls us to do and be something more: to be holy. This is "whole-iness." You are set apart from the world as his own. You are his. Being your own God is a *burden*. It does not set you free. It enslaves you to your own sins and masquerades as freedom. But there's peace in knowing that Christ is not within but is a separate Holy God who became his own creation in the person and work of Jesus to save you. He is the answer to everything. This is not only true but *better*.

Again, being your own God is a burden. But Jesus says for the weary to come to *him* (Matt. 11:28–30). But you have to acknowledge your weariness.

He says to come to *him* if you (spiritually) thirst and streams of living water will flow from you (John 7:37–38). But you have to acknowledge your thirst.

He says to come to *him* if you (spiritually) hunger, for he is the Bread of Life (John 6:35). But you have to acknowledge your hunger.

I think of my reverend friend who's spiritually tired, hungry, and thirsty for Jesus but smiles through it, declaring and affirming her happiness and abundance. This is the fruit of New Thought. It leaves people empty and in denial. The solution to sin isn't denial. It's forgiveness.[5] Jesus invites us to come to him for mercy, forgiveness of sins, rest, eternal life, and for himself—the treasure hidden in the field. Jesus offers an invitation to all to follow him. But some people refuse to come to Jesus for life (John 5:40).

Many people want to focus only on the positive aspects of God and make him solely about love, light, and tolerance. But they ignore what a true relationship with God looks like. Have they fallen on their knees, beating their chest in repentance, confessing their sins to the God that made them? Have they cried out to a holy God, understanding they are separated from him because of sin? Do they understand God became a human being not to show them their inner divinity but to make a way to salvation through his death?

This is the message they truly crave.

I know, because I crave it too. And I find its greatest fulfillment in the truth of the Christian faith.

Call to Action

> Safe? . . . Who said anything about safe? 'Course he isn't safe. But he's good. He's the King, I tell you.
>
> **—Beaver from *The Lion, the Witch and the Wardrobe***

> All you have to decide is what to do with the time that is given to you.
>
> **—Gandalf**

I stood up from my chair. With confidence. I walked over to her.

I know exactly what I'm going to say. It had been many years since my "ugh" epiphany. I had grown significantly in my understanding of the Bible, truth, theology, and different spiritual worldviews. I was at a group Bible study with some incredible people at a church. But it had turned into a "me" study. One woman in particular started talking about the power of our thoughts. Something seemed off.

Hmm . . . that sounds familiar. She's quoting Scripture. But this isn't just from the book of Proverbs, though. She's talking about the Sermon on the Mount but . . . Nope, something is off. Ah, okay. I think I understand exactly what this is. She's fallen for it too. I'm going in.

It was a larger group, and everyone was casually conversing. I went over and sat next to her to ask more questions. As I dug deeper, my suspicions were confirmed. This lovely, intelligent, funny, God-loving woman had been reading *The Sermon on the Mount* by Emmet Fox. A friend recommended it to her. Another victim of New Thought. I couldn't say I blamed her. I remember trying to explain to my Christian friends what New Thought was. They had no idea what I was talking about. Yet *some already believed in New Thought teachings*. Those of us who unknowingly adopt New Thought beliefs desire what we all do: love, belonging, spiritual fulfillment, and to know God. For me, one of the biggest draws to New Thought was personal power. Such blending of beliefs isn't rare. For many people, it stems from a genuine desire to understand God, but people have been lied to on the way there. They end up getting a distorted reflection of reality and who they are.

Imagine a mirror that has infinite reflections of faces. These fragmented faces are bathed in light, whispering, "You are God. You possess the power of creation and control over all things. You are truth." The reflections believe they can shape reality and bend the universe to their will. They appear to perform miracles, command the elements, and reshape the world with a mere thought. Mesmerized by the illusion of omnipotence, the reflections embrace their "godhood." But over time, the radiant reflections darken, revealing only shadows. The once brilliant light is a mere facade, concealing an endless abyss of deception. They find themselves deceived by its hollow promise of power, trapped by the darkness lurking beneath its false glow. We're *all* captives condemned to this "mirror." But Jesus comes to *save us* from this condemnation. He comes to set the captives free.

The remedy is Jesus. He is the Truth. Truth can be uncomfortable. But it's good. One motivation for writing this book was to help people understand where New Thought may have creeped into their life and to equip them to engage effectively, in grace and love, with others who hold New Thought beliefs. This is how we live out Jesus's call to love God and love others.

I spent some time asking my new friend about her beliefs and background. She was inquisitive and eager to talk. Later in our conversation, I shared with her that I was very familiar with Emmet Fox. She was thrilled. But then I shared with her his spiritual background and the New Thought movement he is known for. Her response wasn't one of defense. It was one of confusion. One thing she asked resonated with me:

"But . . . why don't more Christians know this, then?"

Good question. At the time, I could only answer with what I knew. But now the gloves are off. The cover is blown. The code has been cracked. Now I know. And now I hand off the baton to you. I hope you take what I've walked with here in this book and run with it and build on it. Even if you're on the fence about all of this, I hope you see New Thought as entirely different from what Jesus and Scripture teach.

I hope you *lean into it*. Truth is worth it. Our King is worth it. He is good, true, and merciful. Once we know better, we do better. And now you know. What will you do with it? This all matters. This is why I wrote this book. Because New Thought is a different gospel. New Thought teaches a different Jesus. And this means everything. Because a different Jesus is a false Jesus. A different gospel is a false gospel. And a false gospel and a false Jesus cannot save you.

Now that you see what New Thought is, I hope you can't unsee it. I hope it stirs something within you, something refusing to be ignored. Now go tell others.

Tell them the joyful truth so they don't fall for happy lies.

Notes

Chapter 1: What You Don't Know *Can* Hurt You

1. "My Partner Identifies as a Dog | EXTREME LOVE," *Truly*, YouTube, October 11, 2018, https://www.youtube.com/watch?v=h-hz-vjnfI8&t=404s.

2. Editors of Goop, "10 Books That Can Help You Develop Your Intuition," Goop, January 3, 2020, https://goop.com/wellness/spirituality/books-on-developing-intuition/.

3. Caroline Leaf (@drcarolineleaf), "Negative Thoughts Can Make Your Food Less Nutritious," Instagram, July 27, 2020, https://www.instagram.com/p/CDKCIgwgbx0/?igshid=cvxgq3xa7dsy.

4. Brandan Robertson (@revbrandanrobertson), "Did you know that the only person," TikTok, June 2, 2023, https://www.tiktok.com/@revbrandanrobertson/video/7240093094182391083.

5. @adonisbjornson, "Make Your Day," TikTok, accessed August 20, 2024, https://www.tiktok.com/@adonisbjornson/video/7389055142332501291?q=%23ChristConsciousness&t=1724190487270.

6. Katy Rexing, "Advanced Meditation Retreat with Joe Dispenza—My Experience," KatyRexing.com, July 10, 2023, https://katyrexing.com/2023/07/10/advanced-meditation-retreat-with-joe-dispenza-my-experience/?fbclid=IwAR05xEEYI2FiLEvpKUMLtahiJ32UgB01XO0WQBVZEOUGuYWQNd5Ox3obKtI.

7. Mike Winger, "Bethel and Bill Johnson's Bridge to the New Age and Spiritual Fakery," YouTube, January 30, 2023, https://www.youtube.com/watch?v=weHo7pO6cmQ&t=2072s.

8. Joel Osteen, "A Magnet for Blessings," YouTube, November 9, 2023, time stamp 4:32, https://www.youtube.com/watch?v=W25pomHR8Gc.

9. "New Thought Opens Minds to the God Living Inside Us," Maureen Byrne, 2005, https://www.tampabay.com/archive/1999/08/07/new-thought-opens-mind-to-the-god-living-inside-us/.

10. Sherry Evans, *The Roads to Truth: In Search of New Thought's Roots* (Park City, UT: Northern Lights Publications, 2005), 11–12.

11. This book was so controversial that Bethel took it down from their website, as well as the website for the book.

12. Other examples are Phil Mason, foreword by Bill Johnson, *Quantum Glory: The Science of Heaven Invading Earth* and Beni Johnson and

Judy Franklin, *Experiencing the Heavenly Realm: Keys to Accessing Supernatural Encounters*, just to name a few.

Chapter 2: New Thought, Old Lies

1. Sherry Evans, *The Roads to Truth: In Search of New Thought's Roots* (Park City, UT: Northern Lights Publications, 2005), 11–12.
2. John S. Haller Jr., *The History of New Thought: From Mind Cure to Positive Thinking and the Prosperity Gospel* (West Chester, PA: Swedenborg Foundation Press, 2012), 4.
3. Haller Jr., *The History of New Thought*, 8–9.
4. "Swedenborg's Life," Swedenborg Foundation, accessed August 29, 2024, https://swedenborg.com/emanuel-swedenborg/about-life/.
5. Haller Jr., *The History of New Thought*, 34.
6. Ibid., 34.
7. Ibid., 4, 142.
8. John S. Haller Jr., *Swedenborg, Mesmer, and the Mind/Body Connection: The Roots of Complementary Medicine* (West Chester, PA: Swedenborg Foundation Press, 2012), Kindle, Ch 2.
9. Marcia Montenegro, "New Thought: Making the Straight Ways Crooked", http://www.christiananswersnewage.com/article/new-thought-making-the-straight-ways-crooked-a-warning-for-christians.
10. Haller Jr., *The History of New Thought*, 72.
11. Ibid.
12. Haller, *Swedenborg, Mesmer, and the Mind/Body Connection*, Kindle, Ch 3.
13. Ingrid Spilde, "The Placebo Effect: From Mystical Magnetism to Using Our Bodies Inherent Powers," Sciencenorway, March 6, 2020, https://www.sciencenorway.no/history-of-medicine-medical-methods-placebos/the-placebo-effectfrom-mystical-magnetism-to-using-our-bodies-inherent-powers/1650983.
14. Vincent Buranelli, *The Wizard from Vienna: Franz Anton Mesmer* (New York: Coward, McCann & Geoghegan, 1975), 110, https://archive.org/details/wizardfromvienna00bura/page/110/mode/2up?q=laughter.
15. George Barton Cutten, *Three Thousand Years of Mental Healing* (New York: Charles Scribner's Sons, 1911), 259.
16. Margaret Fuller and David Henry Thoreau were also influential in the transcendentalist movement. It's outside the scope of this chapter and book to go into detail about them, but it wasn't just Emerson who had a huge impact on the transcendental movement and New Thought.
17. Ralph Waldo Emerson and Dr. Carol Carnes, *Emerson and New*

Thought: How Emerson's Essays Influenced the Science of Mind Philosophy (Camarillo, CA: DeVorss & Company, 2021), 5.

18. Jason King, "Emerson's 'Self-Reliance'—A Close Reading Lesson Plan," America in Class, last modified September 22, 2022, https://americainclass.org/individualism-in-ralph-waldo-emersons-self-reliance/.

19. Ibid.

20. Many of these essays are required reading for New Thought classes.

21. Haller Jr., *The History of New Thought*, 22.

22. Emerson and Carnes, *Emerson and New Thought*, 11.

23. Dr. Albert Mohler Jr., "Ralph Waldo Emerson at 200: Still Shaping the American Mind," AlbertMohler.com, December 12, 2003, https://albertmohler.com/2003/12/12/ralph-waldo-emerson-at-200-still-shaping-the-american-mind.

24. Ralph Waldo Emerson, "Divinity School Address," emersoncentral.com, accessed August 29, 2024, https://emersoncentral.com/texts/nature-addresses-lectures/addresses/divinity-school-address/.

25. Emerson, "Divinity School Address."

26. Jeff Carreira, "Ralph Waldo Emerson, Spiritual but Not Religious," Philosophy Is Not a Luxury, February 11, 2009, https://philosophyisnotaluxury.com/2009/02/ralph-waldo-emerson-spiritual-but-not-religious/.

27. Haller, *The History of New Thought*, 22.

28. Emerson, "Divinity School Address."

29. Emerson and Carnes, *Emerson and New Thought*, 7.

30. Carreira, "Ralph Waldo Emerson, Spiritual but Not Religious."

31. Haller, *The History of New Thought*, 49.

32. Horatio Dresser, ed., *The Quimby Manuscripts: Showing the Discovery of Spiritual Healing and the Origin of Christian Science* (New York: Crowell, 1921), 9, https://archive.org/details/quimbymanuscript00quimrich.

33. Bruce H. Addington, *Scientific Mental Healing* (Boston: Little, Brown, 1911), 27–28, https://archive.org/details/scientificmental00brucrich/page/34/mode/2up.

34. This isn't to be confused with Scientology either. That's a different religion, though there are some similarities.

35. Haller Jr., *The History of New Thought*, 92, 94.

36. Mark Oppenheimer, "The Queen of the New Age," *New York Times*, May 4, 2008, https://www.nytimes.com/2008/05/04/magazine/04Hay-t.html.

37. Marcia Montenegro, "New Thought: Making the Straight Ways Crooked," http://www.christiananswersnewage.com/article/new-thought -making-the-straight-ways-crooked-a-warning-for-christians.

38. Christian Science is probably the most known group that came out of New Thought. But this book will focus on New Thought in general, not Christian Science specifically, because it has deviated from certain New Thought principles.

39. Gail M. Harley, *Emma Curtis Hopkins: Forgotten Founder of New Thought* (Syracuse, NY: Syracuse University Press, 2002), 6.

40. Haller Jr., *The History of New Thought*, 77.

41. Ibid.

42. Horatio W. Dresser, *A History of the New Thought Movement* (New York: Thomas Crowell, 1919), 84–87.

43. Ibid.

44. Ibid.

45. Haller, *History of New Thought*, 76. This was a phrase coined by New Thought author Prentice Mulford.

46. Here are some influential New Thought teachers and authors that have had a huge ripple effect on our churches and society: James Allen, *As a Man Thinketh*; Wallace Wattles (who influenced *The Secret* by Rhonda Byrne), *The Science of Getting Rich*; Emmet Fox, *The Ten Commandments*; Dale Carnegie, *How to Win Friends and Influence People*; Norman Vincent Peale (who was influenced by Unity and Emmet Fox), *The Power of Positive Thinking*; Napoleon Hill, *Think and Grow Rich*; Joseph Murphy, *The Power of Your Subconscious Mind*; Don Miguel Ruiz, *The Four Agreements*; Neale Donald Walsch, *Conversations with God*; Dr. Helen Schucman, *A Course in Miracles* and many more.

47. Napoleon Hill, *Think and Grow Rich rev. and exp. by Dr. Arthur R. Pell* (New York: TarcherPerigee, 2005), 254.

48. Ibid., 254–255.

49. This is in the foreword to ACIM.

50. Sam Kestenbaum, "The Curious Mystical Text behind Marianne Williamson's Presidential Bid," *New York Times*, July 5, 2019, https://www.nytimes.com/2019/07/05/nyregion/marianne-williamson.html.

51. Haller Jr., *The History of New Thought*, 263.

52. This is the brilliance of the Bible. It wasn't written by just *one* person at *one* time. It had multiple authors over a span of centuries, so not just one person could claim exclusive access to God. Not to mention that ACIM is against what God has revealed in Scripture.

53. Taffy Brodesser-Akner, "The Gospel According to Marianne

Williamson," *New York Times*, September 3, 2019, updated January 10, 2020, https://www.nytimes.com/2019/09/03/magazine/marianne -williamson-2020.html.

54. ACIM has been read and endorsed by Beyoncé, Oprah, and Eckhart Tolle, just to name a few. Williamson claimed ACIM saved her life, made her famous, and inspired her political project. She ran as a democratic nominee in the 2024 election.

Chapter 3: The Teachings

1. Steven Bancarz and Josh Peck, *The Second Coming of the New Age: The Hidden Dangers of Alternate Spirituality in Contemporary America and Its Churches* (Crane, MO: Defender Publishing, 2018), 3.

2. April Moncrieff, *The Principles of New Thought: Tracing Spiritual Truth from the Source to the Soul* (Camarillo, CA: DeVorss, 2013), 8.

3. "Potentials Future Goals," Carlton D. Pearson, accessed December 8, 2023, https://carltondpearson.com/about/.

4. Jon Miller, "What Is New Thought?" Vimeo, May 27, 2015, https:// vimeo.com/ondemand/anewthoughtanewyou.

5. Moncrieff, 3.

6. Emmet Fox, "Affirmation of God's Presence," Pathwork, October 5, 2008, https://thehedge.wordpress.com/2008/10/05/affirmation-of -gods-presence-emmet-fox/.

7. Moncrieff, 80.

8. John P. Newport, *The New Age Movement, and the Biblical Worldview: Conflict and Dialogue* (Grand Rapids: Wm. B. Eerdmans Publishing Co., 1998), 29.

9. John S. Haller Jr., *The History of New Thought: From Mind Cure to Positive Thinking and the Prosperity Gospel* (West Chester, PA: Swedenborg Foundation Press, 2012), 53.

10. Moncrieff, 30–31.

11. Thomas Merton, *Conjectures of a Guilty Bystander* (New York: Doubleday, 1966), 142.

12. Allie Beth Stuckey, *You're Not Enough (And That's Okay): Escaping the Toxic Culture of Self-Love* (New York: Sentinel, 2020), 102.

13. Swedenborg Foundation, "The Lord," accessed August 20, 2024, https://swedenborg.com/emanuel-swedenborg/explore/lord/.

14. Emmet Fox, *Power Through Constructive Thinking* (San Francisco: Harper and Row, 1989), 158.

15. Moncrieff, 14.

16. "Metaphysical Bible Dictionary: Satan," TruthUnity, accessed August 20, 2024, https://www.truthunity.net/mbd/satan.

17. Jack Zavada, "What Do Unity Churches Believe?" Learn Religions, updated September 2, 2022, https://www.learnreligions.com/unity -beliefs-and-practices-700122.

18. Moncrieff, 46–47.

19. Mary Fairchild, "Unity Beliefs and Practices," Learn Religions, last modified May 25, 2019, accessed August 20, 2024, https://www .learnreligions.com/unity-beliefs-and-practices-700122.

20. Marianne Williamson, Facebook post, August 13, 2010, https://www .facebook.com/williamsonmarianne/posts/pfbid022yih5Ts3KZ6t5 xRDamrSio9rM1H1jZFSFsoFTLgLSbzsPpARdszProLqVMsx6EuQl.

21. Moncrieff, 38–39.

22. Ibid., 76.

23. Ibid.

24. Marcia Montenegro, "New Thought: Making the Straight Ways Crooked," http://www.christiananswersnewage.com/article /new-thought-making-the-straight-ways-crooked-a-warning-for -christians.

25. Though there are more, a few others are his omniscience or all-knowing (Ps. 139:1–5, Prov. 5:21), omnipresence or present everywhere but not made out of everything (Ps. 139:7–13, Jer. 23:23), and omnipotent or all-powerful in accordance to his nature (Rev. 19:6, Jer. 32:17, 27). He is sovereign (Ps. 93:1), just (Ps. 18:30, Deut. 32:4), and holy (Rev. 4:8, Heb. 12:29). There's also the veracity of God. The veracity of God says that God is the absolute truth (Ex. 34:6; John 14:6) and that there is no lie in him (Num. 23:19; Heb. 6:18; Tit. 1:2). He is the source of truth and always tells the truth.

26. Sharon Whealy, "Love in a Word," Center for Spiritual Living Tucson, September 13, 2023, https://www.tucsoncsl.org/love-in-a-word.

27. Horatio W. Dresser, ed., "The New Thought Today—The Spirit of the New Thought," Lessons in Truth, accessed August 29, 2024, https:// lessonsintruth.info/library/horatio-w-dresser-new-thought-author /the-spirit-of-the-new-thought-by-horatio-w-dresser/the-new -thought-today-the-spirit-of-the-new-thought/.

28. Moncrieff, 30.

29. Alisa Childers and Tim Barnett, The Deconstruction of Christianity: What It Is, Why It's Destructive, and How to Respond (Carol Stream, IL: Tyndale, 2024), 34–35.

30. Marcia Montenegro, "New Thought: Making the Straight Ways Crooked," http://www.christiananswersnewage.com/article/new-thought -making-the-straight-ways-crooked-a-warning-for-christians.

31. "What We Believe," Centers for Spiritual Living, accessed October 21,

2023, https://www.omcsl.org/copy-of-what-we-believe?fbclid
=IwAR3lmkWWqv79B9-4kOMeSn2t1hTfRQH2fMHK9Z2Qjvpfun
YNFt478Q9a7tQ.

32. Robert Winterhalter, "Phineas B. Quimby, the Bible and Healing," *Phineas Parkhurst Quimby Resource Center*, https://www.ppquimby
.com/winterhalter/winterhalter2.htm.

33. Moncrieff, xv–xx.

34. Ernest Holmes, *The Science of Mind, Definitive Edition* (New York: G. P. Putnam's Sons, 1988), 427.

35. Joel Goldsmith, *The Spiritual Interpretation of Scripture* (San Gabriel, CA: Willing Pub. Co.), https://img1.wsimg.com/blobby/go/a0a7d1c3
-27ec-4f51-862a-ab16bc59e62c/downloads/spiritual_interpretation
_of_scripture.pdf?ver=1619496227099.

36. Charles Fillmore, "Preface to the Metaphysical Bible Dictionary," Truth Unity, accessed December 9, 2023, https://www.truthunity.net
/mbd/preface.

37. Charles Fillmore, "Metaphysical Bible Dictionary," Truth Unity, accessed October 15, 2023, https://www.truthunity.net/mbd/cross.

38. Michael J. Kruger, *Surviving Religion 101: Letters to a Christian Student on Keeping the Faith in College* (Wheaton, IL: Crossway, 2021), 151.

39. A great resource I highly recommend is Marcia Montenegro's work found at https://www.christiananswersnewage.com/. Marcia was a valuable resource for me in giving feedback for Chapters 2 and 3. Her expertise expands into both New Age and New Thought.

Chapter 4: True for Me

1. Greg Koukl, *Street Smarts: Using Questions to Answer Christianity's Toughest Challenges* (Grand Rapids, MI: Zondervan, 2023), 60, 62.

2. Dr. Wayne W. Dyer, "Trust in Yourself: A Conversation with Abraham," Dr. Wayne W. Dyer Blog, September 17, 2015, https://www
.drwaynedyer.com/blog/trust-in-yourself-conversation-abraham-and
-wayne-dyer/.

3. "Metaphysical Meaning of Truth (RW)," Truth Unity, accessed October 11, 2023, https://www.truthunity.net/rw/truth.

4. Rev. Shawn, "What Is a Truth Student?," Unity Center of Norwalk, accessed October 11, 2023, https://www.unitycenternorwalk.org/what
-truth-student.

5. Francis J. Beckwith and Gregory Koukl, *Relativism: Feet Firmly Planted in Mid-Air* (Grand Rapids, MI: Baker, 1998), 20–21.

6. Rod Dreher, *Live Not by Lies: A Manual for Christian Dissidents* (New York: Sentinel, 2020), 61.

7. Norman L. Geisler and Douglas E. Potter, *A Prolegomena to Evangelical Theology* (NGIM, 2016), 70.

8. Lillian Quigley, *The Blind Men and the Elephant: An Old Tale from the Land of India* (New York: Charles Scribner's Sons, 1959). Possible original sources of the story are the *Jataka Tales*, a collection of Buddhist birth stories, and the *Panchatantra Stories*, Hindu religious instruction fables.

9. Keep in mind the "False Self" is what New Thought refers to as the ego or the self-identity that is shaped by external influences, societal conditioning, and negative thought patterns. It is seen as a self-constructed identity that often limits a person's potential and creates feelings of separation from their true, divine nature.

10. Dreher, 212.

11. Sean McDowell and John Marriott, *Set Adrift: Deconstructing What You Believe Without Sinking Your Faith* (Grand Rapids, MI: Zondervan, 2023), 5.

12. Natasha Crain, *Faithfully Different: Regaining Biblical Clarity in a Secular Culture* (Eugene, OR: Harvest House, 2022), 52.

13. Alisa Childers and Tim Barnett, *The Deconstruction of Christianity: What It Is, Why It's Destructive, and How to Respond* (Carol Stream, IL: Tyndale, 2024), 106.

Chapter 5: Identity Crisis

1. spicytweet, "just out here listening to my divine self and no one else," TikTok, September 28, 2020, https://www.tiktok.com/@spicytweet/video/6877576011513400582.

2. MegEmikoArt, "Being my most authentic self means loving myself and allowing myself to explore what it truly means to be me," TikTok, April 27, 2023, https://www.tiktok.com/@megemikoart/video/7226814474647276842?_r=1&_t=8hwDpMw1DSA.

3. Imelda Octavia Shanklin, *What Are You* (Kansas City, MO: Unity School of Christianity, 1944), 12, 15.

4. Carl Trueman, *Strange New World: How Thinkers and Activists Redefined Identity and Sparked the Sexual Revolution* (Wheaton, IL: Crossway, 2022); Trueman draws a connection between the history of Western thought and present-day identity politics with its sexual undertones. In reading his book, I couldn't help but notice the stark similarities between his findings in the Romantic Era and my experience in New Thought. My goal is to add another spiritual connection with transcendentalism to the conversation to further explain how we got to where we are today.

5. Transcendentalism was heavily influenced by Romanticism and vice versa. Both movements existed beside one another and were major early players in how the sexual revolution evolved into what it is today. For more information on this, I recommend *Strange New World* by Carl Trueman.

6. Ralph Waldo Emerson and Dr. Carol Carnes, *Emerson and New Thought: How Emerson's Essays Influenced the Science of Mind Philosophy* (Camarillo, CA: DeVorss & Company, 2021), 9–10, 11, 14, 15, 48.

7. Carl R. Trueman, "What Does It Mean to Be Your True Self?" Crossway, November 25, 2020, https://www.crossway.org/articles/what-does-it-mean-to-be-your-true-self/.

8. An interesting fact is that it's well-documented that Emerson and a fellow transcendentalist, Henry David Thoreau, were both rumored to be either gay or bisexual. I can't help but wonder how much of that informed their beliefs about the inner self. Cited in Caleb Crain, "Bosom Buddies," *New York Times*, June 3, 2001, https://archive.nytimes.com/www.nytimes.com/books/01/06/03/reviews/010603.03robblt.html.

9. Trueman, *Strange New World*, 47.

10. Unity Worldwide Ministries, *Unity: A Positive Path for Spiritual Living* (Lee's Summit, MO: Unity Worldwide Ministries, 2023).

11. Melissa Dougherty, "Oprah is NOT a New Ager," YouTube video, August 22, 2024, https://www.youtube.com/watch?v=9-6KF2E-F_Q.

12. Salvatore Sapienza, "Gay Is a Gift," Unity.org, accessed October 21, 2023, https://www.unity.org/article/gay-gift.

13. Nancy Pearcey, *Love Thy Body: Answering Hard Questions about Life and Sexuality* (Grand Rapids, MI: Baker Books, 2018), 161–162.

14. I took a photo of this on the counter as I went in. They had blank ones too, in case they didn't have your available pronoun.

15. lesbiansnowwhite, "You Are Valid," TikTok, May 20, 2023, https://www.tiktok.com/@lesbiansnowwhite/video/7235467934502522155?q=beep+boop+pronouns&t=1699193600821.

16. "Neopronouns List," Tumblr, accessed January 30, 2024, https://neopronouns-list.tumblr.com/neopronouns-list.

17. Ibid.

18. "A Positive Path for Spiritual Living," Unity Santa Fe, accessed October 9, 2023, https://www.unitysantafe.org/.

19. "CSL Statement: Pride Month," Center for Spiritual Living Redlands, June 25, 2021, https://www.cslredlands.org/csl-statement-pride-month/.

20. Rev. DeeAnn Weir Morency, "What Makes Pronouns Important?," Unity.org, accessed October 21, 2023, https://www.unity.org/article/what-makes-pronouns-important.

21. "'What's in a Pronoun?' Workshop," Affiliated New Thought Network, accessed October 14, 2023, https://newthought.org/event-5434968.

22. Here are the rest of the principles: (1) We affirm God as Mind, Infinite Being, Spirit, Ultimate Reality. (2) We affirm that God, the Good, is supreme, universal, and everlasting. (3) We affirm the unity of God and humanity, in that the divine nature dwells within and expresses through each of us, by means of our acceptance of it, as health, supply, wisdom, love, life, truth, power, beauty, and peace. (4) We affirm the power of prayer and the capacity of each person to have mystical experience with God, and to enjoy the grace of God. (6) We affirm that we are spiritual beings, dwelling in a spiritual universe that is governed by spiritual law; and that in alignment with spiritual law, we can heal, prosper, and harmonize. (7) We affirm that our mental states are carried forward into manifestation and become our experience in daily living. (8) We affirm the manifestation of the kingdom of heaven here and now. (9) We affirm expression of the highest spiritual principles in loving one another unconditionally, promoting the highest good for all, teaching and healing one another, ministering to one another, and living together in peace, in accordance with the teachings of Jesus and other enlightened teachers.

23. "International New Thought Alliance," accessed October 7, 2023, https://www.newthoughtalliance.org/#/.

24. A therian is a human who identifies as a non-human animal to some degree on an emotional, psychological, or spiritual level. Otherkin are humans who identify as not entirely human in a spiritual, emotional, or psychological way. Think of Otherkin as those who identify as mythical creatures such as—but not limited to—hobbits, fairies, or even dragons.

25. Pearcey, 226.

26. "Unconditional Love or Unconditional Approval?" Newbreak Church, accessed August 29, 2024, https://newbreak.church/unconditional -love-or-unconditional-approval/.

27. Laura Perry, *Transgender to Transformed: A Story of Transition That Will Truly Set You Free* (Bartlesville, OK: Genesis Publishing Group, 2019), 172–173.

28. Abigail Shrier, *Irreversible Damage: The Transgender Craze Seducing Our Daughters* (Washington, DC: Regency Publishing, 2020), 218.

Chapter 6: Loving Ourselves to Death

1. "Samuel Smiles," *Encyclopædia Britannica*, accessed December 9, 2023, https://www.britannica.com/biography/Samuel-Smiles.

2. Though this exact title isn't found anywhere, this concept is prevalent

in many New Thought teachings. In *The Game of Life and How to Play It*, New Thought author Florence Scovel Shinn frequently referenced the Golden Rule, emphasizing the importance of positive thinking, affirmations, and treating others with kindness and fairness. She believed that by adhering to the principles of the Golden Rule, one can attract positive circumstances and manifest one's desires.

3. There's a pop-culture term for this: "Main Character Syndrome." This is a term made popular on TikTok to describe someone who views themselves as the lead character in their own life story. These people tend to be rather self-centered, emotionally sensitive, and entitled and have trouble taking constructive feedback from others.

4. Many people know Daymond John from the popular show *Shark Tank*. He has *Think and Grow Rich* on his recommended book list of "books entrepreneurs should read."

5. Kate Bowler, *Blessed: A History of the American Prosperity Gospel* (New York, NY: Oxford Press, 2013), 36.

6. The foreword to Dale Carnegie's book *How to Win Friends and Influence People* misquotes a Harvard University professor who once said that humans have unused mental potential. The self-help movement took this concept and repeated it throughout their teachings to show humans their supposed "true potential."

7. T. J. Raphael, "Morgan Freeman's New Movie Says You Use Just 10 Percent of Your Brain. But Think Again," The World, July 25, 2014, https://theworld.org/stories/2014-07-25/morgan-freemans-new -movie-says-you-use-just-10-percent-your-brain-think-again?fb clid=IwAR0nboXHOfqhgwIvlvDlISWRNllvj32JLbHznBTWoUc _4K0hMiKBwBXOetU.

8. Igor S. Hartford, "What We Were like Emmet Fox and Alcoholics Anonymous," Silkworth.net, February 1996, https://silkworth.net /alcoholics-anonymous/what-we-were-like-emmet-fox-and-- alcoholics-anonymous/.

9. Norman Vincent Peale, *The Power of Positive Thinking* (New York: Simon and Schuster, 2015), 1.

10. Natasha Crain, "Nearly every false idea today can be traced back to the belief that man is fundamentally good," Facebook, April 25, 2023, https://tinyurl.com/ytc4e9wr.

11. Glennon Doyle, *Untamed* (New York: Penguin Random House, 2020), 56–60.

12. Wayne Dyer is also one of the biggest proponents of inner divinity through I AM statements and uses this verse and other "I AM" verses to teach that we all have inner divinity, as well as Eckhart Tolle.

13. Doyle, 122.

14. Brené Brown, *Braving the Wilderness: The Quest for True Belonging and the Courage to Stand Alone* (Center City, MN: Hazelden, 2010) 157.

15. Kristen Padilla, "Brené Brown and the Lie of the Divine Self (Book Review)," The Gospel Coalition, February 7, 2018, https://www.thegospelcoalition.org/reviews/braving-the-wilderness/.

16. Brown, *Braving the Wilderness*, 163, italics original.

17. Wayne Dyer, *Wishes Fulfilled: Mastering the Art of Manifesting* (Carlsbad, CA: Hay House, 2013), 78.

18. Demi Lovato, "Demi Lovato on Instagram: 'Like a serpent in the garden I am truth and I am darkness, I'm an angel, I'm a demon, just depends on what your feeling....'" Instagram, April 30, 2022, https://www.instagram.com/p/Cc_ARbyJhf8/?hl=en.

19. Genesis Rivas, "Jennifer Lopez Shared Her Morning Routine Complete with Daily Affirmations," *Shape Magazine*, April 8, 2022, https://www.shape.com/celebrities/news/jennifer-lopez-morning-routine-affirmations.

20. Swedenborg, as we went over in chapter 1, was a founding father of New Thought.

21. JLo, "#mondaymotivation," Twitter, March 29, 2021, https://x.com/JLo/status/1376581280121323523.

22. Thomas Watson, *The Doctrine of Repentance* (Edinburgh: Banner of Truth Trust, 1987), 63. Originally published 1668.

Chapter 7: Dreams Come True

1. "What Is the Law of Attraction & How Does It Work?," The Law Of Attraction, accessed August 30, 2024, https://thelawofattraction.com/what-is-the-law-of-attraction/.

2. Warren Felt Evans is known for promoting the idea that our thoughts can shape our reality—basically, the concept that "thoughts become things." However, this idea wasn't unique to him. It became a key theme in the broader New Thought movement, with other figures like Ralph Waldo Emerson and Napoleon Hill also popularizing it. Evans played a significant role, but he was one of several who contributed to spreading this concept.

3. Horatio W. Dresser, ed., "The New Thought Today—The Spirit of the New Thought," Lessons in Truth, accessed August 29, 2024, https://lessonsintruth.info/library/horatio-w-dresser-new-thought-author/the-spirit-of-the-new-thought-by-horatio-w-dresser/the-new-thought-today-the-spirit-of-the-new-thought/.

4. This was at a Center for Spiritual Living, or CFSL.

5. Jim Lockard, "Do We Need a New Definition of God? Part 2," New Thought Evolutionary, October 7, 2023, https://newthoughtevolutionary.wordpress.com/2023/10/07/do-we-need-a-new-definition-of-god-part-2/#comments.

6. April Moncrieff, *The Principles of New Thought* (Camarillo, CA: DeVorss Publications, 2013), 65.

7. Moncrieff, *The Principles of New Thought*, 65.

8. D. L. Paulhus, "Bypassing the Will: The Automatization of Affirmations," in D. M. Wegner and J. W. Pennebaker, eds., *Handbook of Mental Control* (Englewood Cliffs, NJ: Prentice Hall, 1993), 573–587, https://www2.psych.ubc.ca/~dpaulhus/research/SOCIAL_COGNITION/downloads/positive%20affirmations%20chap.pdf.

9. Alisha Chinai, "The History of Affirmations," 2 Minute Affirmations, July 9, 2023, https://www.2minuteaffirmations.com/affirmations/the-history-of-affirmations.

10. Sarah Wilson, "Yes! Louise Hay Tells Me Her #1 Healing Trick," SarahWilson.com, September 19, 2017, https://sarahwilson.com/2011/08/yes-louise-hay-tells-me-her-1-healing-trick/.

11. Because we're all a part of the Divine Mind, correct your thinking, then you correct your body. See chapter 2 for more details about how this is defined.

12. Eleve, *Spiritual Law in the Natural World* (Chicago: Purdy, 1894), 181, http://iapsop.com/ssoc/1894__eleve___spiritual_law_in_the_natural_world.pdf.

13. Ibid.

14. Wayne Dyer, a New Thought author, also teaches this approach.

15. *What Is New Thought?*, directed by Jon Miller, released June 13, 2013, produced by Jon Miller, accessed March 2023, https://vimeo.com/ondemand/newthoughtmovie, time stamp 01:26:52.

16. Rabbi Benjamin Blech, "'The Secret' Revealed," Aish.com, accessed August 30, 2024, https://aish.com/the-secret-revealed/.

17. Jennifer Benton, "Positive Affirmations vs Biblical Truth," Rescued Forever, last modified July 6, 2021, https://rescuedforever.com/positive-affirmations-vs-biblical-truth/.

18. Rhonda Byrne, *The Power* (London: Simon & Schuster, 2010), 43.

19. In the book and documentary, this concept is repeatedly insisted.

20. Eric Butterworth, "The Law of Attraction," Unity.org, accessed September 29, 2023, https://www.unity.org/article/law-attraction.

21. Sara Crawford, "Eric Butterworth: A Life Dedicated to Metaphysical Teachings," Unity.org, accessed September 29, 2023, https://www.unity.org/article/eric-butterworth-life-dedicated-metaphysical-teachings.

22. "About Abraham Hicks," Abraham-Hicks Law of Attraction, accessed August 30, 2024, https://www.abraham-hicks.com/about/.

23. The Hicks were also highly influenced by Jane Roberts, a psychic from the 1980s New Age movement who communicated with an entity named Seth. (Isn't it strange that so many of these entities have Biblical names? Why not Ghandi? Or Siddhartha? Or Mohammad? What's up with that?)

24. Jon Clash, *Law of Attraction: A Gateway Drug to Spiritual Heroin* (Why Jesus? Publishing, 2023), 3.

25. Hillary Morgan Ferrer, "Enneagram Shaming Is Not the Way Forward," Mama Bear Apologetics, January 19, 2023, https://mamabearapologetics.com/enneagram-shaming/.

26. Ibid.

27. Rhonda Byrne, *The Secret* (New York: Atria Books, 2018), 164.

28. Ibid., 183.

29. Barbara Ehrenreich, *Bright-Sided: How Positive Thinking Is Undermining America* (New York: Picador, 2009), 177.

Chapter 8: Prosperity Now

1. *What Is New Thought?*, directed by Jon Miller, released June 13, 2013, produced by Jon Miller, accessed March 2023, https://vimeo.com/ondemand/newthoughtmovie, David Alexander, time stamp 00:41:14, 00:43:10.

2. Kate Bowler, *Blessed: A History of the American Property Gospel* (New York: Oxford University Press, 2013), 79.

3. Dr. Robert M. Bowman Jr. is the first that I know of to refer to Kenyon in this manner.

4. Robert M. Bowman Jr., *The Word-Faith Controversy: Understanding the Health and Wealth Gospel* (Grand Rapids: Baker Books, 2001), 37.

5. A lesser-known fact is that the Holiness revivalism in the 1850s may have been influenced by Emanuel Swedenborg's writings (see Bowler, 265).

6. E. W. Kenyon, *Identification: A Romance in Redemption* (Lynwood, WA: Kenyon's Gospel Publishing Society, 1968), 15.

7. E. W. Kenyon, *Jesus the Healer* (Seattle: Kenyon's Gospel Publishing Society, 1943), 26, https://archive.org/details/jesushealer00keny/page/26/mode/2up?q=symptoms; Dan R. McConnell, *A Different Gospel* (Peabody, MA: Hendrickson, 1994), Kindle, Ch 6.

8. Bowman, 44.

9. Kevin Scott Smith, "Mind, Might, and Mastery: Human Potential in Metaphysical Religion and E. W. Kenyon,"(Thesis, Liberty University,

1995), 92–93, https://digitalcommons.liberty.edu/cgi/viewcontent
.cgi?article=1051&context=masters; not all experts agree this is the
case. I tend to believe Kenyon was influenced by Trine because it's
displayed in Kenyon's writing.

10. Bowman, 44.

11. Smith, "Mind, Might, and Mastery," 121–22.

12. Smith, 125.

13. Smith, 125.

14. Smith, 23.

15. Essek William Kenyon, *The Wonderful Name of Jesus*, 26th ed. (Seattle:
Kenyon's Gospel Publishing Society, 1964 [originally published 1927]), 7.

16. Smith, "Mind, Might, and Mastery," 25; note that Kenyon's teachings
and doctrines are in direct opposition to the beliefs of New Thought.
The main point of disagreement lies in the concept of atonement for
sins. While New Thought denies that Jesus died to atone for sin, Kenyon
firmly believed Jesus had to die both physically and spiritually to save
humanity from sin. On the other hand, New Thought teaches that
Jesus's death has no significance when it comes to saving us from sin.

17. Bowman, 38.

18. Bowman, 47.

19. Dan McConnell has documented this well in his book *A Different
Gospel.*

20. Bowman, 93

21. Bowman, 94.

22. Bowman, 89.

23. This isn't confined to just Hagin. William Branham and Oral Roberts,
also considered "fathers" of the movement, had many strange
teachings as well.

24. Bowler, 25.

25. I believe WoF exists in its current form because it was informed by
New Thought metaphysical teachings. New Thought stood on its own
with a unique metaphysical strain focused on health, the power of
the mind, and prosperity, which have occultic and pragmatic origins
that we already went over in chapter 2. The WoF movement, however,
wouldn't exist in its current form if it weren't for the influence of New
Thought. But this doesn't mean the entire movement is *explicitly* New
Thought. Realistically, WoF is a hybrid mix of Pentecostalism, the
Faith Cure movement, and New Thought.

26. Bowman, 38.

27. It's outside the scope of this book to go deeper into other problematic
theological teachings—and there are many other books that have

covered problematic theological teachings extensively, such as *The Word-Faith Controversy* by Dr. Robert M. Bowman Jr., *The Health and Wealth Gospel* by Bruce Barron, *Health, Wealth and Happiness* by David W. Jones and Russell S. Woodbridge, *God, Greed, and the (Prosperity) Gospel* by Costi Hinn, and *Counterfeit Kingdom* by Holly Pivec and Doug Geivett. These are only a few suggestions.

28. This goes all the way back to Emanuel Swedenborg, who taught that sickness is really just ignorance. It was more than just mind over matter. It was mind over *body*.

29. April Moncrieff, *The Principles of New Thought* (Camarillo, CA: DeVorss Publications, 2013), 83.

30. Bowler, 141. See also "Founder's Memorial," Kenneth Hagin Ministries, accessed November 22, 2023, https://www.rhema.org /index.php?option=com_content&view=article&id=8&Itemid=137.

31. Bill Johnson, Kenneth Copeland, and others would agree with this. Benny Hinn, a prominent WoF teacher, says that when people don't receive their healing, "it really is the fault of the person." Bowler, 151.

32. Rhonda Byrne, *The Secret* (New York: Simon and Schuster, 2011), 68, 102, 114, 168.

33. John S. Haller Jr., *The History of New Thought: From Mind Cure to Positive Thinking and the Prosperity Gospel* (West Chester, PA: Swedenborg Foundation Press, 2012), 54.

34. Holly Pivec and Doug Geivett, *Counterfeit Kingdom: The Dangers of New Revelation, New Prophets, and New Age Practices in the Church* (Nashville: B&H Publishing, 2022), 163.

35. Costi Hinn, "Is It Always God's Will to Heal Now?" For the Gospel, accessed August 30, 2024, https://www.forthegospel.org/read/is-it -always-gods-will-to-heal-now.

36. Gail M. Harley, *Emma Curtis Hopkins: Forgotten Founder of New Thought* (Syracuse, NY: Syracuse University Press, 2002), 71–72.

37. Joel Osteen, *Your Best Life Now: 7 Steps to Living at Your Full Potential*, 2nd ed., (New York: Faith Words, 2015) 191.

38. Harley, 73, and Haller, *The History of New Thought*, 102.

39. Harley, 73.

40. Hopkins may have been the first to develop the idea of "the Good," but the first New Thought author to really promote the doctrine of prosperity and abundance was a student of Hopkins, Frances Lord. Prentice Mulford, who was a New Thought author commonly quoted in the book *The Secret*, is also credited with teaching about prosperity (Haller, 72–74). The teaching goes that since you are divine and one with God, you cannot be poor because God cannot be poor. Poverty at its root

is a wrong belief. So change the belief, and it will cure the poverty. By our faith, we are then made prosperous (Haller, 217). It's all in the mind.

41. Bowman, 93–94; Kenneth Hagin, *How God Taught Me About Prosperity* (Tulsa, OK: Rhema Bible Church, 1985), 5, 10–15.

42. Charles Fillmore, *Prosperity* (Kansas City, MO: Unity School of Christianity, 1936), 69.

43. W. I. Hoschouer, *You Can Be Prosperous* (New York: Landau Book Company, 1932, 1947), 83.

44. Emmet Fox, *The Magic of Tithing* (New York: Harper and Brothers Publishers, 1932), 6–11.

45. Gloria Copeland and George Pearsons, "4 Laws of Poverty: How to Become & Stay Poor," Harrison House, last modified December 26, 2022, https://harrisonhouse.com/blog/gloria-copeland-george -pearsons-4-laws-of-poverty-how-to-become-stay-poor.

46. Kenneth Copeland Ministries, "A Three Step Plan for Manifestation," YouTube, December 5, 2018, https://www.youtube.com/watch?v=LWW7j WTz7JM; Kenneth Copeland Ministries, "The Laws Prosperity," YouTube, August 10, 2017, https://www.youtube.com/watch?v=7VixKqtetis.

47. Bowler, 39–40.

48. Like with health, we can see many similarities in these teachings, but there are still important doctrinal differences. The reasons why Christians are poor are different in both WoF and New Thought. For WoF, it's a divine right stolen by Satan. This is true as well with their view of health. When Jesus died and rose again, he gave that dominion back to believers. New Thought does not teach this. Same methods, different reasons.

49. Moncrieff, 66.

50. Ibid.

51. Bowman, 33.

52. Bowler, 20.

53. Smith, 145–46.

54. Bowler, 20.

55. Jon Miller, *What Is New Thought?*, time stamp 00:40:44.

56. Ibid., time stamp 00:40:56.

57. Said by Rev. Sky St. John, minister of Unity Church, in Jon Miller, "What is New Thought?," time stamp 00:39:13.

58. Bowman, 201.

59. I've discussed extensively how and why New Thought teaches humans are divine, so I won't go into detail here.

60. It's well-documented that teachers like Creflo Dollar, Kenneth Copeland, Benny Hinn, and more have taught this doctrine.

61. John G. Lake, *Spiritual Hunger, The God Men, and Other Sermons*, ed. Gordon Lindsay (Dallas: Christ for the Nations, 1994), 20, https://christiandiet.com.ng/wp-content/uploads/2020/06/Spiritual-Hunger-The-God-Men-John-G.-Lake-Christiandiet.com_.ng_.pdf.

62. Bowler, 23.

63. Ibid. This is found in Kemp Pendleton Burpeau, *God's Showman: A Historical Study of John G. Lake and South African/American Pentecostalism* (Oslo, Norway: Refleks, 2004), 152–53.

64. Bowler, 23.

65. John G. Lake, *John G. Lake Sermons on Dominion over Demons, Disease, and Death*, ed. Gordon Lindsay (Dallas: Christ for the Nations, 1949), Ch 2, Ch 9, 90, 91, 94, 119, https://christiandiet.com.ng/wp-content/uploads/2020/06/The-John-G.-Lake-sermons-on-Dominion-Over-Demons-Disease-and-Death-Gordon-Lindsay-Christiandiet.com_.ng_.pdf.

66. Bowman, 32.

67. Kenyon, *Identification*, 60–61.

68. Kenneth Hagin is probably the most vocal WoF teacher who is unapologetic in his belief that human beings are meant to be gods. Hagin says, "Every man who has been born again is an incarnation, and Christianity is a miracle. The believer is as much an incarnation as was Jesus of Nazareth." Kenneth Hagin, "The Incarnation," *The Word of Faith* (December 1980): 14. Hagin plagiarized this statement from Kenyon and the concept is suggested throughout the WoF movement. This same exact wording is found in E. W. Kenyon, *The Father and His Family* (Spencer, MA: Reality Press, 1916), 126, https://archive.org/details/fatherhisfamily00keny/page/126/mode/2up?q=born+again+incarnation.

69. New Thought would not use the term "exact duplicates" of God or "little gods" and doesn't teach God is personal. There are differences here, but New Thought agrees with the idea that being made in the image of God means we're a part of the Divine Mind. We're divine and have creative power. Being in the image of God means we're gods.

70. Kenyon, *The Father and His Family*, 36, 39, 89, 231, 265, https://archive.org/details/fatherhisfamily00keny/page/126/mode/2up?q=born+again+incarnation.

71. Where WoF would part ways with New Thought is how each views "God." As discussed in previous chapters, New Thought has an impersonal view of God, whereas WoF would say the opposite. However, the way they view the teaching of being "made in the image of God" equating with "humans are divine" is comparable.

72. E. W. Kenyon, *Advanced Bible Course: Studies in the Deeper Life*, 5th ed. (Lynnwood, WA: Kenyon's Gospel Publishing Society, 1970), 133. There wasn't an original edition, but this book and quote are found online as well here: https://files.logoscdn.com/v1/files/49566000/assets /11681721/content.pdf?signature=6ldukPg0YY0W1lD9lJiQx59gxJU.

73. Dr. Mikael Stenhammar, "Charismatic Magic," Liberating Faith, YouTube, May 12, 2023, https://www.youtube.com/watch?v=UZjeFQgCx08.

74. Ibid., time stamp 4:50.

75. Carl Tiechrib, "The Labyrinth Journey," Forcing Change, November 2012, https://www.forcingchange.org/the-labyrinth-journe y/?fbclid=IwAR3lLeRxamgNOXvau9srOBfQtoQQEzN9qFBNtZBcx1 K0TGv2i7ihXlOAaMw.

Chapter 9: A Different Gospel

1. This isn't a labyrinth that you get lost in. This labyrinth is made by making a pattern out of rocks on the ground meant for someone to walk in and pray. It's used for meditation, spiritual transformation, and global unity. Historically, labyrinths were used in pagan rituals and later adopted by Catholics. Today, they are promoted by the Emergent Church and others who seek an open spirituality apart from the Bible.

2. It's important I mention that I attended my regular church every week while I attended these other churches. I didn't miss being able to attend my own church. It was important for me to be among believers and in active prayer as I visited these places for my research.

3. The Emergent Church is a movement that aims to merge with contemporary culture and values and is characterized by postmodernism. It questions traditional church practices, encourages dialogue and social justice, and often has a more liberal theological approach, seeking to be more inclusive.

4. John Pavlovitz, "Progressive Christianity—Is Christianity," johnpavlovitz.com, October 5, 2015, https://johnpavlovitz.com/2016 /10/05/explaining-progressive-christianity-otherwise-known-as -christianity/.

5. Jason Jimenez, *Hijacking Jesus: How Progressive Christians Are Remaking Him and Taking Over His Church* (Washington: Salem Books: 2023), 25.

6. "The Core Values of Progressive Christianity," ProgressiveChristianity.org, 2022, accessed August 30, 2024, https://progressivechristianity.org/the-core-values-of-progressive -christianity/.

7. "Social Justice and New Thought," International New Thought Alliance, accessed October 14, 2023, https://www.newthoughtalliance.org/social-justice.html#/.

8. Horatio W. Dresser, ed., "The New Thought Today—The Spirit of the New Thought," Lessons in Truth, accessed August 29, 2024, https://lessonsintruth.info/library/horatio-w-dresser-new-thought-author/the-spirit-of-the-new-thought-by-horatio-w-dresser/the-new-thought-today-the-spirit-of-the-new-thought/.

9. "The Power Of WE," ProgressiveChristianity.org, September 5, 2014, The Association for Global New Thought, accessed August 30, 2024, https://progressivechristianity.org/resource/the-power-of-we/.

10. In many cases, the mind and intellect are seen as a hindrance to personal experience, so contemplative prayer, labyrinth walking, meditation, or other practices are done to quiet the mind to allow for "God" to talk.

11. "What Are Christian Mystics?" GotQuestions.org, accessed August 30, 2024, https://www.gotquestions.org/Christian-mystics.html.

12. Dan Merkur, "Mysticism," *Encyclopædia Britannica*, accessed August 30, 2024, https://www.britannica.com/topic/mysticism.

13. Jimenez, 170.

14. Alisa Childers, *Another Gospel? A Lifelong Christian Seeks Truth in Response to Progressive Christianity* (Eugene, OR: Tyndale, 2020), 76.

15. Artist, David Hayward, @nakedpastor, "From the Gospel Stories It's Quite Evident to Me That What Made Jesus Unique Was That He Was His Most Authentic Self. Profound! And That Goes for You Too!" Twitter, September 26, 2023, https://twitter.com/nakedpastor/status/1706639783772946842.

16. Frank Turek, "Progressive Christians will tell me . . . ," Facebook, July 18, 2021, https://tinyurl.com/4sv22maa.

17. Robert Robinson, "Come Thou Fount of Every Blessing," 1758, in *A Collection of Hymns Used by the Church of Christ in Angel-Alley, Bishopsgate*, 1760.

18. Though I only mentioned Richard Rohr briefly, this book is one of the best books I've read about his beliefs and the origins of the Enneagram. It also played a large role in my understanding of the overall connection between Progressive Christianity and New Thought.

Chapter 10: The Schuller Secret

1. This is a term I first heard from my friend, author, and apologist Greg Koukl.

2. The church growth movement had its beginnings with a man named Donald McGavran. His book *Understanding Church Growth* (Grand Rapids: Eerdmans, 1970) laid the foundation for the church growth movement by encouraging churches to ask themselves four questions: What are the causes of church growth? What are the barriers to church growth? What are the factors that can make Christian faith a movement among populations? And what principles of church growth are reproducible? Men like C. Peter Wagner and George Hunter III contributed to the movement as well. Wagner was a fan of McGavran's emphasis on marketing research. But he was also quite a devoted supporter of Schuller and Peale's "Possibility Thinking," as well as pragmatic marketing strategies and prosperity theology. He thought there should be a therapeutic focus on self-esteem. But Schuller was *the* voice and figure that made the seeker model what it is.

3. Robert Schuller, *My Journey: From an Iowa Farm to a Cathedral of Dreams* (San Francisco: Harper, 2001), 170.

4. Tim Challies, "The False Teachers: Norman Vincent Peale," Challies, April 2, 2014, https://www.challies.com/articles/the-false-teachers -norman-vincent-peale/.

5. Bella Stumbo, "From the Archives: The Time Muhammad Ali Asked for Robert Schuller's Autograph," *Los Angeles Times*, May 29, 1983, https://www.latimes.com/local/california/la-me-schuller-1983 -profile-20150330-story.html.

6. Nelson Searcy, "How Robert Schuller Shaped Your Ministry," Church Leader Insights, July 30, 2015, https://churchleaderinsights.com/how -robert-schuller-shaped-your-ministry/.

7. Julia Lieblich and *Tribune* religion reporter, "Audience of Many Faiths Joins Schuller in Mosque for an 'Evening of Hope,'" *Chicago Tribune*, November 2, 2001, https://www.chicagotribune.com/news/ct-xpm -2001-11-02-0111020131-story.html.

8. Robert H. Schuller, *Self Esteem: The New Reformation* (Waco, TX: Word Books, 1982), 67.

9. Ibid., 104.

10. Ibid., 64.

11. Tim Stafford, "Died: Robert Schuller, Forerunner of the Seeker-Sensitive Movement," *Christianity Today*, April 2, 2015, https://www .christianitytoday.com/ct/2015/april-web-only/died-robert-schuller -forerunner-of-seeker-sensitive-movemen.html.

12. Ibid.

13. Granted, there are toxic legalistic churches distorting the gospel into

a works-based hamster wheel and turning Scripture into a weapon by ridiculing and shaming people. This is *wrong*. But the answer isn't to pendulum in the opposite direction, twisting the gospel entirely by making it all about your self-esteem. That's not a remedy. That's a different gospel dressed in emotional, feel-good language. Both promise control and freedom but give you bondage and pride.

14. Wildred Bockelman, "The Pros and Cons of Robert Schuller," Religion Online, accessed November 10, 2023, https://www.religion-online.org/article/the-pros-and-cons-of-robert-schuller/.

15. Joseph P. Gudel, "A Profile: Robert Schuller," Christian Research Institute, June 10, 2009, https://www.equip.org/articles/robert-schuller/.

16. Stafford, "Died: Robert Schuller."

17. Robert. H. Schuller Institute for Successful Church Leadership, January 24–27, 2005, https://cicministry.org/commentary/Crystal_Cathedral.pdf.

18. "Myths About a Movement: Answers to Common Misunderstandings About Seeker Oriented Churches," *WCA News* 5, no. 5 (September/October 1997): 2.

19. Ibid., 3.

20. Ibid., 6–7.

21. Ibid.

22. Ibid., 4.

23. Michael Nason and Donna Nason, *Robert Schuller: The Inside Story* (Waco: Word Books, 1983), 152.

24. Schuller, *Self Esteem: The New Reformation*, 47.

25. Hartford Institute for Religion Research, "National Survey of Megachurch Attenders," accessed October 19, 2024, http://hirr.hartsem.edu/megachurch/National%20Survey%20of%20Megachurch%20Attenders%20-final.pdf.

26. Ibid.

27. Dennis Allen and Raymond Monroe, "Different Kinds of Gospel Result In Different Kinds of Discipleship," *Kairos: Evangelical Journal of Theology* 17, no. 1 (2023): 49–65, https://doi.org/10.32862/k.17.1.3.

28. "Willow Creek's Huge Shift," *Christianity Today*, May 15, 2008, https://www.christianitytoday.com/2008/05/willow-creeks-huge-shift/; see also "Revealed: Discovering the Strengths of Your Leadership," *Christian Leadership Alliance*, accessed October 19, 2024, https://ym.christianleadershipalliance.org/page/revealed; and Greg Hawkins and Cally Parkinson, *Reveal: Where Are You?* (Barrington, IL: Willow Creek Resources, 2007).

29. This survey was done by Willow Creek. To their credit, they conducted this study and claimed to implement changes moving forward due to their findings.

30. Paul Carter, "Why I Abandoned Seeker Church," The Gospel Coalition Canadian Edition, August 23, 2018, https://ca.thegospelcoalition.org /columns/ad-fontes/abandoned-seeker-church/.

31. Hartford Institute for Religion Research, "National Survey of Megachurch Attenders," accessed October 19, 2024, http://hirr .hartsem.edu/megachurch/National%20Survey%20of%20 Megachurch%20Attenders%20-final.pdf.

32. Morgan Lee, "How 727 Megachurches Spend Their Money," *Christianity Today*, September 10, 2014, https://www.christianitytoday.com/2014 /09/how-727-megachurches-spend-their-money-leadership-network/.

33. Paul Carter, "Why I Abandoned the Seeker Church," The Gospel Coalition Canadian Edition, July 20, 2020, https://ca.thegospelcoalition .org/columns/ad-fontes/abandoned-seeker-church/.

34. Yes, this is a real thing. See Jeffrey Swindoll, "Megachurch Pastor Provides 'User Manual' for Interacting with Him in Case You Want to Climb His Corporate Ladder," Not the Bee, September 1, 2023, https:// notthebee.com/article/pastor-provides-user-manual-for-interacting -with-him-in-case-you-want-to-climb-the-corporate-megachurch -ladder.

Chapter 11: Beyond the Happy Lies

1. Greg Koukl, *Street Smarts* (Grand Rapids: Zondervan, 2023), 172.

2. Ibid.

3. Ibid., 53.

4. Robert Lowry, "Nothing but the Blood" (1876).

5. Red Pen Logic with Mr. B, "The solution to sin isn't denial; it's forgiveness," Facebook, June 8, 2023, https://www.facebook.com/redpenlogic/posts /pfbid02xW9BnCdKDbPbzBkUTtLN9kn1Pwu9cZd8PSzL4AuxHYcYn89 wzXp5upJBKYGgY77kl.

From the Publisher

GREAT BOOKS

ARE EVEN BETTER WHEN THEY'RE SHARED!

Help other readers find this one:

- Post a review at your favorite online bookseller

- Post a picture on a social media account and share why you enjoyed it

- Send a note to a friend who would also love it—or better yet, give them a copy

Thanks for reading!